THE
TAO
OF PEACE

A
GUIDE
TO INNER
AND OUTER
PEACE

THE
TAO OF
PEACE

BY

DIANE DREHER

DONALD I. FINE, INC.
New York

Library of Congress Cataloging-in-Publication Data

Dreher, Diane, 1946–
The Tao of peace / by Diane Dreher.
p. cm.
ISBN 1–55611–151–7
1. Peace of mind. 2. Lao-tzu. Tao te ching. I. Title.
BF637.P3D74 1989
181'.114—dc20 89–45442
CIP

Manufactured in the United States of America

10 9 8 7 6 5 4 3 2 1

Designed by Irving Perkins Associates

The following page constitutes an extension of the copyright page:

The author and publisher gratefully acknowledge permission to use selections and information from the following copyrighted materials:

Jack Canfield, mirror exercise from Full Esteem Ahead workshop in San Jose CA, October 1988. Used with permission of Self Esteem Seminars.
Tina Clare, *Silence in the Heart: Meditations for Inner Growth and Relaxation*. Los Altos Hills: copyright © 1989. Used by permission of Tina Clare.
Jim Dodge, Leonard Charles, Lynn Milliman, and Victoria Stockley, "Where You At? A Bioregional Test," first published in *Coevolution Quarterly*, no. 32, winter 1981. Used by permission of the author and the publisher, now *Whole Earth Review*.
Genevieve Farrow, "A Strange Encounter," originally published in *Science of Mind Magazine*, May 1989, pp. 3–5. Used by permission of the author.
Millard Fuller and Diane Scott, *Love in the Mortar Joints*. Piscataway, NJ: New Century Publishers, © 1980. Used by permission of the publisher.
Suzanne Gowan et al., *Moving Toward a New Society*. Philadelphia: New Society Publishers, copyright © 1976. Used by permission of the publisher.
The Greenpeace Philosophy. Used by permission of Greenpeace USA and Canada.
Dag Hammarskjöld, *Markings*, trans. Leif Sjoberg and W. H. Auden. New York: Alfred A. Knopf, Inc.; London: Faber and Faber Ltd. copyright © 1965. Used by permission of the publishers.
Louise L. Hay, *You Can Heal Your Life*. Santa Monica: Hay House, copyright © 1984. Used by permission of the publisher.
Barbara Howell, "Seedlings of Survival," *Christianity and Crisis*, September 1985. Used by permission of the publisher.
Robert Hunter, *Warriors of the Rainbow: A Chronicle of the Greenpeace Movement*. New York: Holt, Rinehart, and Winston, copyright © 1979. Used by permission of the author.
Gerald G. Jampolsky, *Love Is Letting Go of Fear*. Berkeley: Celestial Arts, copyright © 1979. Used by permission of the author and publisher.

*To all who seek new patterns of peace
and walk the path with heart.*

CONTENTS

V THE WAY OF PEACE

ACKNOWLEDGMENTS

The *Tao* teaches a vision of life as process, which is certainly the case with this book. During the past twenty years many peacemakers have shared with me their wisdom and personal example. You'll find their names throughout these pages and in the notes and resources at the end. I am especially grateful to Linus Pauling, Frances Moore Lappé, Norman Cousins, Mitch Saunders, Gertrude Welch, and Gay Swenson for discussions and interviews during the formative stages of the book.

I would like to thank my agent Sandy Dijkstra and Laurie Fox of the Sandra Dijkstra Literary Agency for their Taoist balance of professionalism, creativity, and personal support. I'm grateful to Brad Bunnin for his valuable legal advice and to my editor, Susan Schwartz, for seeing the book through to completion. Mike Yamashita did the beautiful calligraphy, and Miranda Gan, Richard Henry Gan, Paul Fong, and Henry Chen offered their advice on Chinese characters. Gwilym Stover and Genevieve Farrow read and critiqued early drafts of the work, and Cory Wade lent her poet's ear to the final version. To all of these people and to my friends and colleagues on the path of peace, I am deeply grateful.

The many peace and environmental groups I contacted during the course of my research reinforced my belief in emerging patterns of harmony and cooperation. In the spirit of partnership, some of the proceeds from the sale of this book will help support ongoing work for personal and planetary peace.

INTRODUCTION

"Why did the ancients cherish the Tao?
Because through it
We may find a world of peace,
Leaving behind a world of cares,
And hold the greatest treasure under heaven."

(TAO 62)[1]

S EEKERS for centuries have found inner peace by following the *Tao Te Ching*. Translated more than any book but the Bible, Lao Tzu's volume of 5000 words has helped people live through turbulent times by revealing the deep source of peace within.

Lao Tzu wrote the *Tao* over twenty-five centuries ago as a handbook for leaders. In ancient China, to lead wisely meant to live wisely, to seek personal balance and integration with the cycles of nature. Lao Tzu's teachings assume special importance today as we seek not only peace of mind but peace in our world. Searching for new patterns of harmony in everything from holistic health, psychology, and physics to ecology and social action, people are rediscovering the wisdom of the *Tao Te Ching*.

Peace, Lao Tzu realized, is an inside job. Only when we find peace within ourselves can we see more clearly, act more effectively, cooperating with the energies within and around us to build a more peaceful world. The *Tao* teaches that our actions have far-reaching consequences, stressing the importance of balance and the intimate relationship between ourselves and our environment. Seeing beyond the shifting tides of circumstance, we recognize the patterns of ebb and flow underlying all of nature. The *Tao* teaches patience, precision, and timing. Detaching from problems, we discover solutions. We learn to stop resisting and flow with the natural patterns, bringing greater joy and harmony to our lives.

The *Tao* leads outward, promoting successful action because it first leads inward. If we look beneath the clamor and clutter of our lives, we recognize our inner rhythms, which are part of the overarching rhythms of nature. By honoring these rhythms we bring greater peace to ourselves and our world.

The title of the *Tao Te Ching* underscores the vital relationship between inner and outer peace. *Ching* means simply a sacred book. But *Tao* means "the way," at once a path and principle of order. Translators have called it the single principle underlying all creation, the laws of nature, the truth, and the source of all life. The Chinese character for Tao* combines a head, representing wisdom, with the symbol for walking. A literal translation would be walking the path of wisdom, combining theory with praxis.

The word *Te* means virtue or character. Its Chinese symbol combines the signs for "to go," "straight," and "the heart." Transcending inner conflict, *Te* means living authentically, according to our true character. With the wisdom of *Te* we combine intuition with compassion; our actions are congruent with our deepest feelings. The *Tao Te Ching* is the path that leads straight from the heart.

Lao Tzu wrote that "peace is the goal of the way by which no one ever goes astray."[2] This new discussion of Lao Tzu's classic describes the Tao as the path to inner and outer peace. Drawing from many passages in the *Tao Te Ching,* the book presents the lessons of Tao in thematic order, beginning with peace of mind, then extending outward to the world around us.

Section 1 introduces the Taoist principles of dynamic balance, cyclical growth, oneness, and harmonious action. Section 2 shows how cooperating with these principles brings greater peace to our lives. Sections 3 and 4 describe the principles operating in nature and all our relationships. Section 5 demonstrates how we can use the lessons of Tao to build a more peaceful world.

On the surface, the book follows a linear progression, relating Taoist principles to the individual, to nature, then to problem solving

---

* To differentiate between *Tao,* the shortened title of the *Tao Te Ching,* and Tao, the concept, I have italicized only the former from this point on.

and politics. For the *Tao* teaches that peace grows outward from enlightened individuals. Yet we become enlightened by following the patterns of nature. Transcending linear organization, the *Tao Te Ching* portrays life as a unified process. A recent translator has called its organization "holographic,"[3] each chapter reflecting the greater wisdom of the whole. In this book, too, each chapter echoes the central message of Tao: our participation in an inclusive oneness, a process much larger than ourselves. This is at once the journey and the destination, the key to the *Tao of Peace*.

The lessons of Tao are explained with modern parallels and real life examples, many of them drawn from my own life and work. Personal assessments and exercises will help you apply these lessons to your life.

The Tao is a lifelong path, and I, too, am just beginning. The more I work with its principles, the more I realize their power to release new sources of joy and creativity, new solutions for all of us.

I suggest you read this book slowly, one chapter at a time, applying the lessons to your life by doing the personal exercises. Give yourself enough time to work with each one.

The Tao is a path of reflection and cooperation. You might want to work through some of the exercises with a friend or family member, reinforcing what you learn and sharing the way of Tao.

Each chapter opens with a quote from the *Tao Te Ching*, which you may use as a theme for meditation. How does its message relate to you?

Each chapter closes with an affirmation, reinforcing your oneness with an essential lesson of Tao. It can be a powerful tool in changing your consciousness and bringing greater peace to your life. Say this affirmation out loud to yourself in the morning. Or make a copy and review it throughout the day.

The *Tao* teaches that all life is process. We and our world are continuously evolving. As we follow our path into the future, we can move from turmoil and imbalance to restore our oneness with nature and one another. The *Tao* offers us new sources of power and inspiration, a vision of peace to transform ourselves and our world.

徳

SECTION
I

THE
WAY:
THEN
AND NOW

CHAPTER 1

BEGINNING THE JOURNEY

"A tree that reaches past your embrace grows from
   one small seed.
A structure over nine stories high begins with a handful
   of earth.
A journey of a thousand miles starts with a single step."

(TAO 64)

How did you begin your search for peace? I began mine with political activism in the sixties. My college friends and I marched, protested, and worked for social change. For a while, I felt personally empowered by the protests. We saw ourselves on the evening news and felt we were making a difference. In time our country even pulled out of Vietnam. But by the mid-seventies, most of us were exhausted and disillusioned. Placing all our hopes in some distant cause, we had ignored our personal needs. Many of us even wondered who we were.

So we plunged into the human potential movement, seeking solace in encounter groups, hot tubs, bodywork, and a colorful procession of gurus. The Maharishi, Maharaji, Bhagwan, and Werner Erhard all sold their own brands of inner peace. Blocking out the conflict around me, I went from Gestalt groups to gurus to physical therapies. Hundreds of classes, workshops, and self-help books later, I was a certified massage practitioner, teaching yoga at a holistic health center in northern California. My friends and I tried very hard to be peaceful. But something was missing. The conflict remained.

Most people are still at war with themselves and one another. We run through days of competition, confrontation, and mounting frustration, driven by the fear that we're "not good enough." At home and on the job, our lives are filled with dread. Our economy is troubled, our future uncertain, and the divorce rate has never been higher. Caught in a struggle between our ideals and grim necessity, we wrestle with the contradiction between what we are and what we "should" be. We live in the richest nation in the world, yet we are chronically insecure and defensive. Every day assaults us with new crises and conflicts on the evening news.

My personal search led to the *Tao Te Ching,* which offers a simple yet comprehensive vision of personal and planetary peace. In the *Tao* inner and outer peace are intrinsically related, as we are related to everything in our world.

Instead of waiting for the right guru or political leader to bring us the answer, the *Tao* asks us to take responsibility for our lives, to follow its path of action and contemplation. Through a shift of attitude, we can begin to experience greater peace right now. By seeing the larger patterns, we can take effective action, moving beyond competition to cooperation, harmonizing with the natural principles underlying all existence from the smallest cell to the largest social organism.

Self-Assessment

Let's begin by identifying any areas of our lives where we're not at peace. Do any of these statements sound familiar?

I'm not at peace in my body. It breaks down, knots up in tension, keeps me awake at night, aches, limps, gets into accidents, develops false growths, overeats, craves drugs or alcohol, feels awkward, fat, thin, old, weak, or powerless.

I'm not at peace in my career. It's filled with stress, tension, disappointment, problems, obnoxious people, impossible deadlines. I feel nervous, insecure, angry, closed in, held down, trapped, fearful, unhappy.

I'm not at peace in my relationships. I feel angry, resentful, jealous, fearful, anxious, insecure, bored, trapped, limited, manipulated, dominated, misunderstood, unable to communicate honestly with people I care about.

I'm not at peace in my family. I feel guilty, resentful, angry, bored, restless, exhausted, trapped, sabotaged, manipulated, overburdened with obligations. I cannot be myself with them.

I'm not at peace in my finances. I feel poor, anxious, resentful, limited, overwhelmed by bills and obligations. There's never enough to do what I want. I'm fearful of not having enough or guilty about what I have.

I'm not at peace with myself. I feel frustrated, guilty, confused. My life is filled with conflict. I never do what I want. I'm afraid to try. I procrastinate. I spend all my time pleasing others. I never accomplish anything. I'm often depressed. My life is filled with compulsive working, eating, shopping, drinking, or drugs. I'm not good enough.

I'm not at peace with my world. I feel nervous, anxious, guilty, depressed when I think about the future. I'm afraid of criminals, fascists, or communists. I have nightmares about war. I'm afraid of tomorrow because we're killing ourselves with pollution. There's nothing I can do. I hide behind cynicism or numbness. I feel powerless to change my world or my life.[1]

Becoming a Tao Person

Whatever the conflict in our lives, the first step on the path of peace is to shift our attitudes. According to the *Tao,* what matters is not the situation, but the way we perceive it.

A Tao person is someone who recognizes and works with the patterns of nature. Whatever our religious background or national origin, we become Tao people when we learn to think holistically, seeing our part in the unity of life, respecting the natural cycles within and around us.

Tao people are natural problem solvers. While others often fear conflict and change, a Tao person realizes that conflict is natural, that life constantly evolves through cycles of change. Non-Tao people perceive the world through a reductive dualism that makes them cling to the status quo. Tao people realize life has many options. Creative and resourceful, they flow with change, seeing beyond problems to solutions. One with Tao, they promote greater peace in their world.

Resolving Conflict with the Tao

When we're not one with Tao, we often become defensive, turning problems into blaming games.

I worked for a year during college as a medical receptionist. One day while the office was filled with patients, workmen were laying carpets in the examining rooms.

The phone rang incessantly, patients came and went, when suddenly I smelled smoke. The workmen had gone to lunch, leaving a hot iron plugged in, burning down into the floorboard. I ran into the room, pulled the plug, set the iron upright, and returned to my desk.

Then the commotion began. The doctor smelled smoke and began shouting at the nurses, who shouted at the office assistants. I watched as their faces grew red, their voices strident and defensive. "Whose fault was it?" they shrieked. "Who should have checked the examining rooms?"

I wondered to myself, what difference does it make whose fault it was? The point was to solve the problem.

The *Tao* teaches that

"Wise people seek solutions;
The ignorant only cast blame."

(TAO 79)

In far too many conflicts, both interpersonal and international, people become so busy blaming others and defending their egos that they forget to solve the problem, which in this case was as simple as pulling the plug.

Breathe in Tao

We've all been one with Tao, experiencing a deep sense of peace in meditation, communion with nature, or someone we love. When was the last time you had such an experience?

When confronting conflict, we can find peace within by recalling this feeling and concentrating on our breathing.

- Relax, take a deep breath, and say to yourself as you breath in, "Breathe in Tao." Breathe in that sense of peace and oneness. Let it flow through your body.
- Breathe out any negative emotion: fear, confusion, insecurity, whatever is troubling you.
- When you feel relaxed, affirm "I am one with Tao."
- Then examine the conflict. What would create greater harmony? What would a Tao person do?
- See yourself as that person, doing whatever it is you need to do. Get a clear vision of the process and feel at peace with the outcome. Affirm to yourself again, "I am one with Tao."
- Now apply your vision and take action, drawing upon the infinite source of peace within.

Avoiding the False Dilemma

For centuries Taoists have seen life as the creative synthesis of two opposing forces, *yin* and *yang*. In the *Tao*, all existence is created by this dynamic opposition:

"All life embodies *yin*
And embraces *yang,*
Through their union
Achieving harmony."

(TAO 42)

Recognizing this principle keeps us from falling into the false dilemma that narrows our choices to either/or: right or wrong, us or them, win or lose, all or nothing.

But all too often our vision is narrowed by the dualism so pervasive in western culture. Our options limited by linear reductionism, we perceive reality as two opposite points on a line. Unable to find a synthesis or consider other alternatives, non-Tao people become trapped in the false dilemma of either/or.

When I was a junior in college, my boyfriend offered me a marriage proposal which contained the false dilemma. He was a senior, concerned about his career. "If you love me," he said, "you'll drop out of school and work so I can go to grad school."

How could he ask me this, I wondered. Of course I loved him but I wanted to go to grad school too. Did I have to choose between love and my vocation?

We argued. Love, he said, meant caring about his future, our future together. He wanted to become a college professor. "You're being selfish," he said.

I refused to drop out of school and was angry at him for asking me to. How could he discount my ideals? I wanted to contribute something to the world.

Heartbroken, we each considered the other impossibly selfish, and we broke up. In our immaturity, we overlooked the other options. He could have worked for a year and saved his money. We could have gone to grad school together, working part time, getting student loans or scholarships.

As it happened, we both got Ph.D.s and became college professors. Sometimes I see his name in the alumni bulletin. But long ago our lives took different directions because we were blinded by the false dilemma.

PERSONAL EXERCISE

If you find yourself wrestling with a painful internal conflict, step back. Don't get caught in the false dilemma.

- Look beyond the conflict. Ask yourself, "What would I really *like* to do?" Then think of all the possible ways to get there.
- Brainstorm with a friend who will write down your answers without comment. Later you can decide which ones will work for you.
- Or take out a piece of paper and write down your goal and all the possible options—no matter how outrageous. Free yourself to see the infinite possibilities that lie before you.
- Then review your answers, accepting some possibilities, discarding others. Make an action plan.

Whenever you face a false dilemma, look beyond it. There are always more than two alternatives. Throw off the blinders of custom to reveal the creative wisdom of Tao.

The Strength of Bamboo

The Tao guides us with lessons from nature. For centuries, Chinese calligraphers have painted bamboo as a spiritual exercise. Bamboo is graceful, upright, and strong. Hollow inside, receptive, and humble, it bends with the wind but does not break.

Flexible, resourceful, open to new possibilities, people of Tao are strong in any situation. Avoiding pride and rigidity, they adjust to life's changes, harmonizing in their own patterns of growth. Non-Tao people only resist. The *Tao* tells us:

"At birth all people are soft and yielding.
At death they are hard and stiff.
All green plants are tender and yielding.
At death they are brittle and dry.
When hard and rigid,
We consort with death.
When soft and flexible,
We affirm greater life."

(TAO 76)

The most devastating experience many people face is being fired or laid off. A non-Tao person is often destroyed, unable to move forward, to overcome the shame and confusion. Many have fallen into severe depression, have even committed suicide.

The man or woman of Tao sees crisis as an opportunity. Like the bamboo, Tao people bend and grow, adjusting to the winds of change. They look within, take stock of their lives, and set new goals.

In 1986 a group of women were laid off when Bendel's, a New York specialty shop, was bought out by a large chain. People at Bendel's had been proud of their work, their reputation for creativity and resourcefulness. Some had worked there for 30 years and Bendel's had become another family.

Losing this was a profound shock, yet within months these women began new ventures. Buyers Joy DaRos and Yelena Dieterichs opened successful boutiques, catalogue editor Pat Tennant became director of Monarch Catalogues, merchandising director Jean Rosenberg opened three designer shops, and Bendel's president Geraldine Stutz became publisher and president of Panache Press, a division of Random House. Instead of succumbing to despair, these women took stock of their lives, set new goals, and followed their dreams.

A TAO QUESTION

Is a crisis in your life actually an opportunity to follow through on an unrealized dream? Take some time by yourself. Look within, and you will know.

There's an old saying, "When one door closes, another opens." Tao people recognize that door because they're open to new possibilities.

Opportunities often appear when we follow our natural curiosity. When I was a grad student at UCLA I noticed a new restaurant opening in my neighborhood, "Colonel Beuregard's New Orlean's Restaurant and Gumbo Shop." Intrigued, I walked across the street and looked in the window. The owner peered out at me, asking if I wanted a job. I didn't. I was a research assistant at UCLA, but to make up for my curiosity I signed his register and promised I'd be back to try the food.

Weeks later, the UCLA budget was cut and all the research assistants suddenly laid off. My friend Janette and I were sitting in my apartment wondering what to do when the phone rang. It was the owner of Colonel Beuregard's asking when I'd like to come to work. Two days later I was the cashier, enjoying a job that gave me the income I needed, a free Creole dinner five nights a week, and a pleasant diversion from my studies. Following my curiosity had led me into a new opportunity at just the right time.

The *Tao* encourages us to be spontaneous, to follow our natural inclinations, to keep on learning, and to watch the changing patterns within and around us. Remember, nothing in the universe stands still. We are evolving souls.

Affirmation

I now know my life is peaceful and harmonious.
I see the larger patterns within and around me.
I open up to new insights.
I affirm the strength of bamboo.
I am an evolving soul.
I am one with Tao.
I respect myself and the process.
I harmonize with nature and all others in my world.
I accept greater peace in my life now.
And so it is.

CHAPTER 2

TAO AND TE

"Follow the Tao
And live in harmony.
Cultivate character (*Te*)
And develop your highest potential.
Te and *Tao*
Are the way of life.
Abandon either
And the Tao abandons you."

(TAO 23)

LIFE is dynamic. Like a river it constantly flows, its currents forming new patterns from the interacting elements. To follow Tao is
to flow like a river, to recognize our part in the ever-evolving universe. With our personal currents—our actions and attitudes—we
contribute to the larger process. This is perhaps the most essential
lesson of Tao: that we have the power to make a difference—in our
lives and our world.

There's an old metaphysical saying, "As it is within, so it is without." We renew our outer lives by turning within, by developing
greater *Te* or character.

In Chinese *Te* means personal power, the ability to see clearly, to
act decisively, to be at the right place at the right time. The ancient
Chinese referred to seeds as *Te,* for they have the power to spring
forth as new life.[1]

What Is a Tao Person?

When we release our potential and flow with nature, we become
people of Tao. Centered, creative, and dynamic, Tao people are like

the self-actualizing men and women studied by psychologist Abraham Maslow. Like monks and mystics, they listen to the inner voice and follow the call of their souls,[2] demonstrating how high the human spirit can reach.

Tao people are flexible, spontaneous, and optimistic. They have an active sense of humor, a deep love of life. Sustained by their faith in something larger than themselves, they reach out in creative work and loving service.

We become men and women of Tao when we dare to live authentically and fulfill our greatest potential. How do we do this? By developing *Te*.

Te Is Seeing Clearly

Tao people see clearly, without illusions about themselves or their world. *Te* means seeking the truth in all experience, recognizing nature's patterns and our own. The search for truth frees us from pretense:

"Those who know they do not know
Gain wisdom.
Those who pretend they know
Remain ignorant.

Those who acknowledge their weakness
Become strong.
Those who flaunt their power
Will lose it.

Wisdom and power
Follow truth above all.
For truth is the way of Tao.

(TAO 71)

Many people feel it's a sign of weakness to admit they don't know something. The *Tao* says it's a sign of strength, an opportunity to learn.

When Al was studying at Rutgers, the other graduate students were always asking if he had read this or that learned book. At lunch, over coffee, the uncomfortable questions would arise: "Have you seen the latest book by Stanley Fish? What do you think of Northrop Frye's seasonal theory of genre? Did you see the latest book on deconstructionism?"

His face red with embarrassment, Al would sit in awkward silence, staring into his coffee cup. He not only hadn't read the books, he didn't know the first thing about the authors.

Raised as an Iowa farm boy, Al was the only one in his family to go to college. He'd made decent grades all right, gone to Iowa State, and gotten a graduate fellowship to Rutgers. But with his faded jeans, plaid shirts, and limited knowledge, he still felt fresh off the farm.

His classmates seemed much more sophisticated. They wore tweed jackets, read the *Times Literary Supplement,* and discussed the critics as if they were personal friends.

The next time he faced those questions, Al walked off by himself, turning the problem over in his mind. He hadn't studied Eastern philosophy, but his closeness to nature had given him the fundamental honesty of *Te*.

Te means choosing truth above ego. Al realized the questions were a test of truth. He could lie to protect his ego or accept each question as an opportunity to learn.

Al chose truth. No longer embarrassed, he would answer "No, I haven't read that book. Could you tell me more about it?" and then decide whether to study it for himself.

After completing his graduate work, Al began teaching college English. His best qualities remain his honesty, enthusiasm, and ability to learn. His example encourages others and has made him an outstanding teacher.

PERSONAL EXERCISE

The next time you come up against an area of ignorance in your life, watch what happens when you admit you don't know and ask for more information. Honesty not only provides us with the opportunity to learn, it also removes the strain of defensive egotism, prevents inner conflict, and brings us peace of mind.

Remember: "Those who know they do not know gain wisdom."

Men and women of Tao seek truth above all else. They have no time for pretense.

Te Means Self-Acceptance

Tao people accept themselves as they are. They don't waste their energy in self-criticism.

In nature everything is valuable, everything has its place. Only human beings suffer from low self-esteem. A rose, a daisy, a lark, a squirrel—each manifests its potential differently, yet beautifully. Each form has its own expression, each flower its own fragrance, each bird its own song.

Martha works herself to exhaustion because she hasn't learned self-acceptance. An attractive brunette, she's just begun her career as a sociologist, having earned her Ph.D. after her children were grown.

Mercilessly self-critical, Martha spends all day meeting with clients, students, and colleagues, consuming quarts of Coca-Cola to keep herself alert. Then she works late into the night preparing reports, reading essays, writing lectures and articles in her field.

Martha's schedule is crammed with commitments. She rarely sees her family and hasn't taken a vacation in years. When she has a few days off, she collapses in exhaustion. She slept through Thanksgiving on medication and spent most of Christmas laid up with a bad back.

Any of Martha's colleagues will tell you her workshops are excellent, her work first rate, yet she lives in constant fear of criticism, often overlooking her own strengths. Although she'd rather work with people, she just volunteered to do a complex statistical analysis because it seemed more professional. Now she's stuck doing a job she hates.

Martha's compulsiveness actually keeps her from the success she seeks. Not only does she take on projects that don't suit her, she also reduces her creativity by overloading herself with commitments.

With greater self-acceptance, Martha could be healthier and more successful. As a Tao person, she would respect her own patterns, allowing her real talents to express themselves.

Compulsively proving ourselves only clutters our lives. With self-acceptance comes peace.

"The Tao person knows herself
And makes no display,
Accepts herself
And is not arrogant."

(TAO 72)

Self-acceptance brings humility. The Chinese word for humility, *hsu*, also means emptiness or openness. Tao people express themselves openly, without pretense or posing. Because they're centered, neither criticism nor flattery upsets them. The judgment of others does not disturb us when we know who we are.

TAO QUESTION

Too often we feel inferior because we don't fit some stereotype. *Te* means being more of ourselves, not an imitation of someone else.

Ask yourself: what makes me different from the other people I know? What is my special contribution to this life?

- Are you happier taking a quiet walk by yourself or joining a bustling crowd?
- Are you a people person or more contemplative?
- Do you express yourself with pencils, paints, or colorful yarns?
- Are you a practical person, proud of your home repairs and building projects?
- Are you musical? Mathematical? Good with figures and finances?

We each have some talent that makes us unique. What is yours? Acknowledge and nurture that part of yourself with a special activity today.

Te Means Detachment

Tao people are detached and nonjudgmental. They act with clarity and precision because they don't waste time criticizing others.

"The Tao person, detached and wise,
Embraces all as Tao."

(TAO 49)

My friend Genevieve Farrow is a minister and metaphysical counselor. Gen is over seventy but looks much younger. Years of devotional reading and meditation have brought her serenity and detachment.

She grew up in rural Minnesota, where her Swedish ancestors settled during the last century. At twelve, when her father died and her mother suffered from heart disease, Gen took care of the household. The sickness and poverty sent her on a spiritual quest. She learned to detach, to see herself as part of a larger whole.

Detachment doesn't mean turning a cold shoulder to the world. Far from it. It means transcending ego, caring without getting caught up in day to day commotion. Watching life's changing panorama with patience, acceptance, and good humor, Gen never criticizes others. She accepts them as they are, saying simply, "We're all here to learn."

Often her loving detachment provides just the support people need to take charge of their lives.

One autumn day Gen was walking down the street when a bedraggled young man asked her for a cigarette. While others had merely walked by, Gen paused and answered, "No, I never learned to smoke." Then she looked at him closely, her blue eyes filled with compassion.

Unshaven and dirty, he had undoubtedly lived on the street for some time. He was slumped over, dejected, and his worn green poncho barely kept out the cold. On his feet were old brown oxfords without laces or socks. But he was young and strong.

"Why don't you get a job and buy your own cigarettes?" she asked.

He looked back at her, surprised that someone was speaking to him, then started to tell his story. "Well, I've been down because my girlfriend left me," wandering aimlessly ever since. His voice trailed off.

Looking at Gen, something clicked in his mind. "My mother lives near here," he said. "But I don't want to bother her."

"No mother is ever bothered by her own son," Gen said.

The young man nodded. Perhaps she was right. "I could get a job. I've worked as a house painter," he said, and slowly walked away.

He stopped, turned around, and asked, "Who are you?"

"My name is Gen Farrow," she said.

"Mine is Victor," he replied. He paused for a moment, then suddenly hugged her. "You're beautiful," he said. "Thanks a million. I think I'll go to my mother's and take a bath."

Then he walked off, his body straighter and a new determination in his stride.

Gen had given him nothing but a few moments of attention. Without fear, without guilt, her concern and respect for this lost young man had awakened something deep within him.[3]

Te is this mixture of compassion and detachment. We give emotional support while respecting the rights of others to find their own way. Our detachment frees us from fear, enabling us to participate in the greater harmony.

Te Means Not Trying But Doing

Lao Tzu tells us:

"Tao people never try. They do."

(TAO 48)[4]

Tao people never try. They don't waste time worrying or efforting. They dare, take risks, live with commitment. Family therapist Tom Suzuki teaches his clients the way of Tao. At one group counseling session a woman promised she'd try to communicate more honestly with her son.

"Try?" Suzuki responded in a low, gutteral voice. He paused, rose from his chair, and stood motionless before us, his compact frame suddenly charged with power. He seemed somehow centuries older, venerable, inscrutable, a master of Tao.

Walking deliberately to the center of the room, he dropped his pen on the floor. Repeatedly he bent down, trying to pick it up.

"I'm trying, I'm trying," he said. But the pen remained on the floor.

Then he stood back and said sharply, "Don't try. *Do* it," snatching up the pen in his hand. The lesson was clear: trying is only a half-hearted attempt. The effort without the intention cannot succeed. "Tao people never try. They do."

Non-Tao people hold themselves back, don't give their full effort because they're afraid of change, afraid of making mistakes.

Tao people take risks. They learn by doing. *Te* means living with commitment, realizing that life is continuous change, that even failures bring us closer to the truth.

In the last century Henry David Thoreau moved to a small cabin by Walden Pond, explaining "I went to the woods because I wished to live deliberately, to front only the essential facts of life, and see if I could not learn what it had to teach, and not, when I came to die, discover that I had not lived."[5]

Te means daring to live deliberately. Tao people have no time for halfhearted attempts.

TAO QUESTION

Is there an area in your life where you have been holding back, "trying" instead of doing?

- If so, ask yourself what would happen if you really committed yourself.
- Have you been afraid of failure . . . or success?
- What would happen if you failed?
- What changes would success bring to your life?
- Ask yourself if you really *want* to follow through with this activity.
- If so, stop trying. Do it.

Te Means Thinking Independently

Te means living with the courage of our convictions, transcending social norms. Tao people aren't afraid to think for themselves.

In ancient China there were two great teachers, Lao Tzu and Confucius. Confucius upheld elaborate rituals of etiquette and social duty. He taught filial piety, reverence of ancestors, and conventional rules for business, politics, and relationships.

Lao Tzu opposed rigid rules and enforced courtesy, affirming instead the path with heart. Following the *Tao* means to live compassionately, intuitively, flowing with the present moment. The way of Confucius molds people with social convention; the way of Lao Tzu frees us to be more truly ourselves.

An old story says that once Confucius visited Lao Tzu and was mystified by the source of his power. It was not rational, not predictable. Confucius understood the power in the wings of birds, the fins of fish, the legs of animals, which can be overcome with arrows, nets, and traps. But, he said, "Who knows how dragons surmount wind and cloud into heaven? This day I have seen Lao Tzu and he is a dragon."[6]

Te is the way of the dragon, leaving old assumptions, conventions, and prejudices far behind us.

Today the way of Confucius is strong. Pressures from all sides push us to conform; to please our parents, family, and friends; or to capitulate to an institution. *Te* means never losing ourselves in a group, a job, a relationship. To do so is to lose Tao.

Te Means Expanding our Self

Tao people do not subordinate themselves to a group or institution. They expand outward to encompass all of life. Transcending ego, they experience a spiritual kinship with all the life on this planet. They grieve when someone is injured, rejoice in another's good. Humanitarian work comes naturally to them:

"Through loving service,
They attain fulfillment."

(TAO 7)

Some devote their lives to service, like Albert Schweitzer in his clinic in Lambaréné. Others coordinate service with their careers. *Saturday Review* editor Norman Cousins arranged reconstructive surgery for young Japanese women injured in the atomic blast on Hiroshima. Working with hundreds of concerned readers, he brought the Hiroshima maidens to America, arranging housing, adoptions, and funding.

Today these women live normal, productive lives. After the surgery, they received rehabilitation and training, and began new careers. Most have married and had children. Without the operations they would have been outcasts for life. During their treatment, they became friends with many Americans, once their enemies. One man's shock at the tragedy of Hiroshima helped heal some of the pain between our nations.

Te Means Faith in Life

Tao people have a reverence for life, a faith in the larger process. This faith sustains them, affirming the power of their actions.

Had Norman Cousins lacked faith during the Hiroshima project, the young women would have missed the chance for a better life. Had Albert Schweitzer doubted himself, he would have remained in his secure home in Alsace, never venturing into Africa to fulfill his destiny.

Sustained by their faith, Tao people do not fear change, nor do they surrender to adversity. The complex problems of our age tempt us to pessimism, but pessimism brings moral paralysis. It does not serve us. Norman Cousins once said, "Pessimism is a waste of time."[7] We have to believe we can make a difference. Acting on this belief, we become people of Tao.

Te Means Living Here and Now

Tao people aren't haunted by ghosts of the past or phantoms of the future. They accept the gift of today and make the best use of it they can.

"The Tao person
Lives fully in every moment."

(TAO 14)

Our full attention is the Taoist point of power. When we are totally present, we generate tremendous energy. Yet how rare it is to give our full attention to anything. Most people spend their days in internal monologues of worry, future plans, and self-criticism. Even while listening to others we are rehearsing our answers, slipping back into yesterday, or worrying about tomorrow.

PERSONAL EXERCISE

We can develop *Te* by practicing greater presence. Make it a point today to give full attention to something for at least half an hour, whether it's sharing with a friend, taking a walk, or doing some household chore.

- If you're with a friend, really listen. Tune in to the other person's words, body language, tone of voice. Be present with the energies that flow between you.
- If you're walking, look at the trees, the sky, the houses around you. Notice the colors, the textures, the fragrance of trees and flowers. What about the people you see? Do your eyes meet? What sounds do you hear? At times a simple walk can be as powerful as a prayer.
- If you're at home, slow down. While cleaning, notice the patterns of life in the old oak furniture, the beauty of a hardwood floor. While making a salad, recognize the pattern in each vegetable. Like tiny suns, carrots radiate outward from their centers. Red tomatoes and green bell peppers are filled with the seeds of life.

When you're fully present, fully aware, you can make the most of every moment. The Tao is here and now.

Te Means Embracing Life Joyously

Tao people have more energy because they greet life with enthusiasm. The positive emotions—love, joy, humor—energize us and activate our immune systems. Depression only depletes us.

Many people hide behind defensiveness, afraid to love, to reach out and embrace life. Yet Gerald Jampolsky's work with the chronically ill at the Center for Attitudinal Healing has shown that love removes pain and often works miracles.

Jampolsky tells of one young women named Colleen who was legally blind, having suffered since birth from rentrolental fibroplasia, a painful, progressive blindness. Unhappy and resentful, she joined an attitudinal healing group at the Center.

There she learned to release her resentment and limiting beliefs, to express greater love to those around her. The pain subsided, as she felt more at peace with herself and her world. Then slowly, miraculously, her sight returned. Her eye doctor says he's never seen such a recovery in anyone with this condition.

Colleen now has a joyous new life. Working in the field of holistic health, she's helping others realize the healing power of love.[8]

The Tao of Laughter

As far back as Aristotle, people in the western world realized that laughter releases tension. It can even heal "incurable" diseases, as Norman Cousins demonstrated in *Anatomy of an Illness*. Most of us know how he activated his body's healing energies by watching old comedy movies in the hospital, taking vitamin C, eating healthy foods, and affirming positive emotions.

His example has given hope to millions and led him from the world of publishing into the healing profession. He's now a professor at the UCLA medical school, where he shares his good humor and positive approach with students, patients, and colleagues.

Like Norman Cousins, Tao people retain their sense of humor even while committed to issues of social justice. Is this a contradiction? No, it is the way of Tao. Tao people never agonize over problems but greet life with courage, joy, and good humor. Laughter brings greater detachment, helps us see life's ironies and recognize the larger whole.

For non-Tao people life is a constant struggle because they take themselves too seriously. Tao people can laugh at themselves. The Tao itself elicits laughter because it defies convention. As Lao Tzu tells us:

"When a conventional person hears about Tao,
He breaks into loud laughter.

If there were no laughter,
It would not be Tao."

(TAO 41)

TAO QUESTION

How long has it been since you really laughed at something? Today look for the little ironies of life and enjoy them. Start living more spontaneously. Do something just for the fun of it. See a funny movie, take time out to play. And remember to share your joy with others. Reach out with enthusiasm, compliments, surprises. Give everyone an energizing boost by being more enthusiastically yourself.

Affirmation

I now know my life is peaceful and harmonious.
I manifest greater *Te* in my life.
I live with joy and commitment.
I accept myself and others.
I express myself openly and honestly.
I reach out in loving service.
I do not try; I do.
I respect myself and the process.
I harmonize with nature and all others in my world.
I accept greater peace in my life now.
And so it is.

CHAPTER 3

PRINCIPLES OF TAO

The greatest wisdom
Is to follow the Tao.
The Tao is mysterious, unfathomable,
Yet within is all that lives;
Unfathomable, mysterious,
Yet within is the essence;
Shadowy, intangible,
Yet within are vital principles,
Principles of truth
Informing all creation,
The lessons of life
Inherent in Tao.

(TAO 21)

As we recognize life's patterns and flow with them, we become people of Tao. Yet often these patterns are not what we expect. The *Tao* tells us that:

"The way to greater light leads through the darkness.
Going ahead feels like falling back.
The even path seems rugged and hilly,
The highest power a yielding valley."

(TAO 41)

All is not as it seems. Following the Tao at first feels like self-denial. To find peace, must we abandon our goals and values? No indeed.

The *Tao* asks us not that we deny who we are but that we live more creatively. What seems like surrender actually produces greater success in life.

Tao people are successful because they're at peace with themselves. Free from inner conflict, they have more energy than others. We, too, can achieve this by embracing the mystery of Tao and living its four great principles of oneness, dynamic balance, cyclical growth, and harmonious action.

Embracing the Mystery

Following the Tao requires a fundamental change in our approach to life. We must stop analyzing, stop trying to understand the Tao rationally.

As Lao Tzu tells us:

"The Tao that has been charted is not the eternal Way.
A word we can define is not the eternal Word.
Wu, the eternal, existed before heaven and earth.
We know it as *yu,* the source of ten thousand things."

(TAO 1)

The Tao cannot be reduced to names and formulas. It is *wu ming,* without a name, because it's the source of all existence. In its infinite creative potential the Tao is *wu,* eternal non-being. In its created existence it is *yu,* eternal being. Eternally changing and evolving, it is neither one nor the other: always both.

Like the Tao, we cannot be reduced to categories. Each of us exists in our current state of life and our infinite potential. We are both what we are and what we might be. Herein lies the strength of *wu:* our unlimited capacity for growth and change. Knowing at any moment we may begin a new cycle of creation, we can draw upon the power of *wu* in our lives.

Frank grew up during the 1920s on a small farm in Kentucky. An only child, he was quiet and serious, a skinny blond kid with an anxious smile. His parents were the children of German immigrants, his father a gardener, his mother a devout Catholic who talked about saints and went to church twice a day. Times were hard, they had little money, and dinner was usually coffee, kraut, and potatoes.

A child of the Depression with two paper routes and a variety of odd jobs, Frank had little time for play. Once he saved his money to buy a baseball mitt, but his mother told him this was foolishness and made him take it back. At fourteen, his life was cut out for him. He was to work his way through Catholic high school and become a priest as his mother wanted.

On the long afternoons at school he tried to concentrate but grew increasingly restless. Gazing out the window, he longed for something beyond the small classroom and rigid rules. He shifted in his chair, his leg cramped from hours at the wood and wrought iron desk. Peering down at him in her long black robes, the nun reprimanded him and he wondered, "Was daydreaming really a sin?"

While working in the fields one day, Frank saw a small airplane fly overhead. Soaring above the treetops, free and clear, the plane seemed to beckon as it dipped its wings and circled to land.

Frank dropped his shovel and started running. He'd heard that pilots would give a boy a quarter to tie a plane down. A quarter was a lot of money during the Depression. But he wasn't thinking about quarters as he ran down the dusty country road. He wasn't really thinking at all.

Breathless, he reached the small landing strip two miles away. The bright yellow biplane had just touched down. Its engine still roaring, it seemed like everything he was not. Powerful and free, it could ride the wind, soaring high above the narrow frame houses and the dark Kentucky soil.

Frank had come face to face with *wu*. The limitless potential welled up inside him. He knew he had to fly.

Of course his parents didn't understand. His father was content to work in the soil, and his mother's view of the heavens was far different.

"What's all this crazy talk about flying machines?" she said. "If God had meant men to fly, he'd have given them wings."

The controversy continued. But Frank kept going to the airport, tying down planes, washing and fueling them, anything to get up for short flights. Soaring above the earth into the great unknown, he found a new world of possibilities.

When the discord at home became too much, he moved into the attic of the Louisville Flying Service, where he was adopted by barnstormers and World War I pilots.

Days were long. He still had his paper routes, then school, then back to the airport to do odd jobs and learn as much as he could. After sundown he'd eat his main meal of the day—a bowl of bean soup with as many free crackers as he could manage—at the airport coffee shop while talking to pilots. At 16, he got his pilot's license and was featured in the *Louisville Courier-Journal* as the youngest pilot in Kentucky.

Frank became a flight instructor and an Air Force colonel, flying everything from biplanes to seaplanes to jets and rescue helicopters, and circling the globe many times. At age 72 he remains an active flight instructor, still riding the winds and showing others the way. I admire him for his free and generous spirit, and I'm proud that he's my father.

Frank Dreher's life demonstrates that we need not be confined to what is or has been. By discovering the power of *wu,* by drawing on our unlimited potential, we too can ride the winds of greater possibility.

PERSONAL EXERCISE

- Is there an area of *wu* in your life that beckons to you, daring you to reach out and develop more of yourself?
- What direction does it lead? Close your eyes and visualize what it would be like to follow this path. Are you excited by the prospect?
- If so, ask yourself, "What is the first step I need to get there?" Make a list of these steps and commit to taking the first one. Begin now to release the power of *wu* in your life.

Exploring Wu in Intuition

Recent studies of the human brain have pointed to a significant area of *wu* in our culture. The two cerebral hemispheres perform different functions. The left brain controls speech, analysis, and logical thinking. The right apprehends symbolically and intuitively, perceiving the whole rather than disparate parts.

For centuries, western civilization has emphasized left brain thinking, developing our strength in science and technology while virtually discounting our intuitive capacity. For most of us, the right brain remains *wu,* a frontier of hidden potential. Exploring this frontier brings us closer to Tao.

Lao Tzu tells us, "a word we can define is not the eternal Word" (*Tao* 1). The Tao cannot be defined, apprehended, or articulated by left brain reasoning. But this doesn't mean it cannot be known. We know the Tao intuitively, by transcending rational thought patterns.

The Principle of Oneness

"The Tao person embraces the One
And lives in peace by its pattern."

(TAO 22)[1]

According to psychiatrist Jean Shinoda Bolen, "almost everyone, at some time in his or her life, has had a Tao experience," a flash of insight that takes us beyond ourselves.[2] In these moments of inspiration, we transcend our separateness, becoming one with all life. Poets have written about this experience for centuries.

Whether we find our unifying vision in nature, love, religion, meditation, or even in crisis, at such times we are one with Tao. Perceiving not logically but intuitively, we experience a common bond with all creation. When we return to normal consciousness, glimmers of that vision remain to guide us.

Oneness with Nature

We become one with Tao when we study nature and look within. These two practices are intrinsically linked, for our inner world reflects the world around us. We are one with nature. Its laws are our laws.

The Chinese character for nature or heaven (天) adds two parallel lines to the character for man (人). In Chinese thought, we are part of nature, intimately related to the sky over our heads and the earth beneath our feet. To ignore this bond or defile nature is to injure ourselves.

Western civilization has long ignored our oneness with nature because of a split in consciousness in the late seventeenth century. The powerful logic of René Descartes and the scientific method of Sir Francis Bacon led to tremendous technological progress. But they also left us with a dangerous dualism which separates us from nature and one another. For centuries we have divided our minds and bodies, thoughts and feelings, civilization and nature, ourselves and one another, into disparate and competing polarities.

Modern physics leads us back to the Tao, describing the universe as an integrated whole which transcends polarization. The basic building blocks of existence are not infinitesimal bits of matter as once was thought, but probabilities, dynamic patterns of energy, neither particles nor waves but something in between.[3] David Bohm's concept of "implicate order" describes the universe as a hologram in which each part reflects and contains the whole. The S–Matrix theory, proposed by Geoffrey Chew, portrays the universe as a "dynamic web of interrelated events."[4]

The world is a Gestalt with the whole infinitely more than the sum of its parts. No longer content to understand nature by analyzing separate parts, science has become increasingly interested in the *relationships* between these parts.

By focusing on interdependent energy patterns, the new physics offers a lesson for human interactions. Each of us is more than our ego-bound limits. We know this the moment we enter a room and sense its subtle vibrations. We breathe the same air, share the same energy with others around us. Their energy and attitudes inevitably touch our own. Life does not occur in isolation. We are all one in Tao.

TAO QUESTION

When was the last time you experienced energies beyond your ego boundaries? How did it feel when you entered an office or party full of unfamiliar people? Was there personal warmth? Anxiety? Hostility? We can and do feel these things all the time.

I noticed these patterns when joining a local health spa. Of the two spas in my neighborhood, the first felt friendly, lively, and positive. Although the equipment was worn and the walls needed a coat of paint, the energies were high.

The other place looked better but just didn't feel right. Luxuriously appointed, filled with gleaming chrome equipment, attractive patrons, and a high-powered sales staff, it felt troubled and uncomfortable. I wanted to leave as soon as I arrived. Sensing something was wrong, I joined the other spa.

One month after my visit, the owners of the second spa declared bankruptcy and went out of business, leaving hundreds of patrons with nothing to show for their "lifetime memberships." I still enjoy going to the spa I chose, which has recently gotten more equipment and a bright new coat of paint.

TAO REMINDER

Become more aware of the atmosphere around you. By recognizing the subtle, intangible patterns you can make wiser decisions in your life.

The Principle of Dynamic Balance

"Having and not having produce one another.
Difficult and easy balance each other.
Long and short complete one another.
High and low rely on each other.
Pitch and tone make harmony together.
Beginning and ending follow each other."

(TAO 2)

The Tao teaches that life is composed of complementary opposites: yin and yang. Yang is active, dynamic, assertive; yin is quiet, yielding, receptive. In nature yin and yang combine in patterns of highs and lows, mountains and valleys, turbulence and tranquility.

Pacific coast tide pools are a perfect example. When the forces of *yin* and *yang* are in balance, each small pool becomes a tiny, self-contained world. I've spent hours peering into these microcosms of marine life, watching the surf grass swaying gently to and fro, the pink anemones opening like flowers in bloom. Hermit crabs scurry about, and schools of small fish dart by, glittering in the light of the afternoon sun.

Every day the tide washes in with new sources of water and nutrients, providing the active force of *yang*. The *yin* enclosure in the rocky cliffs protects the tiny world from the pounding waves.

Balance is vital. Pools too far from the rushing waters become stagnant, excessively *yin*. Too close to the *yang* of the turbulent surf, other pools hold only sand and water, too unsettled to sustain life.

Nature renews itself by balancing these forces, but too often modern society drives us to exhaustion with continuous frenetic *yang* activity. As we strive to acquire more, our busy behavior shuts out the wisdom of *yin*. We all need periods of quiet reflection.

Too much stasis and, like the distant tide pools, we experience stagnation. Our lives become dull and monotonous. Without the active *yang* of career commitment, life becomes too *yin* for many retired people. They need to find new interests, new challenges. Some do this in second careers or volunteer work. One friend recently retired from her secretarial job to work full time for peace.

In earlier times, men and women were polarized into stereotyped roles. Men were supposed to be *yang*: strong, active, aggressive; women were *yin*: passive, yielding, nurturing. But not all subscribed to this tradition. Twenty-five centuries ago, the *Tao* condemned rigid roles as unnatural and unhealthy. Lao Tzu must have raised a few eyebrows in his time by telling masculine leaders to embrace the *yin*, the valley, the traditional way of women. But he knew the Tao transcends extremes, affirming the wisdom of wholeness.

We develop greater wisdom and strength by integrating both forces in our lives. If we are too *yang*—active, outspoken, and goal-oriented—we can become impatient and uncentered. Too busy doing, we make mistakes because we don't take time to listen.

If we are always *yin*—listening, waiting, nurturing, putting others' needs before our own—we become timid, passive, and weak.

The Tao person knows when to speak up, when to listen, when to act and when to wait. Balancing the forces within and without, Tao men and women are strong and flexible, courageous and wise.

PERSONAL EXERCISE

Take a few minutes now to get in touch with the complementary opposites in your life.

- What for you is active *yang*?
- What is quiet *yin*?
- If you spend your days working around lots of people and noise, how do you renew yourself? How do you nurture the quiet currents of *yin*?
- If your days are spent quietly, what can you do to bring greater *yang* into your life?

When we take time to live more consciously, we don't react mindlessly to our environment. Our days are filled with active choices, balancing the currents of *yin* and *yang* into greater harmony.

The Principle of Cyclical Growth

"The Tao moves by returning
In endless cycles.
By yielding, it overcomes,
Creating the ten thousand things,
Being from nonbeing.

(TAO 40)

We are part of a universal pattern of growth which renews itself in cycles. Moving from day to night, spring to winter, active *yang* is inevitably followed by dormant *yin,* which gives birth to new *yang*.

The oak table, the walls around you, the roof overhead—may *appear* solid, but are actually composed of billions of tiny particles whirling in cycles of incessant energy, tiny universes unto themselves, continuously evolving. Similarly, every cell in our bodies is constantly changing. We are not the same people we once were. Each year much of our body tissue is renewed through metabolic change. The dance of life goes on within and around us. Nothing in the universe stands still.

The wisdom of Tao is to recognize these cycles and harmonize with them. Often, in our impatience, we ignore this lesson.

Working with plants reminds us to honor the cycles. One year I let a succession of houseguests distract me from my gardening until late summer. In September I went to buy seeds and bedding plants, convinced that California's long growing season would give me time for a good harvest.

The Japanese nurseryman shook his head. "Too late for beans and squash," he said. "Now you plant winter vegetables—broccoli and onions."

But I wanted yellow squash and green beans. The days were still warm, so I ignored his advice and planted some early-germinating seeds. When the plants came up, I laughed to myself and looked for a bountiful harvest.

Two months later, I learned once more to respect the cycles. The squash and beans sprang up briefly, then succumbed to blight and mildew. They needed the long hot summer days to bear good fruit.

The Tao teaches us to conquer our impatience, to work with the cycles. Our projects, like the seeds we plant, have different seasons. Some spring up quickly. Others take longer to germinate, even longer to bear fruit. All the impatience in the world will not change the process.

Our lives, as well, have their cycles. Some people are early bloomers, at their peak in high school and their early twenties. Springing up like corn stalks in the hot summer days, they come to harvest in one short season.

Others grow more slowly. Watching the corn stalks shoot up above them, they often lose heart, wondering if they'll harvest anything of value. The seventeenth-century English poet John Milton wrote a sonnet despairing of how little he'd accomplished by age 23. Yet at 59 he published *Paradise Lost,* the greatest epic in the English language.

While a corn stalk comes to harvest in one short season, an oak tree takes years to mature. But then it towers above the cornfield, its branches reaching toward the sky, bearing fruit for many a season.

Corn stalks, oak trees, green beans, or broccoli: everything that lives has its cycle, its purpose, its part in the Tao.

TAO QUESTION

Take a moment to consider the cycles in your life. Look for the larger patterns.

- Which are the short cycles?
- Which are the longer ones?
- What areas do you need to cultivate more actively?
- Where do you need to be more patient and respectful of the process?

The Principle of Harmonious Action

The *Tao* teaches us to cooperate with the natural patterns in our world. This is the principle of harmonious action or *wu wei:* blending with the energies around us without imposing our will on other life forms.

A good gardener prunes a tree carefully so the effect is natural. When walking in the woods, a Tao person leaves no tracks and certainly no debris. Walking lightly on the earth, men and women of Tao live in harmony with their environment. Respectful of nature, they do not disturb or pollute.

Respectful of their own natures, Tao people do not oppose their personal patterns. Their daily activities and careers are harmonious expressions of who they are. Living the Tao is like working with wood. One must not go against the grain.

Laura learned this lesson when she began her career as a commercial artist. For years she'd dreamed of moving to San Francisco with her fiancé. He'd be a journalist and she'd be an artist, and they'd live in a loft overlooking the bay.

Finally, the opportunity arose. Don got a job with the San Francisco *Chronicle*. After years of night school art classes, Laura left her secretarial job in Los Angeles to seek her fortune.

She had the talent and training to be a good commercial illustrator. Taking her portfolio around, she got a few jobs. So she couldn't understand why she soon became profoundly depressed.

Each day she rattled around the apartment in her bathrobe, trying to get started but working at home drove her up a wall. So she'd get dressed and go out, carrying her portfolio from one art director to another, but that didn't make her feel any better.

She loved Don, she loved San Francisco, and she thought she loved drawing. But she was miserable. She wanted to go home.

Money wasn't the issue. She had her savings and Don had a good income. But she felt so rootless and lonely she couldn't work.

Laura thought nostalgically about the job she'd left behind. Sure, it was boring, but she missed her friends and the little rituals, the coffee breaks, the jokes, the lunches. By becoming a freelance artist, Laura was going against the grain. An extrovert with a strong need for stability, she had run after a romantic dream that wasn't right for her.

She finally became a graphic artist in a large computer company where she developed the friendships and stability she needs. Now Laura sits happily at her drafting table, drawing all day, surrounded by a bustle of people and activity.

PERSONAL EXERCISE

Living the Tao means becoming more aware of our own patterns and harmonizing with them.

Remind yourself of these patterns by contemplating the beauty of natural wood. With its knots, swirls, and tiny lines, each piece is as distinctive as a fingerprint. Perhaps it is a fingerprint: the imprint of Tao.

- Find a quiet corner where you can be alone and observe the grain on a wooden table, cabinet, or other piece of furniture.
- Relax your body, releasing the day's tension with three slow, deep breaths.
- Then run your fingers over the wood. Follow its grain and lifelines. Become aware of the energy patterns coursing through it.
- Know that you have your own patterns, as the Tao flows through your life.
- Glance down at your fingertips, becoming aware of the grain, the patterns of energy there.
- Close your eyes, concentrate on your breathing, and feel the energy of Tao flowing through your body.
- Know that you are a unique expression of Tao. Your patterns are like no other's.
- Ask yourself what you can do now to honor your personal patterns and live more harmoniously.

As you follow the Tao and live its principles, you'll become increasingly aware of the energies within and around you. Your life will be more natural, harmonious, and peaceful.

Affirmation

I now know my life is peaceful and harmonious.
I follow the Tao.
I am one with all there is.
I balance the forces of *yin* and *yang*.
I flow with the cycles in life.
I honor the energies within and around me.
I respect myself and the process.
I harmonize with nature and all others in my world.
I accept greater peace in my life now.
And so it is.

CHAPTER 4

THE WAY OF TRANSFORMATION

"To follow the Tao
In wisdom and stillness
Brings order to the world."

(TAO 45)[1]

THE way of transformation begins within. By renewing ourselves in daily meditation we discover a deep source of inner peace which creates greater peace around us.

The Law of Cause and Effect

Our inner and outer worlds are intrinsically related. As the *Tao* explains:

"Those who focus on Tao
Will be one with Tao.
Those who study its power
Will be powerful.
Those who focus on failure
Will certainly fail."

(TAO 23)

We get what we cultivate in our lives. Like seeds, our thoughts take root in our experience. If we focus on the power of Tao, we become powerful. If we focus on failure, we fail. Even our unexpressed thoughts affect our work, our relationships, our daily lives.

When I was a child, we often spent holidays with my extended family. Each year my aunts, uncles, and grandparents took turns preparing Christmas dinner.

Christmas at my grandmother's was a feast to remember. Her eyes shining, she would run to welcome us in her floral apron. Fragrant spices filled the air, and her love graced every dish from the roast turkey, gravy, and cornbread dressing to the sparkling cranberry sauce and spicy pumpkin pie.

But in one household the turkey was always dry, the dressing and dessert dull and tasteless. Why? This couple had used the same family recipes but something was missing. Years earlier the life had gone out of their marriage. Their meals reflected their boredom as surely as my grandmother's reflected her tremendous love of life.

Our attitudes are powerful, continuously affecting our environment. As we change our attitude, we change our world. Why? Because in the Tao all are one. As my friend Joe Grassi says, the world is not something impersonal "out there,"[2] but as close to us as our breathing, immediate as our next thought.

The Path with Heart

We can transform our world by transforming our attitude. This cannot be accomplished by merely reading or thinking about peace. Living the Tao is more than an intellectual exercise. It is the path with heart.

The Chinese character *hsin* means both mind and heart, the source of all thought, feeling, and motivation. Following the Tao there is no inner split, no agonizing struggle between head and heart. We find harmony by living wholeheartedly.

Returning to Our Roots

The *Tao* tells us:

"Let your roots go deep
Into the source.

With attitude build a firm foundation
Of peace in the Tao."

(TAO 59)

Many conflicts occur when we're not living deeply enough. Dashing frantically from one commitment to another, we lose touch with Tao.

I used to have conflicts between my work and relationships. Over the years people and situations changed but the painful pattern remained. The night before an exam, my college boyfriend would shout angrily, "You'd rather study than be with me!" Years later, when I had papers to grade, other men would complain, "You care more about your students than you do about me." Torn between competing polarities of head and heart, I was never at peace with myself.

Seeking the One

Peace comes from transcending polarities with a vision of the larger whole. Call that vision Life, God, Existence, or Tao. It has many names. Emerson called it the Oversoul. Beyond the surface differences, it is the One that includes us all. Men and women of Tao experience this oneness through regular spiritual exercise.

Each day we meet our physical needs, eating and sleeping at regular intervals. Tao people also make time for spiritual renewal. If we neglect our bodies, they become imbalanced and break down. If we neglect our spiritual needs, we become emotionally imbalanced and our world breaks down in continual conflict.

Moments of reflection enable our roots to go deep to the source, drawing upon the infinite power and wisdom of Tao.

Peace Begins Within

Taking time for reflection may seem like self-indulgence when we face a world of crisis and conflict. Yet it's one of the most responsible things we can do.

When we're confused and uncentered, we project inner conflicts into the world around us. When we're at peace with ourselves, we can see more clearly, act more effectively. Studies have shown that participants in the human potential movement are more socially responsible than the majority of the population.[3] Their quest for health and harmony extends naturally from themselves to others.

The serenity gained from meeting their spiritual needs helps Tao people keep their lives in order. Without the constant drain of emotional crises or burnout, they have more time for themselves and the things they believe in. Balanced, responsible, and at peace with themselves, they radiate peace to all they meet.

Defining Peace for Ourselves

Regular meditation not only restores our inner harmony and vital energy, but provides us with an actual experience of the peace we seek.

The *Tao* describes peace as that inner space so often ignored in the rush of modern life, without which there is no order, no meaning at all.

"Thirty spokes share the wheel's hub;
It is the center hole that makes it useful.
Shape clay into a vessel;
It is the space within that makes it useful.
Cut doors and windows for a room;
It is the holes which make it useful."

(TAO 11)[4]

Cultivating that inner space, we become more balanced, more harmonious, more useful: people of Tao.

No matter where we are, we can find peace in the present moment, within the current pattern of our lives. We need not retreat to a monastery. The inner space is here, as close to us as our breathing, as intimate as our thoughts. Within our daily lives, as within the frame of a window, the clay of a vessel, is the creative potential for peace. We find peace by cultivating the space within.

The Lesson of the Tortoise

There's an old Chinese saying, "the tortoise is good at nurturing energy, so it can survive a century without food."[5]

The early Taoists revered tortoises because they know when to withdraw unto themselves, when to restore their energy. Thus they live to an advanced age. Believed to have mysterious powers, tortoise shells were used in divination, inspiring the hexagram patterns of the *I Ching*. We can cultivate inner peace by following the lesson of the tortoise, setting aside daily periods of withdrawal to nurture the powerful energy of Tao.

Seeking the Silence

Tao people seek out periods of silence. Gandhi kept a day of silence once a week. No matter what happened or who came to visit, he would spend that day quietly, communicating to others only in writing. Most of us are unable to maintain an entire day of silence, but we can establish regular periods of meditation.

There are as many forms of meditation as there are temperaments. Some are elaborate, others simple and unstructured. In alphagenetics people select a number and count down slowly, becoming progressively relaxed. Biofeedback monitors body processes with machines. In transcendental meditation people focus on a personal mantram. Psychosynthesis uses visual images and guided daydreams. Spiritual teacher Eknath Easwaren asks people to meditate on the prayer of St. Francis. Author and counselor Louise Hay just sits quietly, empties her mind, and asks, "What is it that I need to know?"[6]

Slow, conscious breathing focuses our energy; words and images prepare the way. The mind slows down and channels deep beneath the noise and surface clutter. After meditation, we emerge renewed and refreshed, our tension gone, our hearts and minds at peace. We are one with Tao.

You can begin meditating by setting aside as little as fifteen minutes a day, extending that time to suit your needs. Many people meditate the first thing each morning, others do it at the end of the day. Beginning and ending each day in meditation is ideal, but the important thing is to meditate regularly.

PERSONAL EXERCISE: TAOIST MEDITATION

- Find a quiet place where you will not be disturbed. Unplug your phone, loosen your belt, remove all distracting influences.
- Then sit down on the floor or in a straight backed chair, keeping your spine straight. Some people like to lie on their backs. If you do, try not to fall asleep.
- Close your eyes and tune in to your body. Feel the weight of your legs on the surface beneath you, the subtle pressure as your body gently touches the world around you.
- Breathe slowly and deeply, inhaling into your abdomen, the center of your being. With each breath, tune in to the power of *chi,* the vital energy flowing through your body.
- Concentrate on the energy in your toes and gradually trace that energy up your legs and abdomen to your heart. Then feel it flow out through your arms and fingertips, releasing any tension there.
- *Focused breathing:* Now breathe *out* conflict, worry, pain, anywhere you are not at peace in your life. Feel it leaving your body with each breath. Release it. Let it go.
- Alternately breathe out conflict and breathe *in* peace, feeling the new energy flowing in, warming, revitalizing, and renewing you.
- Continue this focused breathing until you feel deeply relaxed.
- With each breath feel more of the healing *chi* energy flow through your body, tingling in your fingers and toes. Deeply relaxed, say to yourself: "I am one with Tao.
- If distracting thoughts cross your mind, dismiss them quietly, affirming "I am one with Tao."
- If you find yourself getting sleepy, try sitting up instead of lying down, remembering to keep your spine straight.
- When you're ready to come back, affirm one final time, "I am one with Tao." Gradually open your eyes, stretch your muscles, and return from meditation refreshed, centered, and serene.

Emptying the Heart

Emptying the heart is an important Taoist practice, necessary to release blocks to inner peace.[7] We do this by breathing out all conflicts or tensions before affirming "I am one with Tao." It's impossible to be at peace with ourselves when in conflict with another. By releasing grudges and negative feelings, we reclaim our own peace of mind.

Inner Peace Breaks

Emptying the heart and meditating regularly will build your inner strength. You'll find yourself growing more balanced, more at peace with yourself and your world.

You'll become more aware of the energies within and around you. Since you feel them more intensely, at times the negative energies of others can set you off balance.

When an angry co-worker takes his impatience out on you, you can't dash off for a half hour meditation. But you can practice one of these brief inner peace breaks.

Energy Release

You can do this one anywhere, any time to regain your peace of mind.

- Slowly inhale, breathing deep into your abdomen.
- Exhale completely, releasing all the jagged negative energy. Say to yourself, "This is not my energy." Let it go.
- Now say to yourself, "I am at peace. I am one with Tao."

Aura Cleansing

Chinese medicine emphasizes prevention, renewing the body's energies to ward off potential illness. For centuries, healers have used acupuncture and medicinal herbs to stimulate the vital energy meridians.

The negative energies of others can pollute your body's aura or energy field. When your energy is high, the aura forms a strong protective shield, but negative energy can wear it thin, weakening your immune system.

When you're assaulted by a blast of negative energy, excuse yourself for a minute. Go off somewhere by yourself (a storeroom or restroom will do).

Rub your hands briskly together. Then move them in an arc over your head and down the sides of your body, visualizing yourself surrounded by a white healing light. Say to yourself, "I am one with Tao."

Years ago, when I worked in a conflict-ridden office, I frequently left my desk to wash my hands. Actually I was cleansing my aura to maintain my personal balance.[8]

Keep a Peace Journal

Another helpful practice is to keep a peace journal. Begin now and record anything that comes up in your inner journey.

- Ask yourself, "Where in my life do I experience the most peace?" Write this down.
- Now ask, "What area do I need to work on?"
- Write down how you have handled conflicts in this area in the past.
- Now ask yourself, "How would a Tao person handle this conflict?" Write this down in as much detail as possible.
- Now close your eyes and visualize yourself doing just that.

Use your journal in the days ahead to record your progress, as well as the lessons you're working on. As you follow the Tao, your inner peace will increase, and the journal will become a valuable record of your spiritual growth.

The *Tao* teaches that we're responsible for the peace in our lives. It's up to us to keep our energies in balance.

When we do this, we not only experience greater peace ourselves but become a source of peace for others. The effect of one harmonious soul is irresistible:

"Cultivated in your soul,
The Tao brings peace to your life.

Cultivated in your home,
It brings peace with those you love.
Spreading to friends and neighbors,
It brings peace to your community."

(TAO 54)

Affirmation

I now know my life is peaceful and harmonious.
I recognize the power of my thoughts.
I use this power wisely.
I renew myself in meditation.
I find the source of peace within.
I express my peace to others.
I respect myself and the process.
I harmonize with nature and all others in my world.
I accept greater peace in my life now.
And so it is.

心

CHAPTER 5

THE WAY BEGINS AT YOUR OWN DOORSTEP

"Know the Tao
Without leaving your doorstep.
See its face
Reflected in the window.
To seek it outside
Is to leave it behind."

(TAO 47)

THE way of peace begins with self-acceptance. To seek peace outside is to leave it behind.

Because of the Taoist principle of oneness, when we accept ourselves, we naturally accept others. Without self-acceptance, people see life as a constant struggle, making war on themselves and others at home, on the job, in relationships. Suffering tremendous emotional ups and downs, they strive to gain approval, but it's never enough, for deep within lurks a nagging sense of inadequacy. Such people can easily lose their balance. When working for political causes, they often fall into fanaticism, swept away by illusions of power and self-importance.[1]

By setting our inner world in order, we gain greater peace. The Chinese character *hsien,* which means peace or quiescence, is made up of two parts: a closed door and the moon.[2] In this chapter we close the door on outside events to increase the inner light of self-acceptance.

The Tao of Self-Acceptance

The Tao tells us that:

"The Tao person knows himself
And makes no display,
Accepts himself,
And is not arrogant."

(TAO 72)

Tao people have no need to hide behind artifice and ostentation. Living the simple truth of who they are, they're beyond envy, competition, and artificial display.

Self-Assessment

How well do you accept yourself? Do any of these statements sound familiar?

- A colleague at work walks by and ignores me. What's wrong with me?
- A new man or woman in my life stands me up. I feel hurt and rejected.
- The person I love is depressed or angry. What did I do wrong?
- My relationship ends and I feel like a failure.
- I'm afraid to ask for a raise.
- I don't make my sales quota. I get turned down for promotion or get a bad evaluation. I'm not good enough.
- I'm afraid to do something new because I know I'll fail.
- I'm afraid to ask others for help.
- Whenever I make a mistake—burn the dinner, spill my coffee, or break something—I feel like a worthless klutz.
- When I look in the mirror all I see are my flaws.
- When people look at me intently, I know they see something wrong with me.

- When someone likes me, I think I've either fooled him/her or this person is an idiot.
- Someone else gets a promotion, a raise, or a new car and I wonder what's wrong with me.
- My tennis or golf game is off and I feel like a failure.
- No matter what I weigh I feel fat and ugly.
- I have to work really hard to feel OK about myself.

The conclusion in all these examples is "I'm not OK. I'm not good enough." People with low self-esteem are quick to blame themselves when something goes wrong because they feel so inadequate.

Betty was a young secretary, eager to please her new boss. She worked hard typing, filing, organizing a deluge of paperwork, and usually received his gruff approval. But one day Mr. Tolliver arrived in a terrible mood. Ignoring her bright "Good morning," he glowered at her and walked by without a word.

Betty was devastated. What had she done wrong? All morning she worried about being fired, ending up with a tension headache and upset stomach.

Actually, her boss' displeasure had nothing to do with her at all. He was upset because he'd gotten a speeding ticket on the way to work.

Betty's reaction is not that unusual. How often do we blame ourselves when things go wrong? But with healthy self-esteem we perceive ourselves as lovable and capable, seeing outside events more objectively. The negative reactions of others usually have nothing to do with us at all.

The Politics of Self-Esteem

California Assemblyman John Vasconcellos has worked for years to promote greater self-esteem. His efforts reflect this essential lesson of Tao: our outer world reflects our world within. The conditions around us reflect how we feel about ourselves.

A longtime veteran of the human potential movement, John has been called "the touchy feely legislator." Tall, with dark curly hair and large soulful eyes, he's a man of deep personal warmth. As chair of the California Assembly's powerful Ways and Means Committee, his days are crammed with activities. Yet he loves to talk about ideas.

He listens intently, his head cocked to one side, often jotting notes to himself on scraps of paper.

He's sponsored legislation on mental health, violence prevention, AIDS research, and international peace negotiation as well as a State Commission on Self-Esteem. On United Nations Day, 1988, Vasconcellos told a college audience that "The future of the world lies in having enough self-esteem to accept others different from ourselves."

A top student in high school and college, John says he suffered from low self-esteem and constantly struggled to prove himself. In the early 1960s, he discovered the humanistic psychology of Carl Rogers, who followed the *Tao,* affirming a vision of life as process. Since then John's personal quest for wholeness has affected his self-concept, his politics, and everything he does.

It's up to us, he says, "to learn how to use our power for life rather than for death, to renew our faith in ourselves, and live each day, each moment, in a way that can truly lead to a world of peace."

The Tao Beyond Appearances

"The Tao person
Never strives to appear great,
Which is how true greatness is achieved."

(TAO 34)

The temptations of ego are great when we suffer from low self-esteem. How many people hide behind pretense, poses, walls of artifice? Tao people dare to be open. Dynamically, spontaneously themselves, they reach out to others to create greater understanding.

My high school government teacher, Miss Sirabian, taught me this lesson of Tao. Unlike other teachers, she never talked down to students. She was the first adult I ever knew who treated me as an equal.

Her class required lots of work, yet was always exciting. Dark-haired and petite, she paced back and forth, challenging us to deal with hard concepts, asking us what *we* thought about politics, power, and world events. Or she'd sit on her desk listening thoughtfully, sharing what she believed.

Born of Armenian immigrants, she took her American citizenship very seriously. In a democracy it's not only our right but our *duty* to participate, she'd tell us, adding, "I've never missed an election in my life."

With her openness and integrity, Miss Sirabian touched this room full of unruly teenagers, making us aware of our destiny and duty as citizens. She took our ideas, our lives, and our collective future seriously and because of this, so did we. Years later, I look back in gratitude, realizing how much her example has meant to me. For she lived the democracy she taught, treating everyone with equal respect and teaching us that we are responsible for the world we create.

Beyond the Walls

We cannot be open with others unless we first accept ourselves. Low self-esteem builds walls of defensiveness, keeping us from the peace we seek.

Carole Price, Religious Science minister in San Jose, California, believes "peace can be consciously attained" by dismantling these walls. Insecure people hide beneath artificial smiles and confident poses, afraid to relax and reveal themselves, but this only increases their insecurity. "We think that we build walls to keep us in peace," says Carole, "and it's completely backward." It's a self-perpetuating cycle. The more we hide, the more fearful we become.[3]

The way out begins with self-acceptance. The Tao person "knows himself, and makes no display" (*Tao* 72). When we stop hiding, the walls gradually disappear.

Our Inner Monologue

Building self-acceptance takes time. At first we notice a monologue of self-criticism. Running through our minds like a radio talk show, it brings up past mistakes, tells us we're "not good enough," and scares us with worries about the future.

The monologue repeats all the criticisms we heard from parents and teachers: "You did it wrong again," "You're a bad girl (or boy)," "You're lazy," "You'll never amount to anything." It undermines our self-esteem, making us feel incompetent, weak, and helpless.

We can turn off the monologue with affirmations or increased attention to what we're doing.

PERSONAL EXERCISES

The next time you hear the monologue, repeat this affirmation:

"I love myself.
I accept myself.
I am one with Tao."

You can also stop the monologue by giving full attention to something. I go skiing, an activity that requires such balance and precision I forget to think. Up on the slopes, surrounded by a magical panorama of snow-frosted pines and miles of bright blue sky, any sense of ego is eclipsed. Dancing with the wind in a silent ballet, I become one with the skis, shifting in subtle rhythm with the gleaming snow around me. There's no room for self-criticism in a communion that embraces body and soul.

You don't have to ski to find such communion. It's possible with anything you really love to do: playing your favorite music, painting, running, walking on the beach, gardening, meditating. Resolve now to do something you love regularly as an important spiritual exercise.

The Self-Fulfilling Prophecy

A few years ago authorities told a group of California teachers that some of their students would have an intellectual growth spurt. By the end of the year, these students' academic performance had improved dramatically. Then it was announced that their names had been selected at random. Because the teachers had expected more of them, the students had expected more of themselves, and their performance matched their expectations.[4] What we believe, we create. This is the power of the self-fulfilling prophecy.

PERSONAL EXERCISE

Because our expectations affect our experience, we need to watch what we tell ourselves. Jack Canfield, President of Self-Esteem Seminars, asks people to practice this simple mirror exercise.

- Go to your mirror, look yourself straight in the eyes and tell yourself some things you like about yourself.
- If this feels strange, it's because you're not used to giving yourself approval.
- For the next week go to your mirror at the end of the day and tell yourself all the things you appreciate about yourself: "I'm really proud of you for exercising this morning, for eating a healthy breakfast, for taking a walk during lunch hour, for breaking out of a bad mood with Tao affirmations, for making a difficult decision, for being honest with a friend," and so on.
- Then call yourself by name and say, "I really love you."[5]

The regular self-approval in this exercise will build your self-esteem and increase your inner peace.

The Tao of Openness

Mitch Saunders, marriage and family counselor in Santa Clara, California, sees honest relationships as a great way to develop self-acceptance. The more we share our feelings with others and find they still accept us, the more our self-acceptance grows. Each moment of openness wears down our defensive walls.

Mitch likens this quest to Gandhi's *satyagraha*. Personally and politically, the force of truth builds greater trust and opens the way to new possibilities. Even when people disagree on issues, trust builds bridges and everyone benefits.[6]

The Chinese have a word for this: *tzu jan,* which means expressing ourselves naturally, without inhibitions.[7] Tao people are as spontaneous as nature itself. Challenge yourself each day to be more open, more natural.

PERSONAL EXERCISE

- Instead of saying things only to please people or hiding behind excuses, begin to say what you really feel.
- Don't use honesty as an excuse to blame or attack others. Instead of saying "You make me angry," say "I feel angry when_____." If the other person cares about you, this will make a powerful difference.
- When other people are more honest with you, remember to listen carefully, respecting their feelings.

Fear builds walls, but truth builds bridges. The Tao is the way of truth. With greater honesty we can build bridges of peace and understanding for ourselves and our world.

Affirmation

I now know my life is peaceful and harmonious.
I love myself.
I accept myself.
I am one with Tao.
I am open and honest.
I have nothing to hide.
I respect myself and the process.
I harmonize with nature and all others in my world.
I accept greater peace in my life now.
And so it is.

CHAPTER 6

FACING YOUR FEARS

"Measuring success
By others' words
Creates anxiety.
What you desire
And what you fear
Are within yourself."

(TAO 13)

THE *Tao* teaches us to take charge of our lives, to face our fears and learn from them.

Fear is a valuable warning signal, our natural response to danger. In an automatic fight or flight response, our muscles tense, heartbeat speeds up, digestive and immune systems temporarily shut down, and our bodies churn out adrenalin and corticosteroids to meet the perceived threat.

But in the modern world, many problems cannot be remedied by fight or flight. With no outlet, our bodies remain stressed and we spend billions of dollars a year to relieve our tension, stiff muscles, indigestion, headaches, and insomnia.[1]

Studies have shown that Americans who regularly watch television news develop an exaggerated view of local crime. Bombarded by violent images, they live in chronic fear of attack, while less frequent viewers have a more realistic perspective.

Harry and Mildred, a retired couple, live in an affluent suburban neighborhood with a guard and security gate. The expansive lawns are well-manicured, new Cadillacs and Mercedes sit in the garages, and crime here is virtually unheard of.

Yet this couple lives in chronic fear. They resent government programs to help the homeless, regarding the poor as a dangerous threat to their security. They don't even trust their neighbors. Their home is a fortress with an elaborate alarm system and two deadbolt locks on the front door. After dinner and three hours of TV news, they venture outside to walk their doberman around the block, each carrying a baseball bat "in case there's trouble."

Chronic fear undermines our health and world view. Driven by fear, we act rashly, aggravating our problems. As anxiety mounts, we feel increasingly helpless, anxious, and defensive. We seem victims of a hostile universe, under constant threat of disaster. Projecting our fears upon others, we perceive them as enemies.

An important step in living a more peaceful life is to face our fears, learn whether the danger is real or imaginary, and take appropriate action.

Tao people stay centered even in the midst of danger. Non-Tao people let their emotions run wild like a herd of frightened sheep. They panic. Wild-eyed and frantic, they often dash off in the wrong direction, injuring themselves and others in their rush to get away.

Avoiding Panic

In *The Healing Heart* Norman Cousins calls panic "the ultimate enemy," explaining how intense psychological stress can damage the heart, undermine the immune system, even cause sudden death. "Nothing," he emphasizes, "is more essential to the treatment of serious disease than liberating the patient from panic and foreboding."[2]

Taking Charge

We can avoid panic with knowledge and foresight. In aviation, one of the first things new pilots learn is the preflight, inspecting the airplane carefully before each flight.

Teaching foresight, the flight instructor tells students to prepare for a forced landing, to look for a field or pasture in case they lose an engine. My father surprises his students by suddenly pulling back the throttle, drastically cutting power, and asking "What are you going to do now?" Students have to show they can handle an emergency before he lets them fly solo.

Anticipating emergencies, a good pilot is prepared. He doesn't panic because he knows what to do. The right response becomes second nature.

So it is with Tao people. They know what to do because they study nature. Understanding the principles of Tao, they make better choices. Like a martial arts master, they see the current crisis in terms of the larger patterns.

Identifying the Danger

Some people think if they just ignore danger it will go away. This is denial, a foolish response to any problem. For the cycle continues. Unsolved problems do not go away: they get worse.

This is true whether our problems are personal or planetary. We cannot afford to languish in denial or give way to despair. Tao people face their fears and respond actively, answering even global crises with positive action.

In *Despair and Personal Power in the Nuclear Age,* Joanna Rogers Macy encourages people to face their fears for the planet, breaking through the conditioned numbness.[3] Only by facing our fears do we recapture the emotional energy they absorb, the energy that otherwise imprisons us. In a later chapter we'll learn how to direct this energy into positive action, becoming empowered by a greater commitment to our future.

Whether our actions are personal or political, taking charge means responding wisely to conditions around us, knowing when and how to act. We do this by following Tao, by studying the way things work and acting in harmony with them.

Dispelling the Shadows

There's an old story told by Chuang Tzu about a man so afraid of the sight of his shadow and the sound of his footsteps that he ran away from them.

But the more he ran, the faster the footsteps sounded after him, the more swiftly his shadow followed behind. Falling into a panic, he ran faster and faster until he finally died of exhaustion.

He didn't realize that if he'd only stopped running, what he feared would stop chasing him. Resting in the shade of a tree would make the shadow disappear and the footsteps cease.[4]

If we stop running from our inner fears, they, too, will cease to torment us. Resting in greater understanding and self-knowing, we will no longer be frightened by shadows.

SELF-ASSESSMENT: WHAT AM I AFRAID OF?

Are you troubled by inner fears? Do any of these statements sound familiar?

- I don't like my home/job/relationship but I'm afraid to change.
- I'm afraid to take chances.
- There's something I'd really like to do, but I'm afraid I'll fail.
- I'm afraid if I really care about something (or someone), I'll lose it.
- I'd like to be more successful but I don't deserve it.
- I'm afraid if I make the changes I'd like, people won't like me.
- I'd like more success in my life, but I'm afraid I can't handle it.

Fear of the Unknown

Many people stay in dead-end jobs and unhappy relationships because they're afraid of change. No matter how bad their situation, at least they know what to expect. The unknown, full of promise, is also full of threat.

My friend Beverly has been in a dead-end secretarial job for over five years. She's bright, creative, and attractive, working beneath her potential in a job that offers only a weekly paycheck.

The work is monotonous, the pay mediocre, there's no chance for advancement, and her boss is unbearable. Yet she hangs on, year after year, afraid to change a familiar pattern.

Beverly fears the great unknown, unaware that no matter how tightly we cling to the familiar, the only constant in life is change.

The Tao Is Dynamic

By following the Tao, we gradually overcome our fear of change. Realizing that our world is constantly evolving in cycles helps us transcend any rigid addiction to status quo. Looming beyond the panorama of changing forms, the Tao itself is eternal. Lao Tzu tells us:

"The Tao is mysterious, unfathomable
Yet within is all that lives;
Unfathomable, mysterious
Yet within is the essence,
Shadowy, intangible,
Yet within are vital principles,
Principles of truth
Informing all creation."

(TAO 21)

The *Tao* portrays life as an ongoing process. This is the truth of our nature, the essence of Tao.

Many people fear failure. Tao people know that even mistakes bring them greater wisdom. Theologian Joseph Grassi tells his students, "Be willing to risk and learn through mistakes. People 'with experience' are those who have learned to profit from their errors."[5]

Some people fear success, afraid it will throw their lives out of control. Roger fears the added pressures a promotion would bring, so he stays in the same predictable job. His wife Doris holds herself back, afraid she'll lose him if she makes more than he does.

Many children of the sixties are afraid they'll lose their balance if they become too successful. One evening, my neighbor, Dave, a former Peace Corps worker, sold his old blue van and drove a new Toyota back to our apartment house.

Concerned about "selling out to the Establishment," he knocked at my door, carrying a six pack of beer. We talked late into the night.

He'd had the van for nearly fifteen years. Decorated with flags and peace signs, it had become part of his identity. But now it was constantly breaking down. Still he wondered, was he getting soft, selling out? Was it OK for him to have a new car when the environment was polluted and people were living in poverty?

Dave's questions were good ones. When making big changes, we need to check our balance, making sure the changes don't betray our values.

Dave tried to live simply and ecologically. Yet the old van had slowly become a big polluter, wasting gasoline and belching black smoke. His new energy efficient car is actually kinder to the environment.

The car would simplify Dave's life, getting him to work and the recycling center without those troublesome breakdowns. He realized he hadn't sold out but made a sensible change.

Tao Question

Living the Tao, we learn to see our decisions in terms of the larger patterns. When contemplating anything new, stop and ask yourself: "Does this choice harmonize with my values? Does it bring greater peace to my life and the planet?"

Personal Exercise: Exploring the Consequences

We're often afraid to change because of unknown consequences. We wonder, "What if I try it and don't like it? What if I fail? What if my friends don't like me?" We can deal with these fears in advance by exploring the consequences.

The next time you face a new challenge, try this simple exercise.

- Go to a quiet place where you won't be disturbed and allow yourself enough time (at least twenty minutes) to relax, go within, and visualize yourself doing the thing you fear.
- Get as clear a picture as possible. What are you doing? What do you look like? Feel like?
- Now ask yourself about the consequences. "What's the worst thing that can happen if I do this?"
- Can you handle it?
- Ask "What's even worse than that? What if everything goes wrong?"

- Can you handle it?
- Ask "What's even worse than that? The worst thing I can imagine?"
- Can you still handle it?

Exploring the consequences helps dispel our fear of the unknown. Most inner fears are shadows that fall away in the light of greater awareness.

But some fears are real. As our lives change, we gain some things and lose others. Perhaps some people will resent our new way of life and leave us. But we'll find new friends to love and support us as we continue to evolve through our choices.

Beyond Followers and Leaders

Affirming an all-pervading oneness, the Tao transcends hierarchy, the frantic struggle of followers and leaders.

Too many people rush around competing, consuming, collecting things in a rush to be bigger and better. But this reveals only inner emptiness, a lack of peace within.

Hierarchical thinking thrives on insecurity. Some hierarchies, of course, designate levels of competence, as in our school system—grades K–12. But Americans have become infatuated with hierarchy, exaggerating its importance and imposing hierarchical values upon our jobs, our possessions, even our social lives. Do we really believe that some people are better than others?

In the Orient, with its emphasis on the process—the path instead of the destination—there are only two ranks in karate: student and master, white belt and black. Unlike our Eastern counterparts, American karate centers advertise a rainbow of different belts: yellow, green, blue, purple, red, and brown. We constantly measure ourselves in competition with others.

Hierarchies do just that. There's always someone to envy and someone to look down upon as we struggle to reach higher and do more. Hierarchies reinforce competition, not cooperation.

PERSONAL EXERCISE

Using your imagination, visualize society as an enormous ladder with people climbing different rungs in their quest for progress.

There's one fellow on top, high and mighty in his seat of power. Beneath him are the higher ups, followed by the upper middles, the middles, the lower middles on down to the lowest.

- Now ask yourself: what's the most secure position on this ladder?
- On top? No, this poor soul is worn out from the climb and fears those below who threaten his position. Those beneath him envy his power and fear those beneath them. Some of the middles look upward in awe, their fear of authority making them perpetual children. Others further down live in constant fear of not meeting their survival needs.
- Now take a piece of paper and draw a ladder of your own hierarchy—at work, school, or in the community. Of all the people you know, who is on top? in the middle? on the bottom?
- Where are you? How does this ladder make you feel?
- Ask yourself, "What limited criteria have I been using to construct this ladder?"
- Close your eyes once more and relax. Replacing competition with compassion, see all of you joining hands. Feel love and acceptance move around the circle.
- Take a deep breath and release it. If you have any remaining animosity toward anyone in the circle, release it with another deep breath.
- Recognize that beneath the differences, we're all part of the circle of life, all one in Tao.
- How do you feel now?

Living the Tao changes our vision of social relationships. Hierarchical thinking cannot lead to peace. Perhaps this is why members of the Society of Friends (Quakers) refrain from using titles, placing respect for our common humanity beyond deference to social differences.

As we seek to live more peacefully, let's look at how often we've let hierarchy affect our relationships. Have we feared others because they seemed "above" or "below" us?

How often have we judged ourselves by externals, scoring points in order to feel "OK"? Points can be anything from grades in school to income, output, consumer goods, sexual conquests, even our weight—whatever we can measure.

The *Tao* reminds us that:

"Standing on tiptoe, we become unsteady.
Stretching ourselves too far, we lack balance.
Showing off, we hide our light.
Competing with others, we lose our way."

(TAO 24)

We must leave competition behind to follow the way of Tao, which transcends our ability to measure.

Building Peace with Compassion

Competitive thinking puts people on the defensive. As Gerald Jampolsky explains in *Love Is Letting Go of Fear*, we often attack others because we perceive them—through our fears—as attacking us. He challenges us to replace "attack thoughts," with compassion. Instead of seeing those who attack us as enemies, see them as frightened and miserable. By recognizing their plea for help,[6] we can break through the destructive cycle of fear and attack.

Every teacher knows that beneath the troublesome student or class bully, there's a fearful, unhappy person. Years ago, two young men constantly interrupted one of my classes with sarcastic comments. As a new teacher I felt attacked and defensive.

Then I realized they were clamoring for attention. I began calling on them, including them in discussion, listening to their opinions. Their attitude changed. Energetic and eager to learn, they became two of my best students.

The *Tao* says when we are at peace with ourselves, we're not vulnerable to the attacks of others:

"The Tao person
Is as pure as a child.
In purity is a strength
That dispels all harm.

If you do not fear others,
They will not fear you."

(TAO 55)

When we're one with Tao, our consciousness subtly transforms people and situations, replacing discord with oneness, fear with compassion.

Trusting the Process

The *Tao* tells us:

"The wisest person
Trusts the process,
Without seeking to control;
Takes everything as it comes,
Lives not to achieve or possess,
But simply to be
All he or she can be
In harmony with Tao.

(TAO 2)

As we follow the Tao, one lesson appears again and again: trust the process. We cannot change the cycles of life to suit ourselves, but we can learn to flow with them.

Harmonizing with Tao requires trust. Arlene Wiltberger, marriage and family counselor in San Mateo, California, sees our lives as "a dance between trust and fear." "When our trust level is higher than our fear level, we have peace," she explains. But "when our desire to control dominates us, then we are victimized by our fears."

To be at peace in any endeavor, we must release our need to control the outcome. We can only do our best, then trust the evolving cycles of Tao.

Gay Swenson, Director of the Carl Rogers Institute for Peace, says she experienced this lesson in 1988 when planning a Central American peace conference in Costa Rica. Strongly committed to a successful project, she was deeply concerned and fearful of failure, wondering "What if the key people don't come?" "What if it doesn't work out?"

Gay recognized that "recovering my peace involves facing my fears." She asked herself, "what's the worst thing that could happen?" In this case it was a small workshop without the principal leaders in attendance, but perhaps this, too, could be a fruitful experience.

Facing her fears led to "a real sense of relief and release." Realizing she couldn't control the outcome, she chose to trust the process and open herself to new insights. Individually and collectively, the workshop was a valuable experience in peace-building.[7]

Letting go of our attachment to the outcome dispels our fear of failure, for success and failure are polarities that emerge when we try to control things. The Tao transcends polarities. Trusting the process, we evolve beyond old definitions, open to new insight, one with Tao.

Affirmation

I now know my life is peaceful and harmonious.
I trust the process.
I look to the larger cycles.
I face my fears and learn from them.
I respond with wisdom and compassion.
I take positive action.
I respect myself and the process.
I harmonize with nature and all others in my world.
I accept greater peace in my life now.
And so it is.

CHAPTER 7

RELEASING TENSION

"At birth all people are soft and yielding.
At death they are hard and stiff.
All green plants are tender and yielding.
At death they are brittle and dry.
When hard and rigid,
We consort with death.
When soft and flexible,
We affirm greater life."

(TAO 76)

FOLLOWING the Tao means keeping our minds open, our bodies relaxed, releasing the tensions of modern life through regular exercise. Taoist yoga, breathing, and *t'ai chi* help regulate the flow of *chi,* the energy of Tao which circulates through our bodies and all creation.

According to Chinese medicine, *chi* moves in continuous cycles from our heads to our feet, nurturing all the vital organs. If this energy is blocked—by stress, negative emotions, poor diet, lack of sleep, or insufficient exercise—we become ill.

Traditional Chinese healers use acupuncture to stimulate points along the meridians. Removing blocks and restoring the flow, they return their patients to a state of dynamic balance. People often consult a healer before they become ill, recognizing that when their *chi* is diminished, they have lower resistance to disease. We, too, can practice preventative medicine by becoming more aware of our energies, strengthening our *chi* with regular exercise and using the techniques in this chapter whenever we feel tired or tense.

Tension and fatigue are all too common in today's world. Author and holistic healer Michael Reed Gach relates our weakened vitality to three unhealthy features of modern living:

(1) shallow breathing and days spent indoors inhaling stale, stagnant air, which results in inadequate oxygen for our bodies. We all need to breathe more deeply and spend more time outside in the fresh air.

(2) chronic tension, which blocks the circulation of *chi*. Taking time to stretch and move around is vital for people who spend all day at a desk or in a stressful, demanding job.

(3) lack of exercise, which slows the circulation of the blood. This deprives our cells of sufficient oxygen, allows toxins to build up, and makes us feel sluggish.[1]

People troubled by chronic fatigue will say they're too tired to exercise. But by releasing tension, exercise increases our energy and builds stamina. Most people feel *more* energetic after an hour of vigorous exercise.

Tension and Emotions

Negative emotions produce tension. Holding onto hurt, fear, anger, frustration, or resentment can cause chronic muscle pain. Tense, tight shoulders result from anxiety, resistance to change, or feeling over-burdened. Middle back pain indicates guilt, lower back pain fear or money problems. Tension collects in the abdomen when we are afraid to be ourselves and in the hips when we're sexually inhibited or afraid of the future. Neck pain indicates frustration or resistance to people or problems, which literally becomes "a pain in the neck."[2]

Depression is related to shallow, constricted breathing. Breathing slowly and deeply for five minutes can often bring someone out of depression. "This sounds simple," says Michael Reed Gach, "but it takes deep concentration." Yet he says that this simple exercise "will completely change how one feels about oneself."[3]

Taoist Yoga

The *Tao* asks us:

"Can you go through your days
Holding fast to the Tao?

Releasing your tension,
As you focus your breathing,
Can you relax like a child?
Can you clear your vision
And open yourself to life?"

(TAO 10)

This passage is Lao Tzu's description of Taoist yoga, or *tso-wang,* a practice which restores us to inner harmony and oneness with Tao.[4] For centuries Taoists have exercised to keep their minds and bodies supple.

Taoist Breathing

Taoist yoga begins with breathing. For the Chinese, life itself begins with our first breath, when the soul or *shen* enters the body. Inhaling is *yin,* taking in new energies and circulating them down past the heart and lungs to our vital organs. Exhaling is *yang,* as the breath ascends from the abdomen past the heart and lungs and out into the atmosphere.[5] This alternation of *yin* and *yang* continues until our last breath, when the *shen* is released at death.

The atmosphere, the air itself, each breath, and the energy they contain are all known as *chi*. In the second century B.C., Taoist master Tung Chung-Shu explained that the "space between heaven and earth," was filled with *chi* in which we were immersed "like fish in water."[6]

As we breathe in and out, what is within circulates around us; what is around us flows back within us. Thus the energy of our thoughts and feelings constantly flows into the atmosphere, continuously affecting our world.

Our buildings become charged with positive or negative *chi*, reflecting the energies of the people there. Areas filled with positive *chi* become wonderful places to recharge. Aikido master Koichi Tohei tells his students to stop by the training hall when they're feeling low, so the accumulated vibrations will help restore their energies.* When irritable or depressed, people can restore their *chi* to positive by exercising for a while, releasing tension, and opening up to vibrant new energy.[7]

TAO QUESTION

Where can you go to restore your energies with positive *chi*? A health club or martial arts center? A local park or quiet chapel? A special place in your home or garden?

Identify at least one place where you can recharge your vital energies. Remember to go there often.

PERSONAL EXERCISE: CHI BREATHING

Our bodies have a natural wisdom in restoring themselves. Many people breathe deeply only when they yawn, a natural reflex which releases stale air and brings in more oxygen.[8] We can cooperate with our body's natural wisdom by practicing *chi* breathing whenever we're feeling tired or tense.

- Sit or stand with your spine straight, inhaling slowly and deeply through your nose, taking the air deep into your abdomen, *not* your chest. Loosen your belt and put your hand on your stomach to feel the air move down into this area.
- Visualize the radiant *chi* energy as a brilliant golden light surrounding you and flowing in with each breath.
- Feel the warm *chi* energy flowing down into your abdomen and through your body.
- Hold your breath and count slowly to three (working up to ten seconds if you wish).
- Now slowly exhale through your mouth, feeling any tension melt away in the warm, golden flow of energy.
- Repeat this three times and you will be deeply relaxed and renewed.

QUICK CHI BREAK

Breathing exercises are wonderful because we can do them any time, anywhere. During a busy day I often take this quick *chi* break:

* Of course, if you're ill, you should seek medical attention from a qualified doctor. Taoist yoga is not accepted by western medicine as a means of diagnosis or treatment, but can be a helpful adjunct to medical care. You should, however, have a physical examination before embarking on any new exercise program.

- Take a deep breath and hold it briefly.
- Exhale slowly, saying to yourself "breathe out tension."
- Inhale slowly, saying to yourself "breathe in peace."

YOGA

Taoist yoga works gently and quietly, increasing the flow of *chi* within us. Some postures activate the acupressure points with the weight of our bodies. These simple postures will help you release stress and become more peaceful.

PRAYER POSE

The prayer pose opens up the heart chakra, increasing our inner peace.

- Sitting in a chair with your spine straight and your feet firmly on the ground, place your palms together, folded as in prayer, and press them against your chest at the sternum, the center of your rib cage next to the heart.
- Closing your eyes, breathe in deeply, concentrating on this point. Feel yourself being filled with new energy.
- As you exhale, feel the energy circulating through your mind and body.
- Continue to breathe slowly and deeply for one minute.
- The prayer posture activates conception vessel 17, an acupressure point that unites all the *yin* meridians, calming the nervous system and renewing our energy.[9]

The *Tao* tells us:

"Twist and become whole.
Bend and become straight.
Empty out and become full.
Expend energy and be renewed."

(TAO 22)

Many yoga exercises or *asanas* work in opposition, contracting and relaxing muscles to release tension, bending the spine to keep it straight. These two *asanas* massage the spine and back, calm the nervous system, and stimulate the flow of *chi*.

Three-Way Stretch

- Lie on your back on an exercise mat or soft rug. Relax your muscles and feel your spine straighten out.
- With your shoulders still touching the floor, raise your hands up toward the ceiling, keeping your arms straight. Breathe in and out slowly and deeply. Then slowly lower your arms to your sides.
- Keeping your arms straight, slowly lift them again and extend them out above your head, letting them rest on the floor if possible. Take another deep breath and let it out. Then slowly lower your arms again to your sides.
- With your arms at your sides, breathe in slowly and deeply, gently pressing the lower part of your back against the floor. Hold it there, then breathe out and release.
- Conclude by lying on your back with your legs straight and arms at your sides, breathing slowly and deeply for one minute, feeling your muscles relax and the energies moving through your body.

Rocking

- Sit on an exercise mat or soft rug so your back won't hit the hard floor. Allow yourself plenty of space to move around in.
- Bend your knees, clasping your hands underneath them, and draw them up toward you.
- Bend your head slightly forward. Keeping your spine rounded, rock back and forth as you would in a rocking chair.
- Rock four to six times, then lie on the floor and relax, breathing deeply.

Yoga teacher Indra Devi recommends this posture to relieve insomnia. Years ago one of her students, a British army officer who had trouble sleeping, told her that after a week of rocking, he'd thrown away his pills and was sleeping peacefully through the night.[10]

When teaching yoga, I conclude each exercise with a brief relaxation period, the *yin* complement to the *yang* movement. We learn from the *Tao* that our energies benefit from alternating periods of contraction and relaxation.

If you enjoy these simple exercises, you might want to sign up for a yoga class to learn more advanced *asanas*. The regular practice of yoga promotes inner peace and spiritual growth, as well as releasing tension, regulating weight, and increasing vitality.

One of my favorite postures, the shoulder stand, stimulates the circulation, regulates the glands and internal organs, and restores vital energy. The yogis say that fifteen minutes in the shoulder stand is comparable to two hours' sleep.[11]

A few years ago, two friends took this lesson to heart. Bill and Allan, commercial pilots, were hired to fly a busy attorney to Bakersfield for a court appearance, then on to Los Angeles, finally returning to San Jose late that night.

They took off from San Jose with their passenger early Tuesday morning and flew him down to Bakersfield, where they waited three hours while he completed his court business. Since they had a long day ahead, they did yoga to recharge their energy.

The sight of these two young men doing shoulder stands on the Bakersfield library lawn must have surprised passersby. But after the yoga and a light lunch, they felt rested and ready to go. They had enough energy to fly down to Los Angeles for the next appointment, then all the way back to San Jose, returning home at four in the morning.

As Tao people, one of our most crucial lessons is managing our own energies. The ancient practice of yoga can be a helpful assert to anyone seeking to live a balanced life.

T'ai Chi

T'ai chi, another ancient exercise system, uses stances and alternating movements to harmonize our energies.

An old Chinese saying, "standing like a pine tree," equates emotional stability with being firmly rooted in the ground.[12] One of the first lessons in t'ai chi is the standing meditation, which restores our strength with nourishing earth energy.

STANDING MEDITATION

- Stand with your feet about a foot apart, keeping your spine straight. Tucking your seat in, bend your knees slightly.
- Hold your hands out in front of you with your elbows bent, slightly above waist level.
- Now inhale deeply into your *hara*, the point of power about two inches below your navel.[13] Feel the earth energy rise up from your feet.
- Exhale, feeling the energy flow out through your hands. You may experience a tingling sensation.

This exercise stimulates the flow of *chi*, strengthens the thigh muscles and "grounds" our energies by reconnecting us with the earth. It's a wonderful way to gain strength when we're feeling scattered.

Janet DeVore, a holistic healer in northern California, taught me this posture long ago. Because it's so strengthening, she recommends practicing it at every opportunity, doing a modified version (without holding out your arms) when brushing your teeth in the morning or waiting in line at the bank.[14] Taking Janet's advice, I have found that secretly practicing the t'ai chi stance has transformed many long waits into opportunities for renewal.

Taoist Movement

The dance-like movements of t'ai chi balance our bodies by alternating the motions of *yin* and *yang*, contraction and expansion, left and right. Spontaneous, fluid, graceful as the wind, the essence of t'ai chi can be modified to fit our modern lives.

Dancing

Al Chung-liang Huang, author of *Embrace Tiger, Return to Mountain*, says whenever he feels emotionally weighed down, he clears his energy by dancing. "When I dance and move," he says, "everything seems to fall in the right place for me."[15]

Movement releases tension, removes blocks, naturally balances our body, our emotions. Dancing, we become fluid, spontaneous, one with Tao. The next time you feel tired or tense, put on some music and start dancing.

Walking

An old Chinese saying compares walking with the flow of the wind. "Walking like the wind"[16] means moving lightly, easily, naturally shifting our weight from left to right and balancing our polarities.

When we're tired or stressed, we can restore our balance by simply taking a walk. A bipolar exercise, walking uses both sides of our bodies. Stimulating left and right brain, it brings us greater balance. Improving circulation and strengthening *chi* energies, it stimulates our own inner rhythms. We tune in to our pulse, our breathing, the sensations of our body, and get a deeper sense of being ourselves.

The *Tao* teaches us to honor the rhythms within and around us. But too often we're pressured by the world outside, losing touch with our own inner music. A barrage of noise, phone calls, deadlines, and demands from others constantly interrupts us, throwing us out of synch. Taoist exercise can restore our inner harmony, returning the rhythms of our lives to more peaceful patterns.

Affirmation

I now know my life is peaceful and harmonious.
Aware of my energies, I remember to nurture and restore them.
Releasing all tension, I relax into deeper awareness.
I follow my own inner music.
I respect myself and the process.
I harmonize with nature and all others in my world.
I accept greater peace in my life now.
And so it is.

CHAPTER 8

SEEKING SIMPLICITY

"Hold to these principles:
Seek simplicity,
Grasp the essential,
Overcome selfishness
And wasteful desires."

(TAO 19)

SIMPLICITY clears our vision, frees us from false values, brings greater beauty to our lives.

The Chinese word for simplicity is *su,* which means raw silk: natural, pure, unadorned.[1] Chinese art has long affirmed the beauty of simplicity.

Years ago I spent many solitary hours trying to achieve the ineffable simplicity of Chinese painting. Practicing the brush strokes takes patience. Made in one fluid motion, the strokes are *wu wei:* they cannot be forced. The painter must achieve a harmony within before portraying it without.

The works of the masters are models of effortless grace: a branch of cherry blossoms, koi in a small pond, a simple stalk of bamboo. There are no extra strokes, no embellishments. All is serene against a plain background. The natural silk or rice paper itself becomes part of the picture. Chinese art teaches the importance of empty space, openness, the wisdom of Tao.

A student of Eastern philosophy, Henry David Thoreau praised the openness of silent reveries, the joy of contemplation. His days at Walden Pond were long and unrushed. "I love a broad margin to my life," he said.

How much margin do we leave in our lives? Are our homes, our closets, our calendars impossibly cluttered? "Our life is frittered away by detail," wrote Thoreau, urging his readers to "simplify, simplify."[2] This chapter will help clear the clutter and confusion from our lives.

Finding Simplicity in a Changing World

Alvin Toffler coined the term "future shock" to describe our disorientation when we experience too much change too often. According to Toffler, rapid changes in the past few decades have eroded our sense of security. We've become a "throw-away society." Fast food wrappers, grocery bags, bottles, cans, paper napkins, plastic packaging, high fashion clothing, disposable razors, cameras, even relationships are quickly discarded when their usefulness is gone.[3]

This pattern has caused not only personal but planetary imbalance, adversely affecting our economy. Planned obsolescence has upset our balance of trade because many American products are unreliable or impossible to repair. It has precipitated an unprecedented pile up of garbage, imbalancing our ecology and poisoning the planet.

Seeking simplicity in a world of impermanence is quite a challenge. Yet scaling down and becoming more conscious of how we use things creates greater peace individually and collectively.

Seeking Simple Solutions

Following the Tao, we realize even our smallest actions have consequences, contributing to the evolving cycles around us. One example is the familiar styrofoam cup. Using these cups at work makes each of us responsible for five cups a week, twenty a month, and within a year 260 non-biodegradable additions to the mountain of trash on this planet.

Bringing your own coffee mug to work and encouraging others to do the same saves money, establishes a more familiar atmosphere, and helps reduce the mindless waste and pollution around us.

Refusing to use styrofoam cups, asking for biodegradable bags and products at the grocery store, avoiding "fast food" restaurants with their wasteful packaging, and scaling down your needs are simple actions with far-reaching consequences.

Creating Patterns of Stability

Simplifying our lives also means keeping our bearings. Tao people take time each day for personal rituals of stability. Some start the day with meditation or exercise. Others take a daily walk at noon or time to unwind after work.

My marriage partner, Gwilym, begins each day with shoto-kan karate and a two-mile run. While it's still dark outside, he does his karate warm-up exercises. Then he runs through the neighborhood at sunrise, watching the changing sky and awakening life around him. The sparrows sing out from the treetops and busy squirrels dance through the branches overhead. Surrounded by this moving panorama, he says his affirmations, recognizing his part in the larger community. His morning ritual combines aerobic exercise with spiritual renewal.

I begin the day quite differently: centering myself with quiet reading and meditation. As the dawn slowly filters through my window, I look over my calendar to see what patterns the new day offers, concluding with affirmations of harmony for the day ahead.

Sometimes when we've had houseguests, I've skipped my morning ritual to join them for breakfast. But then I face the day unfocused, make foolish decisions, and react to events instead of responding from center.

A balanced life takes discipline. We alone can live our lives the way we choose. Now, regardless of what others think, I take time to check in with myself each morning. When my energies are focused, the rest of the day goes more smoothly for everyone.

Tao Question

What is your personal pattern of stability? Do you have a ritual for beginning the day, time to center yourself or unwind in the evening?

If not, choose one ritual of personal renewal that works for you— meditation, exercise, affirmation—and resolve to do it every day at the same time. Then no matter what the universe offers, you'll have one enduring pattern in your life.

Simplifying Sensory Overload

The *Tao* tells us:

"The five colors can blind our eyes,
The five sounds deafen our ears,
The five tastes exhaust our appetites.
Chasing desire can drive us mad.
Therefore, the Tao person
Seeks inner wisdom,
Lets go of excess,
Affirms the truth."

(TAO 12)

Modern life assaults our senses with noise, color, and ceaseless appeals to appetite. It's easy to lose our balance. As Lao Tzu said, "Chasing desire can drive us mad." Research has shown that sensory overload produces symptoms very much like schizophrenia.[4] Too many people race off in a dozen directions at once. They eat, dress, work, and play with no center. Losing sight of the whole, they succumb to fragmentation, illness, and exhaustion.

PERSONAL EXERCISE

We can reduce sensory overload by:

- Seeking out periods of silence each day. Turn off the radio and television, close the door, unplug the phone. Feel the healing sensation of silence.
- Spending some time each day alone, walking, reading, or working, listening to your own thoughts.
- Spending some time in the natural world: working in your garden, walking in the park. Cleanse your senses with natural sounds and

images. Listen to the birds singing, the leaves rustling. Smell the flowers. Rest your eyes with the soft green of growing things and the rich brown of the earth.

Knowing When Enough Is Enough

The *Tao* tells us:

"Great trouble comes
From not knowing what is enough.
Great conflict arises from wanting too much.
When we know when enough is enough,
There will always be enough."

(TAO 46)[6]

Twenty-five centuries ago, Lao Tzu realized the dangers of excess, both individually and collectively. For individuals, excess causes sensory overload, imbalance, disease. Collectively, excess consumption by some causes deficiency for others, perpetuating cycles of poverty, injustice, and warfare. Extreme *yang* leads to *yin,* excess to deficiency. "Great conflict arises from wanting too much."

The Chinese character for wisdom, *hui,* shows a broom held over the mind-heart.[7] For the Chinese, wisdom literally means sweeping away clutter. We can do this in four different ways: by simplifying our possessions, our knowledge, our communication, and our use of time.

Simplifying Our Possessions

Our society seems to encourage clutter. Many of my neighbors must leave their cars outside because their garages are filled with things they've long since forgotten.

Getting rid of things we no longer use helps us find what we have. It also strengthens us emotionally. Releasing old possessions helps us release the past. Old griefs, guilts, grudges, and regrets disappear, enabling us to live more fully in the present.

PERSONAL EXERCISE

You can bring greater order to your life by going through your closets, drawers, and garage, giving away everything you don't need.

- Take one area at a time and go through it systematically, discarding anything you no longer use. You'll probably discover things you didn't know you had.
- Place discarded items neatly in a box or bag and take them to your favorite charity. Recycling what you no longer need produces more to go around, less wear and tear on the planet. Everyone benefits.
- Resolve to clean out one area a month, releasing old possessions, creating greater order, and circulating new energy through your life.

The Politics of Simplicity

Many people mistakenly associate simplicity with poverty, but there's one vital difference. Simplicity is a matter of choice, poverty is not. By simplifying, we affirm greater power over our lives: choosing health, order, and beauty; discarding clutter and confusion.

Because in the Tao everything is related, the political effects of a simpler life are far-reaching. "When we know when enough is enough, there will always be enough" (*Tao* 46). The more people who choose a simpler lifestyle, the more balance and justice in the world.

In the 1950s a woman who called herself Peace Pilgrim began to walk across America on a pilgrimage for peace. Paring down her possessions to the clothes on her back and a few items in her pockets, she chose to live at what she called "need-level," rejoicing in the freedom she found.

By determining their own "need-level," many peacemakers today shun excess as burdensome, unhealthy, and unjust, living simply to affirm their spiritual growth or solidarity with the poor. Many share their wealth with the hungry and homeless. Living simply is liberating and empowering, as Peace Pilgrim explained, "A persistent simplification will create an inner and outer well-being that places harmony in one's life."[8]

There are many advantages to a simpler life. It brings us closer to nature, encourages us to share, decreases pollution, saves money, preserves the environment, reduces tension, promotes better health, and nurtures us spiritually.[9] Consciously simplifying our lives helps us see beyond our society's materialistic values into the enduring wisdom of Tao.

A simpler life improves our mental health, according to marriage and family counselor Mitch Saunders. It restores our wholeness, freeing us from the compulsive work ethic, "the way our culture is structured to value things, not people."

"Peace," Mitch explains, "is staying close to what's natural and simple," returning to the wisdom of primitive societies, which are closer to the earth. Gandhi recognized this as well. Modern industrialized society can easily throw us off balance.

Seeking Security Beyond Our Illusions ✓

Obsessively collecting things has become an emotional crutch for many people, an illusion of security in an insecure world. When Denise's mother died last year, it took my friend months to sort through her possessions.

The kitchen cupboards were stacked full of canned goods, dusty with age, the linen closets filled with new sheets and towels, saved "for company." Eight dozen rolls of toilet paper were stockpiled in closets throughout the house, five sets of dishes neatly stacked in the china closet. Knickknacks filled three display cases and covered all the table tops. The closets were crammed with clothes that hadn't been worn in years.

The Tao teaches that we cannot find security outside ourselves, and certainly not behind walls of clutter. We find it by looking within, following Tao, and living with integrity.

Simplifying Our Knowledge

The *Tao* tells us:

"When seeking knowledge,
Much is acquired.

When seeking Tao,
Much is discarded."

(TAO 48)

The *Tao* teaches openmindedness, freedom from the tyranny of custom and authority. Much of what passes in the world for knowledge is intellectual clutter that keeps us from thinking for ourselves. The knowledge we find in the classroom, in books, newspapers, or on television is mainly the experience and opinion of others. Some of this knowledge may be true, but we forfeit our intellectual independence if we accept it at face value. The *Tao* says not to let anyone else do our thinking for us.

Tao people study life. They listen to others and weigh their opinions. But they make their own decisions, follow inner guidance and the cycles of Tao.

Blind obedience to authority not only violates our integrity but perpetuates violence. In a memorable psychological experiment, Dr. Stanley Milgram asked some paid volunteers to administer electric shocks to people in his laboratory. Standing beside the volunteers, he ordered them to increase the dosage, while the victims (really paid actors) screamed and writhed in pain. Over 60% of the volunteers obeyed.[10]

As this experiment and the many war crimes throughout history attest, many people will obey an authority figure, even when it means hurting others. We can overcome such mindless violence by remaining centered, looking beyond authority to follow conscience and the principles of Tao.

Simplifying Our Communication

The *Tao* says:

"Much chatter brings only exhaustion.
Stay true to your center."

(TAO 5)

The noise of modern life makes it hard to hear ourselves think. Radios drone on in our houses, cars, and at work, following us into the grocery store, stalking us down the aisles. Television invades our living rooms with other people's lives, artificial words and images, leaving little room for our own thoughts.

Many people hide behind the noise, unwilling to face themselves. Phil recently retired from a busy career in merchandising. A widower with two grown sons, he lives alone in a modest Brooklyn apartment. It's time to examine his life and seek new direction, but that's the last thing he wants to do so he fills his days with noise.

He has a TV set in each room of his apartment including the bathroom. Daytime dramas, quiz shows, and commercials drone on all day. When visitors stop by, they have to shout to be heard above the noise. Phil listens to recorded books in the car to keep his mind occupied. Evenings he spends watching movies on the VCR, then drifts off to sleep listening to all night talk shows. When his son Peter visited last month, he was exhausted by all the racket.

PERSONAL EXERCISE: SHUTTING OFF THE CHATTER

Returning to center takes discipline. Tao people seek out daily periods of silence and renewal so they don't forget who they are.

How easy it is to turn on the radio when I'm at home alone. It's easy companionship, but at what cost? The background chatter makes me less likely to meditate, write a friend, work creatively, or attend to my own thoughts. Silence returns us to ourselves and the natural rhythms of Tao.

- The next time you automatically turn on the radio or television, ask yourself why.
- If you choose to watch or listen, leave it on. If not, turn it off.
- Make silent periods an important part of your day. You may miss out on some of the local news, soap operas, or sitcoms, but you'll become better acquainted with an old friend: yourself.

The *Tao* tells us:

"Nature does not waste words.
Neither do people of Tao."

(TAO 23)

How many of us "waste words" each day in meaningless gossip, idle chatter, or telephone addiction? When I was younger, I used to spend most evenings on the phone. Stretched out on the floor, I'd talk for hours. My women friends and I used each other as therapists, analyzing the men in our lives, ventilating our frustrations, massaging our egos, and relieving our loneliness—all on the telephone. After two or three phone calls, with some studying worked in between, another evening had passed.

All through college and grad school this was a regular pattern: long conversations, late nights, and little sleep. But somehow I managed to get things done. For years many of us cried, cursed, laughed, and lived a good part of our lives on the telephone.

Only one woman I knew didn't play this game. Pat told us when she was busy, when she could meet us for lunch or tea. Phone calls with her averaged five minutes at most. Centered and disciplined, she was writing a novel and selling short stories while the rest of us squandered our energies over the wires.

PERSONAL EXERCISE

To simplify your conversations this week, ask yourself:

- Am I communicating honestly? Do I mean what I say? Is my intention to share and not expand my ego?
- Do I listen to others, aware of their body language as well as their words?
- Do I avoid worthless speech—chitchat, gossip, and phone addiction?
- Do I respect the importance of silence in my life and interactions with others? Can I be present with someone without constantly talking?[11]

Simplifying Our Time

The *Tao* says:

"Close your mouth,
Shut your doors,

And live close to Tao.
Open your mouth,
Be busy all day,
And live in confusion."

(TAO 52)

We lose our center when we get caught up in a succession of mundane activities with barely enough time to catch our breath. Simplifying our time means taking charge, putting ourselves back on track.

When we're overextending ourselves, our bodies will sometimes rebel and forcibly simplify things. Once when exhausted by a merciless pileup of classes, conferences, workshops, and deadlines, I lost my voice for three days, forcing me to cancel all my commitments and stay home.

Everything somehow went on without me and I learned a valuable lesson. Now whenever I schedule things, I try not to let commitments pile up that way. Looking at the larger patterns in my life, I leave myself more margin.

Often our schedules clash with our inner rhythms. We feel stressed because we're out of synch. The next time you feel stressed, take a walk by yourself. Rediscover your own rhythm. Then ask yourself how you can better harmonize with it.

PERSONAL EXERCISE: HOW DO I SPEND MY TIME?

Psychologists know the best way to change a stressful pattern is first to become aware of it. This week, monitor your use of time. Ask yourself how much time you spend each day in:

- Eating
- Sleeping
- Exercising
- Meaningful work
- Spiritual growth

- Renewal activities (recreation, reading)
- Sharing with friends
- Routine maintenance
- Social service
- Other

Look at the patterns that emerge. Are your days balanced? Do you allow enough time for exercise, renewal, and spirituality or are you too bogged down with work and maintenance?

Carefully examine the last category: other. What else have you been doing? Are there some things here you can delegate, eliminate, or otherwise simplify?

Is there anything missing from your life? Can you make room for it by scaling down your involvement in other areas?

Think of yourself as an architect designing a beautiful living structure. What changes would help you live a more balanced life? Draw a new pattern incorporating these changes and start living it.

TAO QUESTIONS

Whenever contemplating any new commitment, you can keep yourself on track by asking yourself:

- Is it necessary?
- Is it healthy?
- Will it bring greater peace to my life or the planet?

If it doesn't fit these criteria, then don't do it. Living the Tao means taking personal responsibility for the structure of our lives.

Affirmation

I now know my life is peaceful and harmonious.
I simplify my life.
I release unnecessary possessions.
I follow my inner guidance and the wisdom of Tao.
I communicate simply and honestly.

I use my time wisely.
I respect myself and the process.
I harmonize with nature and all others in my world.
I accept greater peace in my life now.
And so it is.

CHAPTER 9

FINDING YOUR CENTER

"Be still
And discover your center of peace.
Throughout nature
The ten thousand things move along,
But each returns to its source.
Returning to center is peace.
Find Tao by returning to source."

(TAO 16)

WHILE modern life emphasizes the surface of things, the *Tao* teaches that without the center, the surface means nothing. It is not what we look like, what we do, but what we *are* that brings meaning and purpose.

The ocean is a marvelous symbol of Tao: vast, fluid, constantly in motion. Beneath its turbulent surface are the quiet depths. Beneath the restless surface of our lives lies a deep source of peace, power, and inspiration.

We can find this deep center in reflection or meditation. Detaching from particulars, we see the evolving patterns.

Non-Tao people identify with externals. Uncentered, they don't know who they are. When their external supports change or conflict, they're easily thrown off balance.

Who Am I?

Emily was the epitome of an uncentered person. Her life was structured by pleasing others: her parents, friends, employer, and the man she loved.

A pale blonde in her early twenties, she sat huddled in the chair before me, her slender body wracked with sobs. She tried so hard, she said, but faced one conflict after another. Now the problem was Christmas. Her boyfriend wanted them to go skiing, her parents wanted her at home, and her boss had asked her to work overtime.

"What do *you* want to do?" I asked.

She peered up at me, wide-eyed. "I don't know," she said tearfully. "I don't know how I feel . . . about anything."

Years of pleasing others had made her emotionally numb. Even her movements were stiff, almost mechanical. Out of touch with her center, she'd met other people's needs until opposing loyalties turned conflict into crisis. The opposing "shoulds" were pulling her apart.

We slowly sifted through her commitments, separating positive choices from guilt and obligation. Centered in her own feelings, Emily's life has become more harmonious.

PERSONAL EXERCISE

If trying to please others has caught you in conflicting commitments, return to center by eliminating the words "should" and "can't" from your vocabulary. They only reinforce guilt and helplessness. Instead of "I should," say "I choose to." Instead of "I can't," say "I won't."

How does this feel? When you affirm your right to choose, you become more aware of your center, your personal power.

We Are Not the Parts We Play

The *Tao* teaches that all of life is dynamic. Nature and individuals are constantly evolving. Shakespeare wrote that "all the world's a stage," that each of us plays many parts. Never confuse your center with the roles you play.

The Tao cannot be reduced to a simple definition. Neither can we. Roles are rigid and lifeless. The Tao forever grows and changes.

Have you become over-identified with any of the roles in your life? Take this self-assessment and see.

SELF-ASSESSMENT

I *My Job*

1. When I introduce myself, am I proud to say what I do or embarrassed to admit it?
2. Do I find it hard to relax on vacations?
3. When I perform well on the job, do I feel ecstatic?
4. When I perform poorly on the job, do I feel like a complete failure?
5. Is work my number one priority?
6. Do I feel more myself at work?

II *My Family*

1. When I make plans, do I think of my family first?
2. Do I feel my own needs are selfish?
3. Do I do things because parents/children/relatives think I "should"?
4. Is my schedule filled with family obligations?
5. Do I lack time for my own interests?
6. Do I worry a lot about family members?

III *My Partner*

1. When I make plans, do I think of my partner first?
2. Am I afraid to be honest with him or her?
3. Do I do things I don't like to in order to please my partner?
4. Do I react to my partner's moods with emotional ups and downs?
5. Do I neglect my friends and other interests because of my partner?
6. Am I easily jealous? Do I worry about my partner or fear losing him/her?

IV *My Body*

1. Am I uncomfortable in crowds? Do I feel everyone's looking at me?
2. Am I dissatisfied with my body?
3. When I see someone who reminds me of myself when I was younger, do I get depressed or envious?
4. Do I feel I have to be strong/pretty/handsome/thin to be acceptable?
5. Do I fear growing old?

6. Do I spend lots of time compulsively dieting, exercising, or grooming myself?

If you answer yes to three or more questions in any category, go back and examine the implications. If any part of your life has become a source of anxiety, guilt, or radical mood swings, you're over-identifying.

Over-identifying fragments our sense of self. In the next section we'll see how people who over-identify lose their center. We can break this painful pattern by realizing we're always more than the roles we play.

My Job Is Not My Center

For the last twenty years Jim has been searching for the ideal career. A likeable fellow with sandy hair and intense blue eyes, he's been a police cadet, social worker, bilingual instructor, photographer, and law student.

He throws himself into every field with abandon. He was at the top of his police class until falling in love with a social worker prompted him to change careers. To become a better social worker, he learned Spanish, not only mastering the language but teaching it in his spare time. In Mexico for an intensive language course, he became interested in photography, so he quit his other jobs, invested in photo equipment, and moved to a loft in San Francisco. After two years as a commercial photographer, he's decided to become an attorney.

Intelligent and strong-minded, Jim succeeds in every venture until he suddenly loses interest. Once the initial excitement fades, he decides this career isn't right for him and moves on. His center, his identity, always remains outside. The elusive goal beckons, just beyond his grasp, promising *this* time to bring meaning to his life.

Jim keeps searching for his dream career. Others cling to a job for security. Either way, they make their careers their centers. Twenty years ago in Seattle several aerospace engineers committed suicide. Why? They'd been laid off. Without their jobs they felt worthless, unable to face life.

A similar identity crisis often afflicts people at retirement. Without their jobs they wonder who they are. Succumbing to despair, many never live to find out.

Identifying with our careers is strongly encouraged in our society. When introducing ourselves, we usually define who we are as what we do: "My name is Jim Pierce. I'm a law student."

The *Tao* teaches us to see beyond categories. Who we are is always more than what we do.

AFFIRMATION

If you've been over-identifying with your job, restore your balance by reminding yourself, many times a day:

"I have a job, but I'm *not* my job. I am one with Tao."[1]

My Family Is Not My Center

Traditionally, jobs for men and relationships for women have been major sources of over-identification. While men have built their identities around careers, women have built theirs around home and family.

For twenty-eight years Beth submerged herself in her role as the doctor's wife. She met Don in college and worked as a secretary while he struggled through medical school. When he hung up his shingle, she happily quit work to raise children, join the garden club, and become active in the community.

Last summer when the last of their children left for college and Don filed for divorce, Beth went into shock. Suddenly there was no husband, no children, no center to her life.

AFFIRMATION

Our families are sources of love and support, but over-identifying with them is unhealthy. People change. Children grow up. Loved ones can go away. If you've been over-identifying, remind yourself:

"I have a family but I'm *not* my family.
I love my family because I love my life.
I am one with Tao."

My Relationship Is Not My Center

Times have changed, but many women still build their lives around the men they love or waste time waiting for the perfect man.

For over two years Lois has been trying to buy a house. For a single professional woman of 35, this makes sense economically. But one problem after another has blocked her. Her realtor is incompetent, she says, and her current relationship is rocky.

Lois supervises a retail credit department for a large corporation. Her salary is ample, she's saved a down payment, but still can't manage to buy a house.

Through counseling she learned a house was part of her vision of marriage. She'd been holding back because the right man was missing. For Lois, buying a house without a man meant giving up her dream of marriage.

Lois needs to find her own center. She can't keep putting her future on hold, expecting the right relationship to make all her dreams come true.

Many women give away their centers to the men they love. Christa has gone through more identities than I can remember, each a reflection of her current relationship. When she was dating a sportscar afficionado, she came into my office reading *Road and Track*. Her affair with a mystery writer changed her wardrobe to trenchcoats and turtlenecks, her reading material to Ellery Queen and Dashiel Hammett. At present, she's dating a dance promoter, studying ballet, and dressing in a colorful collection of leotards and leg warmers.

What makes an intelligent woman such a chameleon? She keeps placing her center outside, in the hands of the man she loves. Once she gives herself away, Christa becomes compulsively attached to her man, fussing, clinging, and driving him crazy. When he pulls away, strangled by her demands, she's devastated. Who can she be without him?

AFFIRMATION

Once again, the Tao returns us to center. Our relationships become healthier when we stop identifying with them. If you find yourself over-identifying with an important person in your life, repeat this affirmation many times a day:

"I have a relationship, but I'm *not* my relationship.
I love (your partner) because I love myself.
I am one with Tao."

My Body Is Not My Center

Many people identify with their bodies. Struggling to achieve artificial standards of perfection, they're never quite tall enough, strong enough, thin enough.

The Tao teaches that nothing in life stands still. Even if we achieve our society's ideals, we're always changing. Identifying with a body image keeps us from growing up. Too many young athletes become depressed in middle age when they feel they're losing their powers. Women adored as pretty girls can find the midlife transition paved with pain and loss.

AFFIRMATION

If you've been worrying excessively about your physical image, repeat this affirmation:

"I have a body, but I'm *not* my body. I am one with Tao."

I Am Not My Cause

Many people who work for social justice suffer from burnout because no matter how hard they work, how much they sacrifice, the problem remains. Peace workers, like counselors, nurses, and teachers, can become uncentered when they over-identify with a cause.

Problems of hunger, poverty, injustice, nuclear danger, and the environment are so overwhelming it's easy to lose ourselves in them. But in losing ourselves we cannot act. We become paralyzed by despair.

Recently two college students came up to me after a film about Central America. "I feel terrible," one young woman said. "There's so much poverty. The problem's so enormous. There's nothing I can do."

But there is. Each of us can do something, even if we can't singlehandedly solve the problem. The three of us decided to collect clothes for hurricane victims in Nicaragua. Instead of surrendering to despair, we took action and affirmed our hope for a better world.

As peacemakers, we can be more effective if we remain centered, refusing to surrender to guilt or despair.

No matter how important the cause, it's not our center. We must remember to balance concern for our neighbors and our planet with personal renewal.

AFFIRMATION

If you've been over-identifying with your cause, remind yourself:
"I have a cause, but I'm *not* my cause. I am one with Tao."

Centering

Detaching from externals, affirming our center, we are one with Tao. Detaching doesn't mean we can't enjoy our work, our families, our relationships, or commit ourselves to a cause, only that we don't identify with them.

Detachment doesn't mean giving up but opening ourselves up to the Tao, the source of life. For our center is our source of peace, our link with the infinite, the treasure we carry next to our hearts.

Lao Tzu says:

"Rejecting appearances,
The Tao person wears simple clothes,
Lives true to center,
Wears jade close to the heart."

(TAO 70)

Centered, the Tao person looks beyond externals, never flaunting accomplishments or possessions. We can enjoy the blessings of our lives but cannot possess them. They're part of the fluid movement of

Tao, part of the process that flows like a river around and through us.
When we know this, we've found our center and are one with Tao.
Lao Tzu tells us:

"The Tao person embraces the One
And lives in peace by its pattern.
Do not dwell on your ego,
    and you will discover your soul.
Avoid prideful acts,
    and your work will endure.
If you do not compete,
    no one on earth will compete against you.

Follow the ancient wisdom:
'Yield and Overcome.'
True peace is achieved
By centering
And blending with life."

(TAO 22)[2]

Affirmation

I now know my life is peaceful and harmonious.
I am centered, whole and complete.
I have a job, but I'm not my job.
I have a family, but I'm not my family.
I have relationships, but I'm not my relationships.
I have a body, but I'm not my body.
I have a cause, but I'm not my cause.
I am one with Tao.
I respect myself and the process.
I harmonize with nature and all others in my world.
I accept greater peace in my life now.
And so it is.

CHAPTER 10

EXPLORING YOUR DUALITIES: YIN AND YANG

"The Tao is the One.
From the One come *yin* and *yang*;
From these two, creative energy;
From energy, ten thousand things,
The forms of all creation.

All life embodies *yin*
And embraces *yang*,
Through their union
Achieving harmony."

(TAO 42)

THE *Tao* teaches that life is dynamic, its changing patterns comprised of *yang* and *yin,* the polarities found throughout nature. We know them as day and night, heat and cold, male and female, action and repose.

But the western mind too often poses dilemmas, forcing us to choose one extreme over the other: day *or* night, male *or* female, action *or* repose. With our preference of *yang* over *yin,* American culture equates a successful life with day ("early to bed and early to rise"), the masculine stereotype, and the Puritan work ethic.

In the wisdom of Tao, one extreme complements the other. Action and repose *seem* opposite, but wise action includes rest, reflection, and inner guidance, avoiding the extremes of compulsiveness (excessive *yang*) or passivity (excessive *yin*). In our lives and our world, the dynamic balance of these forces brings harmony.

Understanding Yin and Yang

Yin and *yang* are the two polarities of life. They appear as:

yin	yang
darkness	light
moon	sun
night	day
winter	summer
earth	heaven
valley	mountain
water	stone
open	closed
soft	hard
deficiency	excess
interior	exterior
contracting	expanding
passive	aggressive
contemplative	active
feminine	masculine
nurturing	achieving
feeling	thinking
listening	speaking
intuition	reason
unconscious	conscious
repose	action
knowing	doing

The dynamic opposition of *yin* and *yang* is central to Eastern philosophy. The *I Ching*, ancient book of wisdom and divination, is made up of solid lines (*yang*) which combine with broken lines (*yin*) to produce the sixty-four hexagrams depicting all of human experience. The twelfth century Chinese philosopher Chu Hsi explained that "the phase of repose is the *yin*, the phase of activity is the *yang*; and this perpetual alteration of *yin* and *yang* in its turn produces the five elements . . . From the five elements heaven and earth are de-rived, and from them all creation."[1]

The *Tao* teaches that "all life embodies *yin* and embraces *yang*." (*Tao* 42). All existence emerges from the synthesis of these forces. As *yin* simultaneously contrasts with and embraces *yang*, their interaction produces a new creation.

This dynamic paradigm of *yin* and *yang* resembles the Hegelian dialectic of thesis/antithesis/synthesis in which one concept (thesis) inevitably generates its opposite (antithesis) and their interaction produces a new concept (synthesis). The similarity is no accident, for Hegel, too, studied the *Tao*, lecturing on Taoism at Heidelberg early in his career.[2]

Balancing Yin and Yang

Both active *yang* and contemplative *yin* are essential to intelligent living. We all need moments of silent reflection or our actions would have no direction, no meaning. Conversely, without action, our thoughts cannot take form.

Sometimes people get stuck in one extreme or the other, becoming too *yin* or too *yang*. Sunny and Sam grew up as children of the sixties, adopting opposing patterns for their lives.

Sunny embraced sixties idealism. She marched in demonstrations and worked in political campaigns, believing that she could make a difference. After college she joined the Peace Corps, then went on to become a journalist, specializing in social justice issues.

Sunny works long hours at the newspaper, teaches college writing classes, counsels reentry women, does volunteer work at the local shelter, and belongs to a dozen community organizations. They're all good causes, and Sunny just can't say no. Her personal life is almost nonexistent—she's too busy helping others and there's always so much to do.

Racing between commitments, she's like a comet, perpetually in motion, her reddish blonde curls always disheveled, her clothes rumpled, her meals caught on the run. She's almost never home. The tempo of her life ranges from busy to frenetic, excessively *yang*, punctuated with brief periods of involuntary *yin* when she collapses from burnout or exhaustion.

Her brother Sam not only lacks his sister's drive, he seems perfectly happy doing nothing. The sixties introduced him to drugs, cynicism, and passivity. He dropped out of school after the summer of love in San Francisco, drifting from one job to another. But he prefers to live on unemployment.

Whenever he has a few dollars, Sam starts an argument with his boss, gets fired, and goes back on unemployment to enjoy his version of the good life. After sleeping till noon, he spends the day smoking pot and watching TV.

Sam can lie on the couch for hours reading, daydreaming, or dozing off. A real homebody, he putters around the apartment, playing with his roommate's cat or watching the kids next door. Around dinner time he strolls to the corner store for something to eat. He enjoys cooking for his friends, specializing in Indian curries and Tex-Mex.

Sam thinks about going into the restaurant business, but work is such a hassle. So he turns on the TV set and watches another rerun of "Leave It to Beaver" until his dwindling funds force him to take another job.

Sunny never sits still and Sam rarely moves unless he has to. Their parents worry that she's a workaholic, too busy to find a husband, while their son can't seem to hold a job. If Sunny were the passive stay-at-home and Sam the compulsive worker, some people would consider them normal, but they'd still be extremes. A healthy, integrated life combines both contemplation and action, *yin* and *yang*.

Our society needs a better balance as well. Like Sunny, many people in the western world race around constantly, chasing their dreams of a better life without time to reflect, to ask where they— and all of us—are heading.

Duane Elgin writes in *Voluntary Simplicity* that "Our civilizational crisis has emerged in no small part from the gross disparity that exists between our relatively underdeveloped 'inner faculties' and the extremely powerful external technologies now at our disposal."[3] "As it is within, so it is without." An imbalanced world results from personal imbalance. The *Tao* teaches us to slow down, look within, and make wiser choices.

Restoring Our Balance

Without balance, we go to one extreme like Sunny and Sam, or experience alternating highs and lows.

Almost everyone knows someone like Terry. She goes from one diet to another, her weight alternating from 105 to 160. Her closet is filled with clothes in six sizes plus some tentlike caftans when nothing else will do.

Poor Terry is a compulsive eater and dieter, constantly shifting between the two extremes. Between boyfriends, she eats to console herself, indulging in the comfort food she learned to love as a child: fried chicken, fried potatoes, fried ham and grits, or fried pies, ice cream, cookies, and cheese cake.

Then when none of her clothes fit, she throws herself into a deprivation diet, subsisting on celery, bouillon, grapefruit, and salad. When she sheds the unwanted pounds, the cycle starts all over again.

Over the years Terry has lost and gained hundreds of pounds. The *yang* and *yin* extremes of indulgence and deprivation are terribly hard on her body, first flooding her system with fats and cholesterol, then depriving it of essential nutrients. A nutritious diet and regular exercise would help harmonize her life as well as her weight with the right balance of *yin* and *yang*.

To restore our balance, we need to step back, take time to center and get our bearings. Otherwise, like Terry, we'll only zigzag wildly between two extremes. When we recognize the excessive patterns in our lives, we can do something about them.

PERSONAL EXERCISE

Are you experiencing violent alternations in any part of your life: your weight, relationships, health, finances, or career? If so, take a few minutes now to get your bearings.

- Go off by yourself and relax with a few slow, deep breaths.
- Now ask yourself one question at a time. After each one, close your eyes and wait for the answer.
- Where in my life is the point of excess, expansion, the active *yang*? What do I find myself doing too much of?

- Where is the point of deficiency, contraction, the passive *yin?* What in my life do I never have enough of? Where do I feel diminished or deprived?
- How do *yin* and *yang* relate in my life? Is there a causal pattern between the two extremes?
- What can I do to bring greater balance to my life?

Write your insights in your journal. Then review them tomorrow and begin to create a new, more balanced pattern.

The objective, of course, is not to eliminate the highs and lows. That would be impossible. In life there will always be contrasts: valleys and mountains, *yin* and *yang*. But when we're centered, our emotions flow in gentle waves. They no longer plunge from high peaks to deep chasms.

As we become more aware of the natural patterns in our lives, we learn to flow with them. Each of us at times feels outgoing, vibrant, active—*yang*—and at other times quiet, peaceful, reflective—*yin*. The Tao person honors these inner rhythms, enjoys the differences.

Harmonizing with the World Around Us

Sometimes we need to modify our rhythms to harmonize with people and situations around us. One way to do this is with music.

For centuries people have realized that certain sound patterns motivate us, while others calm and soothe our spirits. Psychiatrist Roberto Assagioli prescribed different music for his patients: marches to quicken the energies of depressed people, waltzes to calm the overly anxious.[4]

I find marches invigorating and energizing, the perfect boost when I have a new project or challenge ahead. To slow down and relax, I listen to Bach, Vivaldi, or new age meditation music. The measured rhythms, counterpoint, and gentle tones blend the events of the day into harmonious patterns.

Another way to balance is with color. Decorators create restful environments with cool blue and green or raise our energies with warm yellow, orange, and red. When dressing in the morning, many people unconsciously choose colors that harmonize with their moods.

Students of Eastern philosophy say we're each a walking rainbow. Our seven chakras, the energy centers running through our bodies, range from the passionate lower centers of red and orange, to the yellow solar plexis, the green heart chakra, up to the cool colors of blue (throat chakra), indigo (the third eye), and violet (the crown chakra at the top of the head).

Wearing corresponding colors stimulates the chakras. Red and orange, the lower chakra colors, activate our *yang* tendencies, making us more energetic, assertive, and physically active. I wear red when I want to increase my energy.

Yellow stimulates the intellect and activates our personal power. It's often used in libraries and study areas. Green, the color of nature, has a profound calming effect. Many decorators balance busy offices with the soothing green of tropical plants.

Pale blue or violet activates our contemplative *yin* tendencies, stimulating spirituality, creativity, serenity. My church recently redecorated its sanctuary in soft blue tones, creating a peaceful, meditative atmosphere.

TAO QUESTION

When you get dressed tomorrow, think about the colors you wear. Do you want to harmonize with your feelings or gently modify them, complementing *yin* with *yang*? The choice is up to you but remember, everything in our world gives off subtle vibrations. It's our task to blend them into harmonious patterns.

Transcending Sex Roles

The *Tao* tells us:

"Develop your masculine power
Yet be gentle and nurturing.
Become open like a valley
So the river of virtue
Flows through you,
Returning you to source."

(TAO 28)

Although traditional cultures have reinforced men for active, aggressive *yang* behavior and women for submissive *yin*, we each possess both tendencies. Psychoanalyst Carl Jung realized that beneath the conscious masculine image of every man lies the *anima*, his unconscious feminine potential. Similarly, within each woman is the *animus*, her unrealized masculine tendencies. According to Jung, until we come to terms with our unconscious opposite, life is a continuous quest for wholeness.[5]

Opposites attract. In our youth, we project the *anima* or *animus* upon the person we love, seeking a "soul mate" who embodies our unrealized potential. Athletic, muscular young men are often drawn to petite, "feminine" young women. Emotional women are intrigued by strong, silent men because they're so different.

As we mature, we seek this opposite within ourselves in a process Jung called individuation. Healthy men become more aware of their feelings, learning to listen and nurture others. Adult women learn competence and assertiveness. In seeking out this unconscious potential, we balance *yin* and *yang,* becoming more whole, more complete, more at peace with ourselves.

In the past, too many cultures confined men and women to rigid sex roles, designating men as aggressive, women as nurturing. The wisdom of Tao leads beyond narrow definitions. Men and women of Tao are gentle and strong, patient and assertive, following their own energies and responding appropriately to situations around them.

Years ago it was considered "unfeminine" for American women to have a career. They were supposed to find fulfillment by nurturing husbands and children. Men were expected to work hard and be "good providers," rarely seeing their families. It was an imbalanced life for everyone.

While in grad school during the seventies, I felt sorry for housewives, considering them casualties of a bygone age. After reading Betty Friedan's *Feminine Mystique,* my friends and I rallied around the feminist banner. We joined a consciousness-raising group, meeting in one another's homes to break free of sexist bondage. But some of us went too far. One woman declared all men enemies. Some gave up makeup and jewelry because they "made us into sex objects." Many embraced a feminism that made women as hard-driving and competitive as traditional men, preaching total dedication to careers.

I felt guilty because I had male friends, wore makeup, and liked to do "feminine" things like knitting and needlepoint. Now I realize my *yin* sewing projects helped balance out the competitive *yang* of graduate school, but in those days I kept my "deviant" hobbies to myself.

Decades later, the women's movement has recognized that each woman must seek her own balance between active and passive, *yang* and *yin*. Men, too, are casting aside rigid sex roles, able to be nurturing, sensitive, and strong. Couples can find their own balance, delegating activities according to personal choice, not sex role stereotypes.

In my marriage, we both cook, buy groceries, and take care of household maintenance. Sometimes one of us has more time to handle chores, sometimes the other, but it all balances out in the end. I value my freedom to express myself in many ways from gardening to cooking to laying a hardwood floor. But I also value Gwilym's partnership, his skills, and the delightful meals he cooks for us.

Embracing the Shadow

The *Tao* teaches us to see beyond polarities, pointing out that:

"When people call one thing beautiful,
They see something else as ugly.
By calling one thing good,
Its opposite becomes evil.
Yet having and not having produce one another.
Difficult and easy balance each other.
Long and short complete one another.
High and low rely on each other.
Pitch and tone make harmony together.
Beginning and ending follow each other."

(TAO 2)

With this lesson, we become more tolerant, less quick to condemn someone different from ourselves. For the opposites *yin* and *yang* are part of an ever-evolving pattern. It's foolish to impose our morality upon these differences, seeing one extreme as good and its opposite as evil, for at other times, in other cultures, people have seen them as just the reverse.

Tao people can accept opposing tendencies in the world because they recognize the opposites within themselves. Carl Jung realized that each person has a conscious self and a dark side, the unexpressed feelings and longings called the "shadow."[6] We show our conscious (*yang*) self to the world, but beneath this lies the unconscious shadow (*yin*), our hidden fears, weaknesses, and longings—everything we don't accept about ourselves. A man who prides himself on rationality and order will repress his passionate, sensuous, and impulsive tendencies, which become part of his "shadow." He will criticize anyone with passionate feelings, simultaneously repelled yet attracted to what he's repressed in himself.

Until we accept the unexpressed parts of ourselves, we're vulnerable to someone who expresses them. Our enemies and our lovers are projections of our shadow side.

Francine has finally come to terms with her shadow. All her life Frankie, as her friends call her, has been positive, competent, and successful, the one with the good ideas, the energy, the motivation. She was student counsel president in high school, valedictorian in college, and became an outstanding labor law attorney. An attractive brunette, Frankie succeeded at almost everything—except love.

Why in the world, her friends wondered, was she involved with such a string of losers? Jerry was a temperamental rock musician, Fred an unemployed contractor, Jim an aspiring novelist. None of them could get his act together, so one by one they moved in with her. Frankie encouraged them, supported them, paid their bills, and loved them until they exhausted all her resources.

Why was she drawn to weak men when she couldn't stand weakness in herself and other women? An ardent feminist, she hated feminine weakness because she feared being weak herself, giving in to her shadow side.

Helpless, weak, and needy, Frankie's lovers were the opposite of her competent, dynamic self. They, too, were reflections of her shadow, but being men, they appealed to her. All her life she'd been unable to ask for help, stubbornly doing everything herself. So being helped, nurtured, and taken care of remained *yin,* hidden in her unconscious. Until coming to terms with her shadow she remained vulnerable to weak, needy men.

Fortunately, Frankie joined a new church which offered classes in personal development. There she learned to relax, let down her guard, and accept herself without always having to be competent and in control. As she became emotionally healthier, she attracted healthier relationships. She's now married to Will, a successful architect, enjoying a happier, more balanced life.

PERSONAL EXERCISE: EMBRACING THE SHADOW

We all have our shadows, parts of ourselves that remain unconscious. This exercise will help you begin to recognize yours.

- Go off by yourself where you won't be disturbed and stand with your knees bent, your arms at your side, breathing into your *hara,* the point of power just below your navel.
- Feel the energy flowing through your body and out your fingertips. Experience yourself as a center of power.
- Now close your eyes and visualize someone you dislike standing in front of you. Who is this person? What do you feel about him/her?
- Ask yourself: "What do I dislike about this person?" Get in touch with this message. This characteristic is part of your shadow side, something you cannot accept in yourself.
- Tell this person "I release you. I am one with Tao." As you do so, take a deep breath and let it out.
- Look within yourself for any corresponding weakness and say to yourself, "I accept myself. I forgive myself. I am one with Tao." Take another deep breath and release it.
- Feel renewed energies flowing through you. Then return to your normal activities, more at peace with yourself and the polarities within.

As you follow the Tao you'll become less judgmental of yourself and others, more patient, more forgiving. More aware of the patterns, you'll blend the many levels of *yin* and *yang* into new harmonies, creating greater peace in your life.

Affirmation

I now know my life is peaceful and harmonious.
I'm aware of the patterns within and around me.
I balance the *yin* and *yang* in my life.
I respect myself and the process.
I harmonize with nature and all others in my world.
I accept greater peace in my life now.
And so it is.

CHAPTER 11

CREATING GREATER JOY IN LIFE

"Hold to the Tao within
And joy will surely follow."

(TAO 35)

FOLLOWING the Tao, we become filled with a deep sense of joy. We watch the changing patterns of *yin* and *yang* around us with detachment and peace of mind.

We achieve the joy of Tao by returning to our original nature, affirming *p'u,* which means literally "the uncarved block," natural wood without carving or embellishment.[1] Those who achieve *p'u* are without pretense; therefore, they do not fear exposure or ridicule. Knowing who they are, they're unaffected by flattery or criticism. Holding to the Tao within, they transcend the pitfalls of ego. They enjoy the drama of life without being caught up in it.

Following the Tao often means slowing down, asking if what we're doing makes sense. With excessive haste, we lose our balance and life becomes a dizzy blur. By slowing down, we can recognize life's rhythms and return to harmony.

Too often, people place their happiness outside themselves, which leads to endless straining, competition, and distress. Restless and dissatisfied, they're always searching for something more.

The only son of alcoholic parents, Dennis grew up always feeling he'd done something wrong. Today he owns his own real estate company. A tall handsome man in his early thirties, he looks like the picture of success. He makes over $700,000 a year, drives a customized black Porsche 928, and owns a beautiful home in Miami. Yet he still suffers from low self-esteem.

Constantly driving himself to excel, Dennis works 16 hours a day, six or seven days a week. Two marriages have collapsed because he can't relax long enough to sustain a relationship. His luxurious home has a breathtaking ocean view and a million dollar art collection, but he's almost never there.

Dennis is addicted to making money. He spends most of the time in his car, talking on the cellular phone, racing from one appointment to the next, cutting bigger and better deals. He makes a fortune in commissions, wears imported suits, Gucci shoes, and a gold Rolex watch, but he can't collect enough externals to fill up the emptiness within.

The *Tao* warns us about chasing illusions. The wrong kind of success can bloat our egos and starve our souls. Too much concentration on the world outside can make us lose our balance. Lao Tzu says:

"Great success, like disgrace,
Can bring great trouble.
Success which advances ego
Can make you lose your way."

(TAO 13)

The *Tao* warns us repeatedly not to build our lives upon illusions, the "success which advances ego," but to look within and follow our own rhythms. In this chapter we'll discover how a balance of purpose, detachment, order, adventure, and good humor can fill our lives with the joy of Tao.

The Joy of Purpose

Many people trapped in meaningless routines or jobs they hate become physically ill. To be healthy, we all need a sense of purpose.

Molly, a woman in her early forties, hated her job so much she experienced one illness after another. Depressed and run down, she sought psychiatric help. The doctor said she'd adjust to her work, so she went back, got sick again, and became even more depressed.

Finally, Molly complained to Peace Pilgrim, a woman who walked across America on a pilgrimage for peace from 1953 to 1981. A true mystic, Peace knew we find our purpose by looking within. "What do you really *like* to do?" she asked. Molly liked swimming, playing the piano, and working with plants, but how could she make a living with any of these?

She didn't play the piano well enough to give concerts or teach. She swam well enough to stay afloat but not much more. "Well, what about the plants?" Peace Pilgrim asked, an idea glowing in her bright blue eyes.

So Molly got a job in a florist shop, which she loved. But that wasn't all, for people need more than just a livelihood. Swimming became Molly's regular exercise and playing the piano her path of service. She played old time favorites for people in a local retirement home.

Doing what she loved, sharing with others, Molly became healthy, happy, and strong. She married a year or so later but kept on living her own harmonious pattern.[2]

The Joy of Detachment

The *Tao* tells us:

"The Tao person, detached and wise,
Embraces all as Tao."

(TAO 49)

Living the Tao combines purpose with detachment. Tao people express what the Chinese call *pu shih,* accepting all that comes in the rhythm of life. "The wise man," it has been said, "does what he has to do for everything and everybody but remains independent of them all."[3]

My friend Lyle Farrow practices this principle of Tao. Over dinner one night, Gwilym and I were surprised to hear him say, "There isn't anything I don't like to do."

Lyle's a successful realtor in his early seventies. Fit, energetic, good-humored, with a lively twinkle in his eye, Lyle enjoys a wide range of activities. At an age when many people are living in retirement homes, he plays golf three times a week, meets with clients, and performs maintenance chores around his properties.

But his comment still set me back. "Do you mean you enjoy *everything* you do, even spending all yesterday afternoon fixing plumbing?" I asked in disbelief.

"Yes," he said with a smile. "I've made it a point to enjoy doing whatever has to be done. Yesterday I did plumbing. Today I played golf, and I enjoyed both of them."

Lyle began work early, helping run his parents' theater in Little Falls, Minnesota, and found "there was always something interesting to do." Part of his detachment is humility. Over the years, he's worked with contractors, plumbers, and electricians, doing much of the work himself. "I never felt I was better than anyone I hired," he told us. "Everything is an interesting job, a challenge," and he added again, "I never felt there was anything I don't like to do."

For days we reflected on Lyle's comments, realizing his attitude is not only the secret of his success, but the key to his consistent good health. For he never does anything with resentment, and resentment poisons our minds and bodies.

People like Lyle live with wholeness of purpose, avoiding inner conflict. They embrace everything they do with interest and enthusiasm, the joy of Tao.

The Joy of Order

A joyous life is fluid but well ordered. Peace of mind doesn't just happen. It takes discipline.

There's an old story about a man who approached the Buddha, asking the secret of happiness.

"Did you eat breakfast?" asked the Buddha.

"Yes, master," answered the young man, wondering if the answer was so simple.

"Did you wash your bowl?" the Buddha continued.

"Yes, master," the young man answered again.

"Did you do a good job?" the Buddha asked.

Then the man realized the answer was in the present moment. Happiness comes from attending to whatever we're doing, knowing that in our smallest action we affirm our beliefs.

Like the Buddhist story, Taoist self-discipline means finding value in the everyday. It means to move in harmony, sit up straight, listen intently, speak honestly, and be present in all we do. Living the Tao, we respect our actions, our words, our thoughts, the life within and around us. For all is Tao.[4]

Living harmoniously takes effort. It's easy to fall into lazy thought patterns, succumbing to anger, resentment, self-pity, or the other negative emotions that tug away at us, dragging us into destructive cycles.

Affirmation

To build the joy of Tao, we need to replace negative thoughts with positive affirmations. Try this whenever you find yourself slipping into negativity:

- Take a deep breath and release it.
- Now take another breath to restore your energies, affirming as you exhale: "I choose peace. I am one with Tao."

This mental discipline is especially important for those of us committed to social justice. So much in the world needs changing that we can easily become overwhelmed, depressed, burned out. But then we're no use to anyone. In later chapters we'll apply the principles of Tao to social problems, pollution, and politics, but we cannot change the cycles around us until we change those within us, moving from negative to positive, opening our minds to new possibilities.

The Joy of Adventure

The way of Tao combines discipline and adventure. One person who epitomizes these is Robert William Smith, Ph.D., former professional football coach, now a philosophy professor at Mesa College in Arizona.

A tall, vigorous man in his early fifties, Robert travels extensively, exploring the world, writing books on Eastern philosophy, and living with a zest that makes each day an adventure.

In his life and work he combines the discipline of coaching, the wisdom of the East, and his own hearty enthusiasm. He begins each course by asking students to "give a positive response" to life, which means "learning to spend your days in the proper way."

"Get up early," he tells them, and "greet the day" with a blessing, a song, a chant, a prayer. Make each day your own.

We're each comprised of spirit, mind, and body, he explains, and they all need daily stimulation. For the body, stimulation means exercise: "hit it for a good hour," he says, "whatever your sport." He likes to run. For the mind, Robert recommends "creative daydreaming" to stimulate your imagination. For the spirit, he advises, think empowering thoughts, read inspiring works, and attend to what you're doing. "The secret here," he says, "is in the follow-through." Most people begin projects with good intentions but those who excel in any field are the ones who follow through.[5]

PERSONAL EXERCISE

Robert Smith sees each day as a challenge to excel, to practice what he believes. Take a few minutes now to answer these questions about your own life:

- Finding a meaningful challenge makes any life an adventure. What's yours?
- Can you see each day as a chance to practice what you believe?
- Can you do something each day to renew your sense of challenge?
- Could you benefit from more conscious discipline in following your goals?
- Where in life could you perfect your follow-through?
- Close your eyes and see yourself doing these things, living with greater joy, energy, and adventure. How do you feel?
- When you like, open your eyes but keep the feeling with you. As you follow the Tao, you'll realize more of this potential.

The Joy of Humor

Tao people laugh at life's ironies, finding joy in humor, even laughing at themselves. The *Tao* reminds us that:

"When a conventional person hears about Tao,
He breaks into loud laughter.
If there were no laughter,
It would not be Tao."

(TAO 41)

Too often we forget to laugh, taking ourselves and life too seriously. One friend of mine used to quip, "Don't take life too seriously. You'll never get out of it alive."

With laughter comes the realization that all things come to pass, that life evolves through cycles of change. We can enjoy these cycles or resist them. But resistance brings us pain. It is not the way of Tao.

Have you noticed how much better you feel after a good laugh? Laughter stimulates the production of endorphins, the body's natural painkillers. It also improves respiration, activates our immune system, relaxes our muscles, and relieves stress.

We could all live healthier, happier lives by developing a spirit of play. What do you do for play? One of my favorite things is feeding the squirrels in a nearby park. With their boundless energy and graceful movements, they seem like joy individualized, darting across the ground, walking the telephone wires like acrobats, and jumping from tree to tree.

Gwilym and I take regular walks over to a particular "nut tree," wedging peanuts or walnuts into the grooves between the lower branches and watching the squirrels come to claim their treats. They're still quite wild, so we don't come too close.

One day recently I was standing beside the tree with a bag of nuts when a frisky squirrel came up the other side and stood there looking at me with his large brown eyes, wiggling his nose, and swishing his long bushy tail. Then he scampered up a branch and watched carefully as I left the nuts. The squirrels give me more than I give them: laughter, amazement, and a chance to observe up close some of the wonder of nature.

The joy of Tao is many things, but most of all a realization that we're part of something larger than ourselves, a pattern of infinite beauty that flows within us and around us. We feel this joy revealed in nature, ourselves, and one another when we experience the oneness of Tao.

Affirmation

I now know my life is peaceful and harmonious.
I feel the joy of Tao in my life.
I live with purpose and detachment, discipline and adventure, laughter and play.
I am one with all there is.
I respect myself and the process.
I harmonize with nature and all others in my world.
I accept greater peace in my life now.
And so it is.

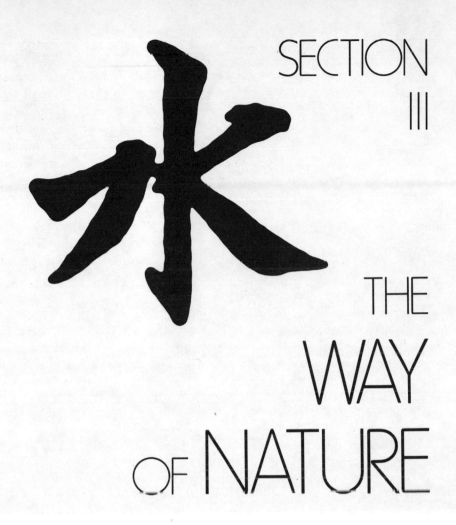

SECTION III

THE
WAY
OF NATURE

CHAPTER 12

NATURAL HARMONY

"When you know nature as part of yourself,
   You will act in harmony.
When you feel yourself part of nature,
   You will live in harmony."

                    (TAO 13)

TAO people stay close to nature. Recognizing the underlying unity of the "ten thousand things," they know that:

"The Tao gives life to the world,
Shaping all things
Into manifest form.

The ten thousand things
Follow its principles,
And the Tao nurtures them,
Providing food and shelter,
Supporting their growth
Through the cycles of life.

To follow the Tao
Is to honor its principles,
To realize:
That we live in nature
But can never possess it;
We can guide and serve,

But never control.

This is the highest wisdom."

(TAO 51)

The unity of the individual with nature is central to Taoist philoso
phy. As we learned in chapter three, the Chinese character for nature
includes the character for a person with arms outstretched to signify
"great," topped by another horizontal line which represents the sky
over our heads. Thus do we become great by recognizing our part in
the harmony of nature.[1]

The ancient Chinese saw each person as a microcosm, a world in
miniature. In elaborate descriptions, they equated our heads with the
heavens, our feet with the earth, our veins with rivers, our many
bones with the 365 days of the year, our changing emotions with the
changing weather.[2] Diseases in humans, like disorders in the world,
were caused by imbalance.

A similar vision once prevailed in the West. From the Middle Ages
to the Renaissance, Europeans saw themselves as microcosms, small
versions of the world around them, believing that a great chain of
being connected all of life. In the thirteenth century, St. Francis of
Assisi celebrated the relationship of creation in his "Canticle of the
Sun," praising "Brother Sun," "Sister Moon," "Sister Water," and
"our Sister, Mother Earth, who sustains and governs us."[3]

Throughout the Renaissance people meditated on nature, applying
its lessons to their lives. Thomas Traherne affirmed in his *Centuries of
Meditations,* "You never enjoy the world aright till you see how a
[grain of] sand exhibiteth the wisdom and power of God: . . . till the
sea itself floweth in your veins, till you are clothed with the heavens,
and crowned with the stars."[4] People saw themselves as part of a
larger pattern. John Donne wrote: "No man is an island, entire of
itself; every man is a piece of the continent, a part of the main. If a
clod be washed away by the sea, Europe is the less, as well as if a
promontory were, as well as if a manor of thy friend's or of thine own
were: any man's death diminishes me, because I am involved in
mankind, and therefore never send to know for whom the bell tolls; it
tolls for thee."[5]

Until the late seventeenth century, people in the West knew a unified sensibility, perceiving body and soul, reason and passion, nature and the individual as part of a larger whole. This unified vision was lost when scientific and industrial revolutions developed a new mechanistic paradigm. God became the Divine watchmaker who left the world to run for itself. Factories reduced individuals to specialized parts, cogs in a machine. The sense of life as a sentient, organic whole was replaced by the frantic pace and fragmentation of modern life. People began to measure their worth in terms of productivity—output—as if we'd all become machines.

The western world is now on the edge of a new paradigm, and science again leads the way, this time affirming a more holistic vision. From physics we learn the world is composed of dynamic energy patterns. Developmental psychologists describe life as a process of continuous growth, and Carl Jung believed we're all part of a universal unconscious. The circle comes around again as we realize once more that no one is an island. We're all intrinsically linked in the dynamic web of life.

A vision of oneness informs the ecological activism of Greenpeace. Risking injury and death, these brave men and women take to the seas in small boats, putting their bodies between endangered whales and their assailants, braving the northern ice to save baby seals from annual slaughter. As the Greenpeace philosophy explains:

> "Ecology teaches us that humankind is not the center of life on the planet. Ecology has taught us that the whole earth is part of our 'body' and that we must learn to respect it as we respect ourselves. As we feel for ourselves, we must feel for all forms of life—the whales, the seals, the forests, the seas. The tremendous beauty of ecological thought is that it shows us a pathway back to an understanding and an appreciation of life itself—an understanding and appreciation that is imperative to that very way of life."[6]

Learning from Nature

Non-Tao people see the world as a collection of disparate parts. Tao people see the underlying unity. By meditating on its shifting cycles they learn personal and planetary balance.

Staying close to nature dispels our illusions of separateness, the excessively developed ego which Taoists call *ying* (literally "being full of oneself")[7] and Christians call the sin of pride. Nature humbles us, making us see we're only part of an infinitely larger whole. From nature's slowly evolving cycles, we learn patience and detachment.

We become more patient by adjusting to the changing weather, unlike Hal who loses his temper when a sudden storm cancels his golf game. Stomping around, red faced and foul-tempered, he pulls his clubs from the trunk of his car, cursing the "bad weather." But the Tao teaches that weather is neither "good" nor "bad." It just is. The rain that upsets Hal's plans is welcomed by farmers a few miles away.

Like a Taoist monk, the nineteenth-century writer Henry David Thoreau watched for the lessons of nature. One rainy day he learned patience, seeing beyond ego to the larger pattern: "The gentle rain which waters my beans and keeps me in the house today is not drear and melancholy, but good for me too. Though it prevents my hoeing them, it is of far more worth than my hoeing. If it should continue so long as to cause the seeds to rot in the ground and destroy the potatoes in the low lands, it would still be good for the grass on the uplands, and being good for the grass, it would be good for me."[8]

By living close to nature, Thoreau recognized his oneness with the life process. Taking us beyond our limited, linear view of life, nature celebrates growth and perpetual renewal.

Like Thoreau, men and women of Tao find beauty in all weather and seasons. They learn the folly of clinging to one moment or possession. For objects, too, pass into different forms. Days, moments, are steps on the path, and the pattern evolves with continuous change, creating the wonder of ten thousand things.

Peace Is Harmony with Natural Laws

The *Tao* tells us:

"To live in harmony is to follow Tao.
To follow Tao is enlightenment.
Excessive striving

Leads to exhaustion.
Competitive struggle
Is contrary to Tao.
Whatever violates Tao
Will not endure."

(TAO 55)

Tao people harmonize with natural laws, following the underlying principles that support life. Physical laws are easily observed: the law of gravity, for example. Drop an object and it falls to the earth. Following their own patterns of cause and effect, Taoist principles of dynamic balance, oneness, and cyclical growth hold true for individuals, nature, and societies. When we follow the Tao we have harmony; when we work against it, we have problems.

Whenever we see a problem, we can be certain the order of Tao has been violated. Author Dorothy L. Sayers has called war "a judgment that overtakes societies when they have been living upon ideas that conflict too violently with the laws governing the universe."[9]

Wars and social conflicts are symptoms of an imbalanced society, diseases caused by an unhealthy social order. By following the principles of Tao, we can create a healthier, more peaceful life for ourselves and our world.

We'll learn about Taoist political action in the final section. But first let's consider how the Tao works in nature. This chapter explains two Taoist principles: dynamic balance and oneness. The next chapter focuses on the principle of cyclical growth. We create harmonious action by cooperating with these principles.

The Principle of Dynamic Balance

Taoists have long equated peace with balance. The hexagram for peace in the *I Ching* is made up of three horizontal lines divided in the center above three solid horizontal lines, the *yin* of earth balanced by the *yang* of heaven.[10] Peace results from the dynamic balance of opposites within and around us.

Following this principle, Taoists teach moderation, realizing that one extreme invariably leads to the other. Chuang Tzu knew that "all rise and decay are interrelated. When something reaches a limit, then it reverses its direction; when the end is reached, the beginning begins."[11] The Greeks discovered this principle as well, calling it the Aristotelian Golden Mean, the balance between excess and deficiency.

Excess of any kind brings imbalance and disaster. Economist E.F. Schumacher criticized the western world for extreme materialism: "a life devoted primarily to the pursuit of material ends, to the neglect of the spiritual. Such a life necessarily sets man against man and nation against nation."[12] Imbalance causes personal and political disorder.

Twenty-five centuries earlier, Lao Tzu taught the same lesson:

"When people do not follow Tao,
Their horses are harnessed for war,
Their energies are used for destruction,
And many go hungry.
Great trouble comes
From not knowing what is enough.
Great conflict arises from wanting too much.
When we know when enough is enough,
There will always be enough."

(TAO 46)[13]

The Principle of Oneness

For peace to exist, societies and individuals must understand the interrelatedness of microcosm and macrocosm, recognizing their unity with nature and one another. Aware of this underlying oneness, Tao people respect nature and other people, exploiting neither their neighbors nor the environment. They see our ecosystem as an integrated whole, realizing that any action has wide-ranging effects.

Many mistakes are made when people ignore this lesson. In the 1950s the World Health Organization tried to eliminate malaria in northern Borneo by using the pesticide dieldrin to kill mosquitoes carrying the disease. Initially, the project seemed a great success. Not only did the mosquitoes and malaria disappear, but villagers were no longer bothered by flies and cockroaches. But then their roofs began falling in on them and they faced the threat of a typhoid epidemic.

How did this happen? First hundreds of lizards died from eating the poisoned insects. Then the local cats died from eating the lizards. Without the cats, rats ran rampant through the villages, carrying typhus-infested fleas on their bodies. To add insult to injury, the villagers' thatched roofs were collapsing. Why? The dieldrin killed wasps and other insects which ordinarily ate the caterpillars that fed on the thatched roofs.[14] The *Tao* teaches that everything in life is interconnected, a lesson World Health workers were forced to acknowledge in Borneo. After staving off the typhoid threat, they began to consider the larger implications of their actions.

Another more global example of our interrelatedness is the greenhouse effect, caused by increasing amount of carbon dioxide in the atmosphere. This excess is raising the earth's temperature, threatening to turn agricultural lands into deserts, burn up temperate forests, and flood coastal areas as polar ice melts and sea levels rise.

Until this century, nature maintained a balance of oxygen and carbon dioxide, for humans and animals inhale oxygen and exhale carbon dioxide while plants do just the reverse. Taoists would call this a perfect balance of *yin* and *yang*.

The greenhouse effect stems from the enormous use by industrialized societies of fossil fuels and chlorofluorocarbons but also from something that at first seems completely unrelated—the increased consumption of hamburgers in fast-food restaurants.

To produce more low-priced beef, entrepreneurs in Central and South America have been cutting down rain forests, converting them into pastures for beef cattle. In Costa Rica alone, between 125,000 and 175,000 acres of forest are destroyed annually.[15] Such action is unwise both locally and globally. Because the thin tropical soil lacks humus, it's eroded away in a few short years, leaving the region desolate and poorer than before.

Globally, the effects are ominous. With their lush vegetation, rain forests have always served as the planet's "lungs," converting enormous amounts of carbon dioxide into oxygen and purifying the atmosphere. Now, while producing more carbon dioxide, we're sabotaging this natural balancing process by destroying the rain forests.

If this pattern continues, the buildup of carbon dioxide would cause a massive global warming with dire effects in the United States. The American midwest would become a parched and arid desert, with a warmer Canada and Soviet Union taking our place as the world's food producer. Coastal cities from New York to Miami, New Orleans, San Diego, and Seattle would be flooded as the earth's temperature increases, melting the polar ice caps and raising the sea level all over the planet.

Once again, the lesson is clear. Because we're all part of a larger whole, shortsighted action can produce imbalance on a grand scale. We must remember to look for the larger patterns, to stay in balance, for

"Whatever violates Tao
Will not endure."

(TAO 55)

Living in Harmony with Our Neighbors

American naturalist John Muir was a Tao person in the highest sense. Wandering the mountains of the west, he concluded that "Pollution, defilement, squalor are words that never would have been created had man lived conformably to nature."[16] Non-Tao people are often shortsighted. They pollute and destroy life because they don't see the larger patterns.

Pacific Grove, a lovely coastal town in northern California, is known for its monarch butterflies. Every year the brilliant orange monarchs return to Pacific Grove and have become the town symbol. Their pictures appear on street signs, maps, and promotional material.

But lately, there's been a dramatic decrease in butterflies. Why? Increased development has destroyed the shrubs and flowers which are their natural habitat. The expanding human population has driven these natural creatures out of their homes.

For years, people have come to Pacific Grove to see the monarchs. If unrestrained development continues, the town will lose its special character, becoming just another collection of streets, houses, shopping centers, and fast food restaurants. The only butterflies left will be on postcards and plastic souvenirs.

How often do we do this, unwittingly, to our non-human neighbors? As developers replace the natural landscape with layers of grass and concrete, something precious is lost. By destroying natural habitats we threaten the vital links in life's chain and rob ourselves of their beauty.

PERSONAL EXERCISE

How well do you know the natural landscape in your area? Take this self-scoring quiz and see.

1. What trees grow in your local area? Name or describe five.
2. What wild flowers grow in your area? Name five.
3. Name five edible plants native to your region.
4. Name five locally-grown fruits and vegetables.
5. What birds are native to your region? Name five or more.
6. Which birds migrate and which are year-long residents?
7. What other non-human neighbors are native to your area? Name five (or more, if possible).
8. What has happened to your local environment in the past fifty years?
9. Are any birds or animals in danger of extinction?
10. If so, what is the cause?[17]

If you scored 9 or 10, you have an excellent awareness of your environment. If your score was 7 to 8, you're more aware than most people.

If you scored less than 5, you, like most Americans, are out of touch with your environment. Many of us don't even know the names of the plants in our yard, let alone the native plants and animals around us.

But we can learn. Begin answering these questions by walking around and observing your neighborhood, talking to longtime residents, reading natural history in the local library. You'll develop a deeper understanding of your habitat and learn about threats to your environment. With that awareness comes the possibility for solutions, for the more we know about our problems, the sooner we can begin to solve them.

Transcending Dualism

The increasing number of endangered species on the planet is a sad testimony to the current level of human ignorance, unkindness, and lack of respect for the other lives that share our world.

The *Tao* tells us:

"Those who dominate nature
And seek to possess it
Will never succeed,
For nature is a living system, so sacred
That those who use it profanely
Will surely lose it;
And to lose nature
Is to lose ourselves."

(TAO 29)

The *Tao* teaches a vision of oneness that transcends dualism, affirming the necessity of cooperation. We realize that "nature is a living system," that by abusing it we destroy the source of our own life, for "to lose nature is to lose ourselves."

Our old mechanistic paradigm with its ingrained dualism and separation has made people see the world as a collection of objects to exploit. Such a vision is not only inaccurate but destructive, making our relationship with nature and the rest of the world into a struggle for dominance. Our ecological problems should teach us that what we dominate we inevitably destroy.

The Tao takes us beyond anthropocentric dualism, the mistaken illusion of separateness from one another and our environment. Ecologist Robert Aitkin Roshi sees this limited mindset as responsible for racism, sexism, nationalism, and other forms of alienation and exploitation.[18] Affirming our oneness, the holistic wisdom of Tao transcends dualism and the violence it engenders.

PERSONAL EXERCISE

We can experience the oneness of Tao by taking a slow, meditative walk through nature. To do justice to this exercise, set aside enough time to explore a nearby natural landscape alone and unrushed.

- Wear comfortable clothes and shoes, carrying no more than you need. Leave your calendar, purse, briefcase, and all they imply far behind you. You may want to take a small knapsack with drinking water and a snack, but the point is to travel light.
- Slow down, focusing on the rhythm of your breathing.
- Remain in the present. Don't let your mind wander.
- Tune in to your senses. Feel the earth beneath your feet and say to yourself, "I am one with the earth."
- Feel the warmth of the sun on your skin and say to yourself, "I am one with the sun."
- As the wind caresses your body, say to yourself, "I am one with the wind."
- Look closely at the green plants around you, noticing the varieties and all the different shades of green. Affirm your oneness with the plants.
- Hear the rustling of the leaves in the trees above you. Affirm, "I am one with the trees."
- Smell the fragrance of the trees and flowers. Affirm your oneness.
- Listen for the melody of a stream or lake. Affirm "I am one with the water."
- See and hear the birds and other creatures around you. As you notice each one, affirm your oneness.
- Feel how the rhythms of your body interact with the natural rhythms around you.
- When you're ready, slowly return the way you came, retaining this

sense of natural harmony as you re-enter the mechanized world. For beneath all the bustle and noise is the enduring oneness of Tao.

If you enjoyed this exercise you may want to try a variation. Following the same guidelines, share a silent walk with someone you love. Resolve to look, listen, and feel, but do not talk. As you walk along you may point out the natural wonders to one another, sharing a meditative communion with nature.

Becoming One with Nature

Recognizing our oneness with nature expands our vision and gives us a deeper sense of ourselves. Ecological activist John Seed explains how his work has taken him from an individual protecting nature to oneness with the entire life process. " 'I am protecting the rain forest' develops to 'I am part of the rain forest protecting myself. I am that part of the rain forest recently emerged into thinking.' What a relief then! The thousands of years of imagined separation are over and we begin to recall our true nature." "The change," he says, "is a spiritual one."[19]

To study nature is to follow the Tao; to follow the Tao is to know ourselves. Looking back, John Muir described his work at the end of his life, saying, "I only went out for a walk, and finally concluded to stay out till sundown, for going out, I found, was really going in."[20] Going out into nature is going into ourselves, reaching far beyond the brittle surface of life to become one with nature, one with Tao.

There are many ways to study nature, from camping and hiking to working in your garden. This chapter can only set you on your way. Nature, for Taoists, is a living system. It must be experienced. The best way to do this is to put down this book and go outside, take a walk, feed the birds, or tend a tree. Get close to living, growing things, take a deep breath, and participate in the infinite harmony of Tao.

Affirmation

I now know my life is peaceful and harmonious.
Each day I learn more about the life around me.
I am one with nature.
I honor its principles.
I respect myself and the process.
I harmonize with nature and all others in my world.
I accept greater peace in my life now.
And so it is.

CHAPTER 13

NATURAL CYCLES

"The Tao moves by returning
In endless cycles.
By yielding, it overcomes,
Creating the ten thousand things,
Being from nonbeing."

(TAO 40)

THE Tao flows within and around us in cycles of energy known as *chi*, giving life to the "ten thousand things," *wan wu*, the Chinese symbol for all creation.

Tao people work with these cycles. Non-Tao people work against them. Driven by ignorance, ego, or unbridled appetite, they upset the balance of nature.

As we learned in earlier chapters, *chi* energy circulates in continuous cycles through our bodies. In Taoist meditation, we focus our breathing in cycles of *yin* and *yang,* helping the *chi* circulate and renew us. Ancient Taoists taught that the earth itself breathes in alternating patterns of *yin* and *yang*. The way plants and animals exchange oxygen and carbon dioxide in our atmosphere parallels this Taoist teaching.

Chinese painting portrays the movement of *chi* throughout nature. The Taoists believe that the *yang* energy of heaven meets the *yin* energy of earth at points known as "dragon veins." Chinese artists have portrayed these energies for centuries. With great sweeping curves, streams of *chi* flow across the landscape, connecting clouds and mountains, earth and sky.[1]

Cycles of Energy

The *Tao* teaches a vision of life as process, constantly moving, changing, and growing as the *chi* energies circulate throughout all existence:

"Something infinite,
Older than heaven and earth,
Silent, solitary, and vast;
Eternal, unchanging,
Yet ever evolving
Throughout ten thousand things.
Not knowing its name,
I call it Tao.
A mystery beyond words,
I call it great."

(TAO 25)

The evolving energies of Tao have been compared to the quantum theory in physics. Subatomic energy patterns—the scientific equivalents of *chi*—are the creative force beneath all existence. This energy is not quite a particle, a predictable, solid form of matter. It's not quite a wave, an action or process, but a combination of the two. Like the Tao, the essential energy of existence is both principle and process, moving in cycles known as probability waves.[2]

This dynamic view of existence is intrinsic to Chinese and other primeval cultures. In Chinese and Welsh, the ancient Celtic language, words are simultaneously verbs and nouns: existence and process combined in one concept. Such languages convey a sense that "objects are also events,"[3] that life is comprised of dynamic patterns.

The Cyclical Rhythm of Nature

Cyclical patterns occur throughout nature from the infinitesimal world of the atom to the infinitely larger world above our heads. In our solar system, planets trace expansive cycles in space. In the cosmic immensity of time, stars go through their own life cycles. They're born, grow in brilliance, then slowly die after bringing light to our universe for millenia.

Nothing in the universe stands still. The *Tao* explains:

"Throughout nature
The ten thousand things move along,
But each returns to its source."

(TAO 16)

We experience these cyclical patterns by getting close to nature, watching an orchard tree blossom in springtime, bear fruit in summer. In autumn we see its leaves fall to the ground. Slowly disintegrating into humus, they enrich the soil, bringing new energy to the tree in spring.

Even the cold winter weather is part of the pattern. The "chill factor," a prolonged period of temperatures below 45 degrees, is essential for these trees to blossom and bear fruit.[4] Fruit trees must spend enough time in a state of dormancy (*yin*) to spring forth with new life (*yang*). Reconciling opposites in endless harmony, the seasons turn and the cycle begins again.

The Chinese calendar portrays the cyclical alternations of *yin* and *yang,* winter and spring, death and rebirth. At the winter solstice, the height of *yin,* active *yang* lies dormant. The world is cold and dark. Animals hibernate, trees are bare, the fields buried by blankets of snow. Yet with this eclipse of *yang* comes its inevitable rebirth. The sap rises, tiny buds appear. *Yang* gradually awakens into spring. At the summer solstice, *yang* begins another decline as the seasons move into a new phase of *yin*. With these alternations flows the rhythm of nature, combining polarities, creating new life from dynamic opposition.

The Cycles and Ourselves

Like the seasons, we undergo cycles. The *Tao* teaches us to be still and watch the evolving patterns:

"The wise person follows the earth;
Earth follows the sky;
The sky follows Tao;
And Tao follows its own nature."

(TAO 25)

By observing the cycles of nature, we know ourselves; by observing our own cycles, we know nature. Following the cycles, we are one with Tao.

The natural cycles of sun and moon have figured prominently in the world's oldest religions. For centuries the Chinese have honored the lunar cycles with new year's and moon celebrations, moon cakes, and fireworks. Ancient Egyptians celebrated the seasonal cycles of the Nile with the myth of Isis and Osiris. In Europe the Druids observed solstices and equinoxes, charting the changing patterns of light in the sky. With candles and bonfires they brightened the darkness of winter and celebrated the return of life in the spring.

We can become more aware of our own diurnal cycles, recognizing the patterns of *yin* and *yang*. Psychologists say that we all have peak periods during the day when our energy flows the most strongly. This is our prime time, *yang*. During our lag time our energies diminish. The cycle turns to *yin*. We feel tired and withdrawn. Things slow down.

PERSONAL EXERCISE

- Take a few moments now to identify your own daily cycle. When is your prime time? Are you a morning, afternoon, or night person?
- What time of day do your energies decrease?
- Can you plot your daily cycle? Where are *yin* and *yang* for you?

Becoming aware of our daily cycles can help us live more creatively. My friend Bill, a research physicist, plans his day around his energy cycle. He does his research in the morning during his prime time and saves routine work like opening the mail for his lag time, 3:00 in the afternoon.

More subtle but equally powerful is the lunar cycle. The waxing and waning of the moon influences the tides, women's monthly cycles, human emotions, and physical energies. For centuries the full moon has been equated with restlessness and impulsiveness, giving rise to the English word "lunatic" (from the Latin, "luna," for moon). Policemen know that more crimes of passion happen during a full moon than at any other time.

For centuries farmers have planted seeds by the cycles of the moon, recording its changes in their almanacs. Some organic gardeners I know recommend planting vegetable seeds two days before the new moon, and flower seeds two days before the full moon, which is also the best time for transplanting.

PERSONAL EXERCISE

How aware are you of the natural cycles around you? Take this self-scoring quiz and see.

1. When is the next solstice? Equinox?
2. What phase is the moon in now?
3. What changes do the plants in your area go through during the different seasons of the year?
4. Do any birds in your area migrate? If so, when?
5. Do any animals in your area hibernate? If so, which ones and for how long?
6. Where does your water come from?
7. Where does your water go when it leaves your house?
8. Where does your trash go?[5]

How many answers do you know? What does this tell you about your knowledge of natural cycles?

Cyclical Work

For centuries, Taoist and Buddhist monks have regarded cyclical work—gardening, cooking, housecleaning—as spiritual exercises. In our daily lives we too can participate in the cycles of renewal by doing something cyclical. We can:

- plant a garden—on a rooftop or patio if we don't have a yard.
- plant a tree and tend it.
- recycle our cans, bottles, newspapers—returning them to the source to be renewed again and again.[6]

• make a compost pile or box—recycling kitchen scraps into natural nutrients for the soil.

Each of these practices affirms our membership in a pattern far larger than ourselves. Each physically benefits the planet while renewing our vision of the life process.

One Buddhist practice is to plant a tree every few years and tend it carefully. This combines personal renewal with real pragmatism, for as we learned in the last chapter, trees are vitally important in preserving the ecology of the planet. Without trees, the world as we know it would cease to exist.[7]

Last year, my friends Eric and Brendan gave me a Japanese maple for my birthday. That evening when I came home from dinner, I was surprised to find a small graceful tree standing in a pot on my front porch, its green leaves sparkling in the gentle spring rain.

I've known the tree for nearly a year now, transplanted, trimmed, watered, and fed it. I've seen its leaves droop and berated myself for neglecting it during a hot spell last summer. Last fall I watched its leaves turn scarlet and worried as it stood dormant all winter. Had I watered it enough? Was it still alive? This spring, during a water shortage, I've been giving the tree a bucket of water from my shower, more aware of conserving and sharing.

Now it's March and the small tree has burst forth with a profusion of delicate green leaves and some tiny red flowers, filling me with joy and a deeper awareness of the cycles that shape our lives.

The Water Cycle

The *Tao* tells us:

"The best people are like water.
They benefit all things,
And do not compete with them.
They settle in low places,
One with nature, one with Tao."

(TAO 8)

In Chinese art and philosophy, water is the symbol of the Tao. It is fluid, nurturing, ministering to all, yet possesses great strength, able to cut through the hardest rocks.

Water, like the Tao, "moves by returning/ In endless cycles." (*Tao* 40). The water that existed a million years ago is still here today, neither increasing nor decreasing. We always have the same amount of water on earth.

Water moves in an endless hydrologic cycle, beginning with evaporation from the sea, which comprises 97 percent of the world's supply. The heat of the sun turns this water into vapor, which rises into the atmosphere, forming clouds, which then return to the earth as rain or snow, replenishing our freshwater supplies.

Precipitation soaks into the ground or runs into lakes and rivers, which take it back to the ocean, where the entire cycle begins again. Plants, animals, and humans intercept the water in its cycle, use it, excrete it, then pass it on, often polluting it along the way.

As the years go by, we interfere more and more with the natural cycle, diverting water from its original channels, drawing great quantities out of the ground, and contaminating it with sewage and chemicals.

Our freshwater supply—a mere 3 percent of the earth's water—comes from rivers and lakes, or from ground water, which is naturally purified as it percolates down through many layers of sediment into deep underwater lakes known as aquifers. We drill wells to get this pure drinking water. But too often we abuse our water supply by violating the principles of Tao. Ignoring the cycle, we use water as a product, not a process, polluting and wasting it.

Ignoring the Cycle

Most western countries have been using their limited freshwater supply with little understanding or respect for the natural cycle. Whenever a city's population increases, water departments drill more wells, draining the local aquifers, or they build massive aqueducts, importing water from distant lakes and rivers, doing untold damage to natural habitats.

Aquifers all over the world are being drained by overconsumption. The Ogallala Aquifer, in the American midwest, dates back thousands of years, to Pleistocene times. If current consumption rates continue, it will be dry in forty years, taking thousands of years to fill up again.[8] Draining the aquifer would radically alter life throughout Kansas, Nebraska, Iowa, and other midwestern states, causing not only severe drought, but massive subsidence.

Subsidence, sinking of the earth after ground water removal, is already widespread in California. The town of Alviso, near the south end of San Francisco Bay, has sunk ten feet, putting the whole area below sea level, and subjecting it to recurrent flooding. California's central valley has subsided even more dramatically—up to 100 feet in some areas.

When ground and surface water is insufficient, many cities import water through large aqueducts. Urban water projects have rearranged the natural landscape, flooding land with artificial reservoirs, drying up rivers and lakes.

Mono Lake, a million year old saline lake in northeastern California, is being drained to provide water for Los Angeles. Extending over sixty-one square miles, the lake is a bird refuge, filled with brine shrimp. Every year 50,000 California gulls, 85 percent of the state population, raise their young on its volcanic islands. Over a million other birds stop there during annual migrations.

As the water level drops and salinity increases, Mono Lake is slowly dying. The streams that replenish it have been diverted 388 miles south through the Los Angeles Aqueduct, and soon the lake will be too salty to sustain life.

In 1978 and 1989 the receding water exposed a narrow strip of land connecting the islands to the mainland. Coyotes and other predators attacked and killed the nesting birds and their young. The water level continues to drop, leaving a border of white dust around the lake, now over a mile wide. When disturbed by the strong winds of the area, this alkaline layer kills local vegetation and could become a health hazard to nearby residents.

Local citizens have developed a grassroots movement to save Mono Lake, supported by other concerned individuals across the state and around the nation. Confronting the powerful interests of a huge utility company, they're asking why the lake and its wildlife must be sacrificed to further development and fill the swimming pools of their wasteful neighbors to the south.[9]

The story of Mono Lake and the problem of subsidence dramatically illustrate the Taoist principle of oneness. As we learned in the last chapter, the *Tao* teaches that:

"Nature is a living system, so sacred
That those who use it profanely
Will surely lose it;
And to lose nature
Is to lose ourselves."

(TAO 29)

Pollution

Nature is an interconnected web, a complex integrated system. When we meddle with one part, we cause inevitable repercussions. Every year developed countries fill rivers and lakes with industrial chemicals, petroleum products, solvents, road salt, garbage runoff, household detergents, pesticides, and organic waste. A few miles downstream, the water is pumped out, treated with chlorine and other chemicals, then sent back through the pipes as drinking water.

In a kind of aquatic karma, what we give out comes back to us, threatening our health. Chemical fertilizer containing nitrates (converted by the human body into nitrosamines, which cause stomach cancer) often seeps into our drinking water. Hormones and contraceptives excreted in urine have found their way into urban rivers and may result in reduced fertility among the population. Industrial chemicals contaminate the ground water in many areas with lead, mercury, cadmium, arsenic, dioxin, and other poisons, endangering life many times over.[10]

This increasing water pollution is threatening our health and destroying other life forms. In the past few years, fish and marine mammals have been dying of mysterious diseases, their immune systems weakened by polluted waters.

Even our misguided attempts to stay clean can damage the environment. The phosphates contained in most detergents run out into the waterways, encouraging the massive growth of algae, which turns the water green and slimy, depleting the oxygen so that fish die of suffocation.

PERSONAL EXERCISE: REDUCING WATER POLLUTION

As conscious participants in the water cycle, we can help reduce pollution by taking positive action in these areas:

- *Avoid or reduce your use of phosphates.* Use soap or biodegradable non-phosphate detergents. They're available in some health food stores, and Switzerland has had them for years. Until you find alternatives, at least reduce the quantity. Half a cup of detergent will still get your clothes clean.
- *Don't overuse bleach and scouring powders.* Some health food stores and mail order catalogues sell biodegradable cleansers. Look for them, and until you find them use less of the commercial variety.
- *Don't use water fresheners* in the bathroom. They merely pollute the water with chemicals and artificial perfumes.
- *Don't use garden chemicals.* Artificial fertilizers, like phosphates, cause uncontrolled growth of algae and put nitrates into the water. Pesticides get into the water chain, harming many other forms of life. Garden organically, fertilizing with compost and using natural pest controls. You can learn how by reading the next chapter.
- *Don't dump oils, paints, and chemicals down the drain.* Engine oil, battery acid, car polish, turpentine, paint—all these need to be disposed of safely. Some towns have a special dump for such wastes. Call your local refuse disposal company for advice.
- *Share your ideas with others.* The water we use belongs to all of us, our descendents, and the many life forms on this planet. The more people who use it wisely, the healthier our collective future.[11]

Each day most non-Tao people abuse the water cycle through waste. In nature, nothing is wasted. Everything is used, recycled, returned to the source. Native peoples who live close to the earth have always honored its cycles, cooperating with nature. As they leave their natural roots behind, industrialized people replace cooperation with conquest.

In North America, the plains Indians offered a prayer before killing buffalo and then used every part: the meat for food, the hides for clothing and shelter, the bones for tools or decorations. When the transcontinental railroad stretched westward, other Americans began shooting buffalo for sport. Firing rifles out the windows, they killed hundreds of buffalo as the train sped by, leaving their bodies to rot in the dust. Like the buffalo, the Indian nation vanished in the wake of westward expansion, and we never stopped to learn their wisdom.

In America this attitude of conquest and exploitation still distorts our relationship with nature. We take it for granted and we take from it in large quantities, wasting resources with reckless abandon. In 1975 each person in the United States used 1595 gallons of water a day: for personal use, to grow our food, and to support business, power plants, and manufacturing. If the present trend continues, we face widespread water shortages in the United States by the year 2000.[12]

But still the waste continues. Heedless of natural cycles, Americans act as if there were a limitless supply of water every time they turn on the tap. And our technology encourages this waste. One fourth of all domestic water goes straight down the toilet, polluting five to seven gallons of pure water with every flush.[13] To sustain our typical meat and potato diet, agribusiness uses enormous amounts of water each year: 2500 gallons to produce one pound of beef. A pound of rice uses only 500, a glass of milk 100, a pound of flour seventy-five, an ear of corn eighty, an egg only forty.[14] Eating less meat and more complex carbohydrates would not only reduce our use of water, but lower our cholesterol, bringing greater health to ourselves and our planet.

Changes in business and technology would reduce water waste and cut down on pollution. Swedish inventors have developed a composting toilet that returns organic waste to the soil without polluting the water supply. Authors John Seymour and Herbert Girardet recommend a dual water system, with one set of pipes bringing fresh water to the house for drinking and washing, another to flush the toilet, wash the car, water the lawn, and use for industrial purposes.[15] But until our society makes large scale changes, we can each begin voluntarily conserving our water.

A recent drought in my area has made water conservation mandatory. Most of my friends have complied with water rationing, but some people still ignore the regulations. To save their manicured lawns, they water excessively, letting hundreds of gallons of water run down the street.

Along with many neighbors, last summer Gwilym and I began voluntary conservation, installing water-saving shower heads, putting bottles in the toilet tanks to reduce waste, and checking our faucets for leaks. This year we have a collection of buckets all around the house—one for each shower, washbasin, and one for the kitchen sink. We catch this "gray water" and carry it outside to water our garden. The lawns—never very popular with either of us—we're not watering at all. We plan to replace them with edible landscape, native plants, and drought-resistant rosemary.

Though many people complain about drought restrictions, they might be a blessing in disguise, making people more aware of the environment and their use of water. Perhaps we'll all be less likely to take nature for granted, more aware of our place in the larger cycle.

PERSONAL EXERCISE

Even if you don't have a drought in your area, you can conserve water by using it more consciously. Personal conservation *does* make a difference. You can begin by:

- Turning off the faucet when brushing your teeth, shaving, or washing dishes.
- Using the dishwasher and washing machines only with full loads.
- Repairing all leaks quickly.
- Putting a plastic container filled with gravel or a plastic bag filled with water in your toilet tank to reduce waste. If every toilet in America had one, we could save 60 million gallons a day.
- Installing water-saving shower heads.
- Not using the garbage disposal, which wastes water in large quantities. Compost your kitchen waste instead.
- Taking shorter showers.
- Washing your car with a bucket, using the hose briefly and then shutting it off.[16]

You can also call your local water district and find out where your water comes from. I did this and they sent me some information about my local water system.

The *Tao* encourages us to keep learning about nature, looking for the larger patterns and becoming more aware of the cycles in our lives. For the more we understand, the more we can harmonize with them.

By respecting our water cycle, tending a tree, or planting a garden, we become personally attuned to the wisdom of Tao. Familiar with the cycle of the seasons, we learn that spring inevitably follows winter, that with every decline comes a corresponding renewal. This principle of Tao brings enduring wisdom, patience, and hope.

Since all life is dynamic, we realize the futility of holding on too tightly to any object or experience. We know that every organism, every situation, even the worst of problems, has its own cycle of birth, growth, and decline. We learn the importance of timing. By observing the cycles around us we know when to combine our energies with those of others. Is the season ripe for change? Study the Tao and you will know.

Affirmation

I now know my life is peaceful and harmonious.

I am more aware of the cycles within and around me.

I watch the changes in the sun, the moon, the water, and the earth and cooperate with them.

I respect myself and the process.

I harmonize with nature and all others in my life.

I accept greater peace in my life now.

And so it is.

CHAPTER 14

TAOIST PROBLEM SOLVING

"Wise people seek solutions;
The ignorant only cast blame."

(TAO 79)

B Y studying nature, we learn the principles of Tao. By cooperating
with these principles, we can solve problems more effectively.
The first step in Taoist problem solving is to see our place in the
larger pattern. Responding with humility and detachment, Tao people don't let ego demands narrow their perspective and lead them into
foolish action.

All around us, we see people reacting from an ego space: blaming
others, having tantrums, making demands, or seeking revenge—
doing everything but solving the problem. In March 1989, angry
northern Californians sued the Marin County water district for imposing mandatory 35 percent rationing and restrictions on new development. Calling themselves "Citizens Against Irrational Rationing,"
they accused their district of using an emergency clause to impose
rationing when there was no "real" emergency—an earthquake or
broken dam—just a water shortage. Arguing over legal techni-
calities, they were resisting the problem, not solving it. Whatever
happens in court will not change the growing water shortage in parts
of this country.

In our litigious society, many people believe the best way to solve a
problem is to sue someone. Yet this merely strains the already over-
crowded courts and shifts money around, much of it into lawyers'
pockets, often leaving the original problem unsolved.

Tao people look to the larger patterns, seeing beyond the artificial

147

dualism of "us against them." From courtrooms to combat, too many people in this world have wasted their energies casting blame, perpetuating conflict, making enemies instead of solving problems.

Intellectual myopia—nearsightedness—is a bane of modern existence. Not only are we distracted by dualism, but we succumb to overspecialization. Concentrating our knowledge in one area, we ignore the entire picture.

Taoist problem solving means thinking holistically, working with the larger patterns found in nature. Specialized knowledge cannot solve our complex global problems. Academic specialists have advised presidents for years. But in 1979 many academic leaders told the Washington *Post* that they didn't know how to solve global problems. At New York University a professor of urban values resigned because he didn't have "anything to say anymore."[1]

The *Tao* teaches us to look for the natural cycles. Problems arise when we seek short-term solutions, ignoring these cycles. In March 1989, a consumer panic spread through the United States when the Natural Resources Defense Council announced the carcinogenic danger of alar, a chemical sprayed on commercially-grown red apples to improve shelf life and appearance. The council's report led to outcries by concerned citizens, the banning of apples in school lunchrooms, and a Senate hearing on the safety of our food.

The alar scare has subsided and the company involved has stopped producing it. But the lesson remains. Until recently, commercial growers have been so concerned with improved appearance and shelf life, that they've ignored the larger implications of their actions. This example and others like it demonstrate the Taoist principles of oneness and cyclical growth. For agricultural chemicals become an irrevocable part of the food cycle, affecting not only the treated produce but everyone who eats it. As the cycle continues, these chemicals enter our soil and water supplies and could poison the earth as well. The Tao teaches us to be more careful about our choices.

Working with the Cycles

Tao people recognize the consequences of their actions. As we'll see in this chapter, Taoist problem solving works *with* the cycles, preventing problems before they arise and solving current problems by cooperating with nature. Thinking cyclically and globally while acting locally, we can bring greater harmony to our world.

The Wisdom of Prevention

The *Tao* tells us to:

"Deal with the difficult,
While it is still easy.
Solve large problems
When they are still small.
Preventing large problems
By taking small steps
Is easier than solving them.
Therefore, the Tao person
Anticipates and lives wisely,
By small actions
Accomplishing great things.

(TAO 63)

We practice the wisdom of prevention by seeing our actions in perspective, looking to the larger cycles. By eating more whole foods, we can help prevent disease as well as hunger and pollution on the planet. How is this possible? Let's consider all the cycles involved.

To begin with our own life cycle, a simpler diet of grains, legumes, fresh fruits, and vegetables is much healthier than the heavy load of meats, fat, sugar, and processed foods consumed by average Americans. This unhealthy diet has led to an increase in obesity and "diseases of affluence," heart disease and cancer among the general population.[3] We can improve our health by reducing or eliminating meat, obtaining protein by combining complex carbohydrates, grains, and legumes. In 1988 *The American Journal of Clinical Nutrition* reported that a vegetarian diet greatly reduces the risk of obesity, heart disease, high blood pressure, lung cancer, adult–onset diabetes, gallstones, and digestive disorders.[4]

Because all life is interrelated, our daily choices affect our neighbors on the planet. If more of us reduced our intake of meat and animal products, there would be more than enough food to go around. This was Frances Moore Lappé's astounding conclusion nearly twenty years ago in *Diet for a Small Planet*. Eating the animals who consume tons of grain and soy protein vastly reduces the amount of available food.

The traditional American diet perpetuates cycles of scarcity. Half our harvested acreage goes to feed livestock: it takes at least seven pounds of grain and soy feed to produce one pound of meat. A heavy meat diet wastes water as well. A day's food for the average American takes 4,200 gallons of water per day, 80 percent of which goes to produce meat (2,500 gallons for each pound of beef).

Lappé says that "a diet based on grain-fed meat is like driving a gas-guzzling car," a waste of resources and an intolerable burden on the environment.[5] Raising beef, pork, lamb, and veal on large scale commercial feed lots produces tons of excremental waste which pollutes the water supply. To keep the animals healthy in such crowded conditions, breeders fill them full of chemicals and hormones, which are then passed on to people who eat the meat.

Without artificial additives, whole foods are easier on our bodies. Because they produce less waste, they're also easier on the environment. Unlike their processed counterparts, whole foods like oranges and potatoes don't need fancy wrappers. Grains and legumes can be sold in bulk without wasteful packaging.

Commercial processing creates mountains of waste each year in disposable packaging, much of it not even biodegradable. With increased processing, the nutrition value of food decreases. Transporting food from farms to processing plants to individual stores pollutes the air and consumes enormous amounts of petroleum. Heavily processed foods are unhealthy for our bodies and our environment.

PERSONAL EXERCISE: MAKING WISER CHOICES

We can make wiser choices, cooperating with the natural cycles to prevent disease, hunger, and pollution. Here are some helpful guidelines when buying food:

- Decrease or curtail your use of meat. Eat more whole grains and legumes, buying in bulk when possible. Books like *Diet for a Small Planet, Laurel's Kitchen,* and *The Pritikin Diet* offer helpful advice and recipes.
- Buy fresh produce. It's much more nutritious than processed versions which contain salt, sugar, and chemical additives.
- Avoid over-packaged fruits and vegetables needlessly wrapped in layers of plastic. Some studies claim that plastics give off unhealthy residues.[6] They may not be healthy for us and they most certainly pollute the planet.
- Buy local fruits and vegetables whenever possible. Eliminate the waste and pollution involved in shipping foods in from other areas. Find out what foods are produced locally and buy them in season, living in harmony with the natural cycles.
- Buy organic produce when possible, reducing personal and planetary pollution by chemical fertilizers and pesticides. If your store doesn't have organic produce, ask for it. The greater the demand for organic fruits and vegetables, the greater the supply, and the healthier life will be for all of us.

Growing Your Own

Another way to cut down on pollution is to grow your own produce. A garden gives us fresh, naturally ripened food while putting us back in touch with the soil and natural cycles.

Using only compost and natural fertilizers, organic gardening does not pollute or exhaust the soil but actually improves it. Plants grown organically are healthier and less susceptible to pests and disease. Organic farmers rely heavily upon prevention: companion planting, crop rotation, and natural inhibitors such as garlic and onions to repel aphids. When problems do occur, they resort to natural pesticides such as soapy water, killing pests without poisoning the garden. John Jeavons' book, *How to Grow More Vegetables* is an excellent guide to organic gardening.[7]

Although you may not be able to "live off the land" in a city or suburb, you'll be surprised at how much you can grow in a small space. The Chinese have gardened manually and organically for centuries, using only fertilizers produced on the farm. They've been able to feed up to twice as many people per acre as modern methods. John Jeavons says that biodynamic intensive gardening with small raised beds produces at least four times more vegetables per acre than mechanized chemical agriculture.[8] It's also kinder to the environment, pollution free, and uses only half the water and one percent of the energy of commercial farming.

Some people have taken to organic gardening with a passion. Richard Stevens, a professor at the University of Colorado, Denver, grows all his own vegetables in his 6,000 square foot back yard. Each fall he and his family can forty pounds each of peas, beans, squash, and corn, storing carrots, onions, and other root crops in the cellar. What they don't put away for winter, they sell at a nearby farmer's market.

While most of his colleagues are doing academic research in the library, Stevens uses his garden as a laboratory to see how much food people can grow in their yards. The professor smiles and says, "The idea is to show city people they can grow groceries instead of grass."

The garden provides more than food. When he leaves his classroom and enters his natural laboratory, Professor Stevens feels a strong sense of peace. "There's a feeling about the plants and the soil," he admits. "I can walk out there and my worries all go away."[9]

After spending yesterday double-digging my own small garden for spring planting, I understand what he means. My muscles were sore this morning, but I awoke with a sense of anticipation. Running to the window, I looked out at the freshly turned soil with the small green plants set out in careful patterns. In the coming weeks, I'll watch for emerging seedlings, physical evidence of the power of nature—right in my own back yard.

If you live in an apartment or condominium, you can still grow fresh vegetables and herbs in containers on your patio or rooftop. Tomatoes, lettuce, peppers, and strawberries grow well in pots or planter boxes. Ask your local nursery which plants grow best in your area.

My cousin Norma always has something edible growing on her patio. One year it was cucumbers, another year a variety of herbs. A few years ago, she and her coworkers started a community garden at work, growing fresh vegetables in the lot behind the office. With a little ingenuity, you too can find the right growing space for your garden.

Organic gardening reconnects us to nature's cycles. We learn to work with the seasons, the earth, air, sunlight, and water—all the elements that support life. Cooperating with nature, we are one with Tao, preventing problems in our lives and world by harmonizing with natural cycles.

Solving Problems with the Cycles

Taoists rely on natural cycles not only to prevent problems but to solve them. One excellent example of this is recycling, a natural solution to the growing waste and depletion on the planet. The *Tao* tells us:

"The Tao person helps others
So no one is lost,
And uses things wisely
So nothing is wasted."

(TAO 27)

The Chinese gardener "uses things wisely." In 1970, when Peter Chan and his family moved to their new home in Oregon, the yard was filled with hard clay soil and large stones, enough to make another man throw up his hands in dismay. Peter saw the yard not as a problem but an opportunity. Today his beautiful gardens have won awards and been featured in *Sunset Magazine Better Homes and Gardens* and on national television. The clay soil has been enriched with compost, and the once troublesome stones now form neat pathways between the raised beds of his vegetable garden.[10]

"Nothing is wasted." So deeply ingrained is this principle to the Chinese that they have a hard time understanding what we mean by garbage. To them, "the byproducts of something are potentially good materials for something else."[11] In Chinese philosophy, everything is part of an ongoing process. To recognize that process and cooperate with it is to be one with Tao.

Yet depletion and waste are all too common in the western world. Industrialized countries—one fourth of the world's population—use

80 percent of the earth's resources. [12] Our demand for low cost beef, hardwood, and paper is destroying the planet's tropical rainforests at the alarming rate of ninety-five acres a minute, aggravating the greenhouse effect. To produce our daily deluge of print media—newspapers, magazines, catalogues, and brochures—we kill thousands of trees. One print run of the Sunday New York *Times* uses 75,000 trees. [13]

We also pile up mountains of waste. In industrialized countries each person discards up to 165 pounds a month of paper, glass, metal, plastic, and kitchen waste. In the United States, this amounts to a personal average of 1,930 pounds per year, with city dwellers producing over a ton of waste apiece. [14]

Since our landfills can't contain all this trash, refuse companies are looking for new dumping grounds, transferring the problem to other locations instead of solving it. Garbage barges are creating bad feelings and bad smells on the international scene, as the United States attempts to unload its garbage on the Third World. In 1988 Philadelphia shipped 14,000 tons of toxic waste through the Caribbean, rejected in turn by Guinea-Bissau, Honduras, the Bahamas, Bermuda, and the Dominican Republic, finally surreptitiously dumping its cargo on a beach in Haiti, which lodged an unsuccessful protest. [15]

According to the Taoist principle of oneness, every action has inevitable ripples and repercussions. America's irresponsible waste disposal not only contributes to planetary pollution but could lead to new cycles of hostility in international relations.

America, like other industrialized countries, creates tremendous waste from excessive packaging. Just one generation ago, most people bought food in bulk at local stores, carried the sugar, tea, rice, flour, and other dry goods home in reusable cotton bags, and stored them in kitchen canisters. My mother and grandmother had canister sets although I rarely see them in modern kitchens. We've evolved into a disposable society which creates massive piles of paper, cardboard, and plastic every time we go to the market. At least one tenth of the average grocery bill is spent on packaging. [16]

Some packaging is not even biodegradable. Those plastic wrappers, bags, and bottles we use every day are made of nonrenewable petrochemicals and don't break down naturally. The earth is already cluttered with plastic debris which not only pollutes the planet, but harms wildlife. Seals and fish are injured, often strangled by discarded plastic nets, wrappers, and six pack bands from soft drinks.

When we're asked at the checkout stand if we'd like our groceries in "paper or plastic." I used to wonder what responsible choice we could make: using paper destroys trees while plastic pollutes the planet. Lately I've been avoiding this dilemma by bringing my own canvas bags when I go to the store.

The other day I asked a friend who works at the health food store if they could do something to reduce packaging waste and pollution. "We use so much plastic," she agreed, shaking her head sadly, "I don't know if plastic is *ever* environmentally safe, biodegradable or not." Two weeks later the store announced a new policy: discounts for customers who return bags for reuse or bring their own.

The next week a local grocery clerk noticed my bags. "What a great idea! We need to do more of this," she said, offering to tell the store manager they should offer low cost canvas bags with the store logo as an ecological alternative.

Taking canvas bags along when I shop is a small step, really, but it's a direct action I can take to help reduce waste and pollution. And I've found that most people I know do care about the environment. They just need a tangible expression of that caring.

If enough of us look to the larger cycles, we can come up with new solutions to our global problems. Meanwhile, we can help by not using so many grocery bags, reaching for products in glass instead of plastic, and asking local stores for biodegradable alternatives.

Turning Problems into Resources

Often what seems like a problem can be a resource when seen from another perspective. A few years ago, a scientist at the 3M Corporation developed a new glue, which didn't seem at all promising. It had very limited adhesion, sticking to things only temporarily. Yet today this glue has become nearly indispensible in offices across the country, for it's used to make the small removable notes called Post-Its.

Recycling turns our mounting waste problem into a resource, creating new sources of glass, metal, and paper materials. Glass can be recycled in two ways. Returnable bottles have a short cycle of use, return, and reuse. Nonreturnable glass is used, recycled (melted down and made into new glass containers), and reused. Cans can be used, recycled (melted down and made into new cans), and reused; and paper can be used, recycled (de-inked, immersed in a chemical solution, made into new paper), and reused.

For years I saved all my bottles, cans, and newspapers, hauling them to the local recycling center in the trunk of my car. Last year my town initiated curbside recycling, dropping off three brightly colored plastic bins and a set of instructions at each house in the area. What recycling possibilities exist in your community? Call your local refuse company and find out.

Composting

For those of us with gardens, kitchen waste can be composted, returned to the soil, and used to grow new food or other plants. Grass clippings, fallen leaves, and other garden waste can also go into the compost pile. After a few months, the materials decompose into rich dark humus, perfect for transplanting and adding nutrients to the soil.

Shocked by the garbage barges America was sending around the Caribbean last year, I decided to take greater responsibility for the waste in my household. Since we already had curbside recycling, the only other easily recyclable trash was kitchen and yard waste, which comprises twenty to thirty percent of our garbage. So I invested in a compost bin which its makers claimed would speedily break down kitchen and garden waste while remaining odor free. With some trepidations, I drove to Palo Alto to pick it up, wondering if I was out of my mind to pay $100 for a compost bin. But I've found it both odor free and effective. After a couple of months the garden clippings and kitchen scraps turn into dark, crumbly humus that looks (and smells) like potting soil. My garden is growing better than ever, thriving on its diet of natural nutrients that otherwise would have wound up in the municipal dump.

Of course, you don't have to buy a compost bin. Many people build them themselves of wood or chicken wire. Other people prefer old-fashioned compost piles. Stu Campbell's *Let It Rot* is a helpful guide to making your own.

The Principle of Return

Many communities have their own composting projects, collecting kitchen and yard waste in special containers and converting it to organic fertilizer. New York State and New Jersey have recently begun local leaf composting and mulch programs. Composting has become a large-scale project in many European countries. France has one hundred composting plants, while Sweden composts one-fourth of its solid waste each year.[17]

Whether small or large scale, composting cooperates with the natural cycles. Stu Campbell sees it as one way we can give back to the land after taking from it for so long.[18] The Tao "moves by returning in endless cycles" (Tao 40). By composting and recycling, we participate in these cycles, becoming more consciously one with Tao.

Cycles and Solutions

The Tao teaches that everything is part of a larger process. The byproducts of one thing are valuable components of something else. Taoist problem solving makes us more conscious of the process, involving us more actively in solutions. By heeding the cycles, we come up with creative new possibilities.

One major problem facing farmers around the planet is soil depletion. Each year they add more chemical fertilizers, which slowly seep into the water supply and out to sea, leaving the soil depleted. As authors John Seymour and Herbert Girardet have explained, "the metabolism of our species is at present linear" when "it should be cyclical." We mine phosphates in North Africa to grow one crop. When the food is eaten, the refuse is carried off to the sea and lost. Before modern sewage systems, organic waste was composted, then returned to the soil to renew the agricultural cycle.[19]

Thinking cyclically, Swedish engineers have been separating sewage from other waste water. They send the gray water to purification plants and compost the sewage, treat it, and return it to the land. This has been going on since 1959. In China, each village has its own sewage treatment plant, which produces fertilizer as well as methane gas used to light and heat the village.[20]

The Swedish people, like the Chinese, have always lived close to nature. Entire families walk in the woods together on Sundays, pointing out native herbs and flowers. Perhaps this is why Swedes are so good at thinking cyclically, emulating the natural cycles. One favorite example of mine is the pneumatic pipeline system, used in Swedish cities since 1969 to dispose of household garbage. Pneumatic tubes, installed in each unit in an apartment building, carry trash down to the cellar, where it's separated into recyclable glass and metal, with remaining waste burned in an incinerator. The heat from incineration rises in another set of pipes to warm the building. Thus, each apartment house is a small closed system, with its own heat supply created from household waste.[21] Instead of a problem, trash in Sweden has become a solution: part of an ongoing cycle and a source of radiant energy.

Thinking Globally, Acting Locally

Like the resourceful Swedes, we can work for more local solutions to the closely related problems of increasing waste and decreasing natural resources. By thinking globally, we see how our actions fit into the planetary picture. By acting locally, we help restore order and balance to the planet. Here are some things you can do:

- Separate and recycle your garbage. Ask your refuse company to begin curbside recycling if they haven't already done so.
- Start a compost pile or bin to recycle kitchen and garden waste if you have a yard. Or ask your refuse company to begin a local composting project.
- Avoid overpackaged products and ask businesses to use less packaging, especially fast food restaurants, which use tons of paper, cardboard, and styrofoam.
- Avoid plastic packaging. Choose products in glass or metal containers whenever possible.
- Ask stores to use biodegradable packaging.
- Reduce waste and raise consciousness by bringing your own shopping bags.
- Use returnable bottles when possible—*and* return them.

- Find out which companies are big polluters and ask them to change, boycotting when necessary.
- Write to political leaders expressing your views and recommending more responsible waste management.
- Join a local ecology action group.
- When you've established more positive cycles at home, move on to the workplace. The average office employee throws away over 3½ lbs. of waste paper a day, which amounts to over 900 lbs. a year. Recycling office paper and using recycled paper products helps save trees, energy, and water, while reducing trash and chemical pollution, especially from sulfur dioxide which produces acid rain.[22]

In Taoist problem solving the most important resource is your consciousness, your awareness of natural cycles. By actively participating in these cycles, you'll come up with new ideas, new insights of your own. With this awareness comes the responsibility to take action and share your concerns with others. Encourage the people around you to come up with healthier solutions to collective problems.

Our consciousness *does* make a difference. During 1989, Berkeley and Santa Cruz, California banned styrofoam packaging, requiring local businesses and government offices to use biodegradable alternatives. In West Milford, New Jersey a group of high school students convinced their school to offer paper lunch trays as an alternative to disposable plastic ones. Proclaiming "Put your money where your mouth is," students chose the paper trays although they cost five cents more. In the spring of 1989, these teenagers told a United Nations environmental forum in New York what they were doing to promote a healthier world.[23]

Public concern about dangerous pesticides has prompted lettuce growers in Salinas, California to use a safer form of pest control. With a new invention called the salad-vac, they literally vacuum the bugs out of the lettuce. More economical than pesticides, this invention actually saves the company money. Lately I've found salad-vac lettuce in local markets. It's often cheaper than the pesticide-sprayed variety and certainly healthier for both people and planet.

These are just a few positive changes emerging from our growing concern for personal and planetary health. What's happening in your area? What can you do to support positive change close to home?

Our daily lives, our daily choices, can make a tremendous difference. By following the Tao we can "by small actions accomplish great things" (*Tao* 63). Living in harmony with the natural cycles we can release new streams of creativity to heal ourselves and our world.

Affirmation

I now know my life is peaceful and harmonious.
I recognize the natural cycles and work with them.
I practice the wisdom of prevention.
When faced with problems, I look to the larger cycles
    and cooperate with Tao.
I think globally, act locally.
I respect myself and the process.
I harmonize with nature and all others in my world.
I accept greater peace in my life now.
And so it is.

CHAPTER 15

THE IMPORTANCE OF TIMING

"The Tao person
Lives fully in every moment."

(TAO 14)

F OR centuries Taoists have modeled their personal lives after the
cycles of nature. In fact, the Chinese word *tzu jan* means not only
the natural sciences but living in harmony with nature.[1]

Following nature, Tao people learn the vital lesson of timing. They
enjoy every season of their lives, practice the wisdom of beginnings
and endings, and prevent problems by making careful choices. Recognizing the cycles within and around them, they know which action
is best at every stage.

The Seasons of Our Lives

We all go through cycles of growth: physically, emotionally, spiritually. Psychologists Carl Jung and Erik Erikson described the stages of
human life, an approach popularized by Gail Sheehy in *Passages*. For
developmental psychologists, each season of life has its own lesson or
"crisis." In childhood we learn to trust ourselves and others, developing physical and intellectual competency. Adolescence brings the
quest for personal identity and intimacy. In adulthood, we learn
lessons of responsibility, integrity, and spirituality.

Tao people accept each season of life and the opportunities it offers.
They don't fight the cycles by resisting or looking back. But our
culture's strong emphasis on youth often obscures our perception of
adulthood, making many people lose their balance.

Accepting Our Changing Seasons: Adulthood
and Spiritual Maturity

Our physical cycle continues and the seasons change from youth to maturity. Without spiritual growth, adult life becomes shallow and meaningless. We must keep developing our minds and souls. The great religious traditions of East and West have long recognized this. Christianity tells of the midlife conversions of St. Paul and St. Augustine. Hinduism, too, acknowledges the watershed of middle life. In early adulthood, most Hindus become householders with family and community commitments, but later many become *sannyasin,* renouncing their worldly responsibilities. Retiring to the country, they devote their time to quiet contemplation, service, and spiritual growth. Combining spirituality with political service, Mahatma Gandhi followed this path.

Like their Hindu counterparts, Taoist masters seek the path of spiritual maturity. Combining strength with compassion, they devote their lives to contemplation and service.[2]

Beginning a New Cycle: Renewal in Retirement

My friend Gertrude Welch has chosen such a path. In the householder tradition, she has been the typical American woman—wife, mother, grandmother, active in her church and community. For years she worked as a secretary, first at San Jose State, then at Santa Clara University. But in 1984 she retired from her job to work full time for peace.

Softspoken and gracious, Gertrude radiates a personal warmth that breaks down barriers. With her ready smile, she immediately puts people at ease. Over the years she's worked at migrant camps and shelters for the homeless, marched in demonstrations, organized classes and discussion groups for her church, and traveled at her own expense to the Soviet Union, the Middle East, and Central America, led by a vision of peace and justice.

She's lived with Nicaraguan peasants, spoken on TV and radio talk shows, shared her views with politicians and people on the street. A peacemaker wherever she goes, she quietly witnesses for her beliefs, reaching out to her neighbors, the homeless, and the oppressed. "I believe that peace is a way of life," she says. "You have to live it in your home, your community, and your world."

In retirement, she welcomes the extra time to work for peace. A longtime leader in her church, in the Women's International League for Peace and Freedom, the Fellowship of Reconciliation, and the local Peace Center, she combines organizational work with service and contemplation. She volunteers one night a week at a shelter for the homeless and spends some time each day praying for peace, guidance for world leaders, healing, and understanding.

There's an old Chinese adage: "flowing water does not decay."[3] In our society, many people stagnate when they reach middle life. The challenge is gone. Bored and dissatisfied, they fill their emptiness with artificial stimulants or consumer goods.

Tao people know life evolves in cycles, that without renewal comes stagnation and decline. Only when we face new challenges, begin a new cycle, are we revitalized. After raising her family and earning a living, Gertrude Welch now works to build a powerful legacy of peace and justice, affirming a new cycle of hope for all of us on the planet.

Respecting the Cycles

Following the Tao helps us work with the cycles in life, not against them. This means honoring not only life's seasons, but our own energy cycles so we avoid being driven and compulsive, exhausted by "efforting." Sometimes this means stepping back and assessing what's going on, focusing on our energies as well as the larger process.

In college I could study for only so long until reaching a point of diminishing returns. Then I made mistakes or had to read a page over and over again to understand it. Even if I hadn't finished my work, I learned it was better to honor my energies, not to fight them. It actually took *less* time to finish an assignment if I rested when I was tired, then completed the task when my mind was fresh.

PERSONAL EXERCISE

- The next time you reach the point of diminishing returns, don't fight the cycles.
- Take a break. Rest, take a walk or do something different for a while. Then return to your project with new energy and insight.

Beginnings and Endings

Aware of the cycles in life, we realize that for every project, every process, there's a beginning and ending. The *Tao* teaches us to take special care in these times of change:

"If we know the wisdom of beginning
And ending,
We will never fail."

(TAO 64)

The Wisdom of Beginning

There's a special wisdom to beginnings. We must have faith in ourselves and the process. Otherwise we procrastinate. Afraid of failure, we postpone it by not getting started.

Writing a long term paper sends many students into tailspins of self-doubt. They put off doing anything until the last minute, concluding with frantic efforts and poor performance until they break out of this destructive pattern.

Many people are intimidated by long-term projects, overwhelmed by the thought of all that work. Yet if we divide the work into manageable units, we can handle it. Writing a 300-page doctoral dissertation once overwhelmed me too. But then I made an outline and convinced myself I could do it—one chapter at a time.

Following the Tao, we develop faith in the process. We don't give up because we can't see immediate results.

My neighbor Jack is a successful engineer in his early thirties. He runs through the neighborhood each day after work and participates in local marathons. One day I learned that he'd lost 150 pounds. He showed me a pair of pants and a belt he'd saved from the old days. They were enormous.

The change was incredible. "How did you do it?" I asked.

Overweight from childhood, Jack had faced his problem, consulted a doctor, changed his diet, and taken up running. But results didn't happen overnight.

"One day at a time," he said.

Sarah is a counselor at my church. Ten years ago her life was sabotaged by alcoholism. She lost her job, her husband, and her self-respect before hitting bottom. Today, you'd never know she'd been there.

How did she do it? She smiled and said, "It took courage, prayer, and living one day at a time."

Committed peace workers like my friend Gertrude also live one day at a time. Whether they volunteer at local shelters, teach classes, write letters, distribute petitions, or participate in political action, they take steps to end the poverty, injustice, and imbalance in our world. Instead of worrying themselves to despair about planetary problems, they take positive action.

The *Tao* reminds us that:

"The journey of a thousand miles starts with a single step."

(TAO 64)

We need to take that step, then another, but remember to be patient with ourselves. For our goals are achieved one step at a time. As in nature, everything has its own growth cycle. Our seeds will sprout when they're ready. We cannot rush the process. Even if we see no results, we must not succumb to self-doubt.

The *Tao* also tells us to:

"Be careful with commitments.
Do not begin something
You may not want to finish."

(TAO 63)

How many of us fill our lives with tension and conflict by saying yes to too many people, too many projects? An important lesson in timing is knowing when to say yes, when to say no.

Don't be reactive, doing whatever other people ask without considering your own cycles. Take time to look within before answering. The *Tao* says:

"The wise person chooses what is real
And looks beneath the surface,
Chooses the fruit and not the flower,
Not reacting, but responding
In harmony with Tao."

(TAO 38)

TAO QUESTIONS

If you have difficulty saying no, as many people do, ask yourself these questions before making another commitment:

- Is it necessary?
- Will it bring greater good to my life or the planet?
- Will it fail to happen without my participation?
- Do I really *want* to do it?
- Do I have the time?

If your answer is yes to at least three of these, including the last one, then you're making a meaningful commitment. If not, then why do it?

The Wisdom of Endings

There's a special wisdom to endings. Many people spoil a project when it's nearly completed because they get impatient. They see the end in sight and get excited. Rushing to finish, they make mistakes.

Life offers many chances to learn these lessons. Working in my yard last week, I realized once again the cost of impatience. The long meandering pumpkin vines were taking over my garden, and I'd heard that pinching off some of the flowers produces better fruit, so I set out to do some pruning. I'd nearly finished when I made a false move, slicing off the best vine with one slip of the knife. I looked down at the severed vine and the pumpkins that would never ripen, realizing how much damage is done in one instant of impatience.

I love to finish projects. I always have. Completing anything gives me a sense of exhilaration. Yet all too often I've been driven by my passion for closure and gotten careless near the end.

Following the Tao teaches patience. Without it, our stubborn will overpowers the process and we make mistakes. I'm learning to slow down and focus my attention so my passion for closure won't sabotage my timing.

Timing Means Prevention

Working with the natural cycles, Tao people practice prevention in their personal lives, taking action before things get out of hand. They learn this lesson by studying nature.

Stella, a successful graphic artist, lives a life filled with conflict and upheaval because she hasn't learned this lesson of Tao.

On first impression, it seems no one is more put together. Her hair is elegantly coiffed, and she's always stylishly dressed. But beneath that impeccable veneer, she goes from one crisis to another. When she comes home at night, she checks the lights to see if the electricity is still on, picks up her phone to make sure it hasn't been cut off. Why? Because for all her professional polish, she can't manage to pay her bills on time. She makes more than enough money but chalks it up to her artistic temperament. She forgets, and so her mailbox is filled with past due notices.

Through all the cycles of our lives, the *Tao* tells us to handle events before they reach the crisis stage. In this way much trouble is averted in our relationships with one another and our environment, much violence can be prevented in our world.

The principles of Tao operate on all levels from the personal to the planetary. As we saw in the last two chapters, our environmental problems are the direct result of carelessness and mismanagement. Like Stella, we haven't been taking care of our domestic responsibilities—on the global level. And unless we do so, our power and water will some day be cut off

The *Tao* reminds us to:

"Deal with the difficult
While it is still easy
Solve large problems
While they are still small."

(TAO 63)

Living the Tao means honoring the cycles within and around us, cooperating with them in the many choices we make each day. For by choosing wisely, we perfect our timing, bringing greater harmony to our lives.

Affirmation

I now know my life is peaceful and harmonious.
There's enough time for everything I need.
I live in the present, accepting the changing seasons of life.
I practice the wisdom of beginnings and endings.
I prevent problems by working with the cycles.
I respect myself and the process.
I harmonize with nature and all others in my world
I accept greater peace in my life now.
And so it is.

CHAPTER 16

TRANSCENDING HOSTILE CYCLES

"A plant that grows deep in the earth
Cannot be uprooted.
Hold fast to the Tao
And nothing will defeat you."

(TAO 54)

OUR thoughts, our attitudes, our emotions are all forms of energy, constantly influencing the world around us. Physicists no longer consider themselves detached observers. They know their very presence influences the properties of the particle/waves they study.[1] Our attitudes affect the cycles within and around us. Aware of this, Tao people live consciously, respectfully, knowing they exert a powerful influence on their world.

Recognizing Energy Drains

Not only do we influence people around us; we're continuously affected by the actions and attitudes of others. Spending time with other people means breathing the same air, sharing the same energy field. Some interactions are energizing. Others deplete us.

Do you know someone who drags you down? If you're always exhausted after being together, this person is an energy drain. Imbalanced, uncentered, out of touch with the source of *chi* in their lives, such people subsist on energy transfusions from others.

Energy drains are constantly clamoring for help. Whenever something goes wrong, they run to a strong friend to rescue them, acting so helpless that others feel guilty saying no. Attaching themselves like barnacles, these people become increasingly demanding and dependent.

In college I met Michael, the dark, brooding young man I chose to love. Perhaps it was my desire to make things better, to improve the world. After all, it was the sixties, and we were an idealistic generation. Determined to make him happy, to "let the sunshine in" to his life, I ministered to his ills, listened to his tirades about social injustice, helped solve his problems, mended his clothes, and brought him bags of groceries when he ran out of money. Michael's negative moods exhausted me. I got very little sleep trying to keep up with him as well as my job and classwork, but to make him happy I thought it was worth it.

Yet despite all my efforts, Michael only grew worse, becoming jealous of my friends, my classwork, my parents, anything that took me away from him. He complained constantly, called me at all hours, insulted my parents, and picked a fight with my friend Peter. His demands increased until we finally broke up.

Later I realized I'd attracted him because I was insecure. I "needed to be needed" to reinforce my own self-worth. People with low self-esteem often get caught up in the negative energies of others. Their insecurity and confusion make them vulnerable to manipulators.

PERSONAL EXERCISE

Do you have an energy drain in your life? Does being with a particular person leave you exhausted? If so, you need to get centered.

- Before you see this person again, go off by yourself and do the centering exercise in this chapter.
- When you feel yourself being drained, put your hand over your *hara,* your center of power just above your navel.
- Say to yourself (about the other person's negativity), "This is not my energy. I am one with Tao."
- After seeing this person, do a centering exercise, cleanse your aura, or wash your hands.
- Ask yourself why you've attracted this unhealthy relationship. What is there in you that created this pattern?

• Take steps to change the pattern, beginning a more positive cycle. This chapter will show you how.

The Path to Transcendence

We can transcend hostile cycles in our personal lives—in relationships, health, careers, and finances. We can also help overcome hostile cycles in society. Whether these cycles are large or small, personal or planetary, the way to transcend them is the same combination of Taoist principles: 1) centering, 2) nonresistance, and 3) taking positive action.

Centering

When facing another hostile cycle, first take a few minutes to get centered. Centered in the strength of Tao, we're not thrown off balance by the jagged, negative energies of others. We don't react from guilt, fear, or anger but draw upon a deeper source of wisdom.

The *Tao* says:

"To keep your center is to endure"

(TAO 33)

Martial arts students practice this power of centering. Focusing on the *hara,* an aikido master generates incredible force. He can't be moved even when pushed by several individuals over twice his size. Centered, he endures.

Aikido teaches that a wise person reaches out in fluid movements, integrating apparently hostile energies into a larger whole. Using an aggressor's own force and direction, an aikido master draws him into a circular pattern in which the aggressive energy is neutralized and the opponent left unharmed.

Aikido masters resolve conflict externally because they first do so internally. Stressing the importance of centering, they believe we get caught up in hostile cycles when we're stuck on the surface of life. Distracted by details, we fail to see the larger cycles.[2]

Too often problems catch us off balance because modern life fragments our consciousness. With our minds overburdened, our bodies stiff with stress, we experience life only from the neck up. Divided from ourselves, we cannot act with wisdom.

PERSONAL EXERCISE: CENTERING

How long has it been since you felt the sensation of your feet planted firmly on the ground? Aikido masters teach their students to "keep the one point," to stay centered.[3] You can regain your center with the standing meditation:

- Stand with your feet about twelve inches apart, keeping your spine straight. Bend your knees slightly.
- Hold your hands out in front of you with your elbows bent, slightly above waist level.
- Now inhale deeply into your *hara,* the point of power about two inches below your navel. Feel the energy rise up through your feet as they're planted firmly on the ground.
- Exhale, feeling the energy flow out through your hands.
- Now go back to what you were doing, centered and strengthened by the energy of Tao.

The next time you feel yourself caught up in a hostile cycle, do the standing meditation and remember this lesson from Lao Tzu:

"A plant that grows deep in the earth
Cannot be uprooted.
Hold fast to the Tao
And nothing will defeat you."

(TAO 54)

Nonresistance

Centered, Tao people do not become hostile, fearful, or angry when confronting negative events. They know that an angry response will only create another violent cycle with inevitable reprisals and further aggression. Succumbing to fear or guilt only empowers manipulators, who draw us into negativity.

What we give out inevitably comes back to us. The cycles of Tao are like the Buddhist law of *karma*. Every action produces a corresponding reaction. Violence begets further violence, negativity begets negativity. The Buddhists believe that a person repeats his karmic lessons until he finally *learns* from them, a process that may take hundreds of incarnations. They transcend the frustrating cycles of *karma* through *nirvana,* a mystical unity with life.

The *Tao* teaches that the consequences of our actions occur in this lifetime. We're subject to recurrent, often vicious cycles until we transcend them with the wisdom of Tao.

If we react violently to a violent person, we create more violence, initiating another negative cycle. This is true with individuals and true with nations. Our aggressive reactions keep us in bondage to further aggression. And unless we transcend this violent pattern, it will ultimately destroy us.

The *Tao*'s alternative to continuing hostile cycles is the principle of nonresistance, or *wu wei*. Nonresistance neutralizes negative cycles. Instead of emotionally reacting to the turmoil around us, Lao Tzu says initially to do nothing, to step back and watch the cycles. When our heart-minds are no longer troubled by negative emotions, we can act wisely, defusing negativity with the wisdom of Tao.

We can practice nonresistance every day: at work, at home, even driving our cars. Caught up in their own stressful cycles, many people express their frustration behind the wheel. A friend of mine who owns a Porsche finds himself continually challenged by aggressive drivers. The other day as he got onto the freeway, a battered truck cut him off on the ramp, then slowed down and challenged him to race. Instead of joining another dangerous cycle of "car wars," my friend practiced nonresistance, letting the other driver go. He doesn't need to prove his masculinity every time a car cuts in front of him.

PERSONAL EXERCISE: NONRESISTANCE

We can practice nonresistance by following these guidelines.

- The next time someone is hostile to you or tries to manipulate you with fear or guilt, don't react emotionally and escalate the negative cycle. Take a deep breath and get centered.

- This doesn't mean to subject yourself to injury or abuse. If necessary, stand aside, take evasive action. The important thing is not to overreact or fight back.
- From a centered space, listen and observe. What's going on with this person? What does he or she really want? What are you feeling? Look for the larger cycles.
- When you're ready, respond. Listen to your intuition, and act from center. Drawing upon the infinite wisdom of Tao, you'll know what to do.

Nonresistance helps us shift from negative to positive. When no one overreacts, the hostile cycle winds down. The other person's anger burns itself out and a new, more peaceful pattern can begin.

Taking Positive Action

The final step in transcending hostile cycles is taking positive action. It needn't even be directed toward solving the problem. The important thing is to affirm your faith in life and set new healing energies into motion.

Marsha Sinetar writes in *Elegant Choices, Healing Choices* that we become healthier when we make positive choices, bringing beauty, order, goodness, and joy to our lives. As a teacher in an inner city elementary school, she brought fresh flowers, artwork, and classical music to class, awakening a new cycle of self-esteem in her students. They kept their desks and the classroom more orderly, paid more attention to their work. Her small affirmations of beauty began a new, more positive cycle for all of them.[4]

Tao Question

When was the last time you did something positive for yourself—an affirmation of your own self-worth? It needn't be expensive or extravagant. One veteran I know used to suffer serious depressions and post-Vietnam stress syndrome until beginning a healthy new cycle. As part of his therapy he was told to develop a ritual act of caring for himself. He chose to eat a salad every day as a way of saying, "I'm OK. I deserve a healthy, happy life." Now wherever he is, he has a salad, even if it's only a piece of lettuce on the side of his plate, and he's grown much healthier emotionally and physically.

Yin and Yang Positive Acts

Taoists have a tradition of spontaneous positive action, advocating good deeds as a means of spiritual development. Master Hua-ching Ni describes two kinds of good deeds: the *yang* actions that everyone notices and the more subtle *yin* actions that pass unobserved.[5] *Yang* deeds enhance our reputation and bolster our egos, but *yin* deeds, done simply for the joy of affirming the good, strengthen our spirit. One way to end a cycle of boredom or depression is to do something unexpected, perhaps even anonymous, for the fun of it. I've put coins in expired parking meters, mended books from the public library, sent encouraging notes to public officials, and other small acts of *yin* for which I've never received any response—and yet, the spontaneous joy of these acts has cleared many a cloudy day for me.

Taoist Action: Responding with Clear Vision

When we follow the Taoist formula: centering ourselves, practicing nonresistance, and taking positive action, we respond to hostile cycles with greater wisdom and clarity. Then our minds become like a mirror. Clear and centered, we can act successfully in all situations.[6]

When our vision is clear, right answers are there when we need them. We act harmoniously, affirming the good of the whole, following the intuitive wisdom of Tao. The Chinese call this wisdom *hui*.[7] It's always with us, but buried deep within, often obscured by the troubled surface of life. When we clear our vision by following the three steps in this chapter, we return to the inherent wisdom within and become vessels of celestial light, transcending hostile cycles with the enduring wisdom of Tao.

Transcending Hostile Cycles for Yourself

Whenever circumstances drag you down into a negative cycle, you can recover by centering yourself, practicing nonresistance, and taking positive action.

Marsha Sinetar tells of one man who came for counseling after losing his job in a corporate takeover. Usually confident and energetic, he became uncentered, falling into a reactive depression. Resisting this change, he felt emotionally drained, too exhausted to do anything. Rumpled and unkempt, he admitted that even his household was a mess. He didn't have the energy to make the bed, hang up his clothes, or wash the dishes.

Aware that positive action would rebuild his self-esteem, Sinetar asked him to go home, take the sheets off his bed, wash them, and make the bed carefully. He was then to clean the entire kitchen, beginning with the dishes piled up in the sink. The next day, he was to wear his favorite suit, taking extra time to shave, shower, and dress, so he left the house looking confident and successful. She told him to maintain this standard of order until his next appointment. The following week he returned, feeling more like himself again. The negative cycle was broken. No longer depressed, he found another job.[8]

A wise friend once told me, "order is the first law of the universe."[9] The *Tao* teaches us to respect the natural order within and around us. When we find ourselves surrounded by confusion, we need to stand back, look within, and work on our consciousness.

We can begin a more positive cycle by affirming greater order and beauty in our lives. Putting your affairs in order has a subtle, healing influence. The peace and tranquility of a simple, well-ordered room with the sun shining in the windows restores my soul when I'm exhausted by the noisy world outside. A silent hour working in the garden, pulling weeds, propping up the snow peas, even cutting the grass, can be an affirmation and spiritual exercise.

TAO QUESTION

Is there something you can do to affirm greater order and beauty in your life? It can be as simple as making your bed every morning, a personal ritual I adopted years ago when working through old cycles of self-doubt. My unmade bed, littered with cast-off clothing, used to confirm my cluttered, directionless life. Now just walking into my room and seeing the bed made up with its plain white sheets and ivory comforter is an affirmation of beauty and order.

Transcending Hostile Cycles and Reaching Out to Others

Sometimes the action we take to heal our lives also brings healing to others. After an auto accident in 1983 that killed his wife and left him disabled, Richard Woolstrum took positive action. With insurance money from the accident he bought a three-story hotel in his home town of Lodi, California, and opened it as low-income housing and a shelter for the homeless. He also bought forty undeveloped acres in nearby Amador County as a wildlife refuge.

"Everyone told me I should take the money and leave, go make a good life for myself somewhere else, have fun. But I didn't want to leave here," he said. So he stayed in Lodi, reached out to others, and built a new life for himself. His neighbor Joani who came to help during his recovery became his second wife, sharing his commitment to social justice. By reaching beyond himself and taking positive action in the face of adversity, Richard Woolstrum began a creative new cycle for himself and his community.[10]

Transcending Hostile Cycles in Society

Every day, hungry people wander down America's streets, searching garbage cans for scraps, lining up outside crowded shelters and soup kitchens. Somehow the cycles of supply in the richest country in the world are by-passing hundreds of thousands of people, who walk our city streets, suffering from neglect, malnutrition, and despair.

One man I know who took positive action is Frank Olson, co-owner of Ernesto's, an elegant Mexican restaurant in Los Gatos, California. When I visited the restaurant last week, Frank told me how he began feeding the homeless. An energetic man in his late forties with bright blue eyes, silver gray hair, and mustache, Frank explained that his family background had always stressed "people taking care of people." He'd heard news reports about the hungry and homeless in our area and wondered what he could do to help.

On Christmas day 1987, Frank went down to the National Guard Armory, a temporary shelter for the homeless, to see what he could do. The place was full of hungry people. Up to two hundred a night had been crowding inside during the winter months. Frank brought back some food from the restaurant and a hundred one dollar bills for Santa Claus to distribute to the children. He's been helping out ever since.

Frank makes daily food deliveries to the armory between 4 and 5 P.M., the slow time for restaurants. And these are not scraps or luftovers, but the same foods his customers enjoy: fresh enchiladas, meat cooked with tomatoes and spices, green beans with herbs, Spanish rice, crisp green salad—a well-balanced meal.

"It's pretty hard for anyone to do anything, to pick themselves up and go for a job interview, on an empty stomach," he said. "How can that person feel good about himself?" So he serves them delicious hot meals and a generous helping of hope.

Recently, Frank's efforts have made their way into the local papers and many of his customers have given money to support the dinners. He's contacted other restaurants and wants to organize a network of people in the food business to help the hungry.

Frank said, "I've always believed it's so much better to do something yourself, to get out there and do the job. When you give your time, you're giving of yourself, and that's a lot more meaningful than just writing a check." Frank's a very busy man, active with his business, his family, and the local Lion's Club, with its many community service activities. But he's taken the time to bring hot meals to his homeless neighbors, initiating a new cycle of caring, commitment, and hope.[11]

Lao Tzu tells us that

"The Tao person helps others
So no one is lost,
And uses things wisely
So nothing is wasted."

(TAO 27)

As a nation, we've long ignored this lesson of Tao. We waste our resources, we waste our time, and we waste more food than any other country. As a result, we've created negative cycles of pollution, frustration, poverty, and despair. There are more hungry and home-less now than at any time in our nation's history. If more people had the vision and dedication of Richard Woolstrum and Frank Olson, we could overcome these hostile cycles and begin a new cycle of hope for all.

Affirmation

I now know my life is peaceful and harmonious.
I recognize the energy cycles in my world.
I affirm the order of Tao in my life.
I overcome the hostile cycles within and around me.
I center myself, practice nonresistance, and take positive action.
I respect myself and the process.
I harmonize with nature and all others in my world.
I accept greater peace in my life now.
And so it is.

CHAPTER 17

LEADING WITH THE TAO

"The best people are like water.
They benefit all things,
And do not compete with them.
They settle in low places,
One with nature, one with Tao."

(TAO 8)

THE Chinese character for wise leader is made up of three symbols. The lower part means "ruler," a person centered between the planes of heaven and earth. Above this, the symbols for "ear" and "mouth" indicate that not only has the leader attained personal balance, but that he or she listens before speaking, taking in before giving out.[1]

Tao people evolve naturally into responsible leaders. Becoming more peaceful within themselves, they recognize possibilities for greater peace in the world. Eighteenth-century Master Liu I-ming wrote that for generations of Taoists, personal balance and social responsibility have been synonymous: "The Great Way is not transmitted to people without social conscience."[2]

Materialism and ego too often fragment our world into opposing factions, making us lose sight of the whole. Personally balanced, Tao people transcend the demands of ego. They see beyond materialistic values which trap many people in cycles of competition and scarcity.

Ch'iang, the Chinese term for a stubborn ego also means proud, headstrong, stiff, or rigid. To be stubborn and inflexible is to lack the fluid wisdom of Tao. Tao people practice *hsu* or humility, which also means open-mindedness or emptiness.[3] Getting their egos out of the way, they can take appropriate action and change course when needed. Humble and flexible, they're always ready to ask themselves, "What if I am wrong?"[4]

Transcending Old Stereotypes: Leading with the Tao

Lao Tzu rejected leaders who rule by force, intimidation, or personality, reducing other people to "followers." Recognizing the destruction wrought by combative egos, the danger of blind devotion to charismatic leaders, he asks us to discard our old stereotypes, affirming instead a wisdom beyond competition, a leadership of caring and humility.

The Tao leader is not a superstar who mesmerizes others with the force of rhetoric or flashy deeds. While lesser people crave power and dominance, Tao leaders reject competitive hierarchies as unnatural. They build networks, realizing we're all part of the interlocking web of life. As we'll see in this chapter, Tao people lead with a new combination of talents: cooperation, awareness of the cycles, courage, and facilitation. Affirming what Lao Tzu called "the spirit of the valley," they draw upon the infinite wisdom and power of Tao.

Leading Through Cooperation

Progressive leaders in any field never hide behind elitism and hierarchies. They lead through cooperation. Living the Tao, working with others,

"The wisest person
Trusts the process,
Without seeking to control;
Takes everything as it comes,
Lives not to achieve or possess,
But simply to be
All he or she can be
In harmony with Tao."

(TAO 2)

Eleanor Roosevelt exemplifies leadership through cooperation. As America's first lady, she traveled around the country, later throughout the world, becoming the eyes and ears of her husband. She walked through Nebraska cornfields and urban slums, visiting migrant workers in California, unemployed workers in Detroit, miners in West Virginia, and black children in Alabama, her eyes shining with kindness and concern.

Throughout the Depression, she kept FDR informed of people's problems. Building friendships and cooperative networks, she discovered talented people and invited them to the White House to work with the President. During World War II, her efforts spanned the globe. She visited with soldiers and heads of state, carrying her message of reassurance and understanding throughout a war-torn world.

In 1945, after FDR's death, President Truman made her a delegate to the United Nations. At first she hesitated, wondering if she was qualified. But her competence, personal warmth, and cooperative spirit soon made that clear. During a debate with Andrei Vishinsky of the Soviet Union, Eleanor Roosevelt addressed the General Assembly, defending the rights of displaced persons. The Assembly voted to give the refugees their rights, but for years Vishinsky protested. Yet, in 1954, Ambassador and Mrs. Vishinsky attended Eleanor Roosevelt's seventieth birthday party, confirming her ability to differ strongly on political issues without personal animosity.

In 1946, she became chair of the United Nations Human Rights Commission. Her tireless work and cooperative spirit resulted in the *Universal Declaration of Human Rights,* approved after long debate by the General Assembly in 1948. In 1952, when President Eisenhower failed to reappoint her, she began working as a U.N. volunteer. When Eleanor Roosevelt returned as a U.N. delegate in 1961 by appointment of President Kennedy, the entire Assembly rose to acknowledge her. No other delegate has received this honor, a demonstration of cooperation on a global scale.

Observing the Cycles: Watching and Listening

Tao leaders spend their time watching and listening. In order to see clearly, we must look beyond ourselves. In order to listen, we must first be still.

In their stillness, Tao people learn the wisdom of nature, realizing:

"When you feel yourself part of nature,
You will live in harmony."

(TAO 13)

The cycles of nature occur within and around us. To act wisely is to harmonize with these cycles. This is the basis for all harmony, personal or planetary. Wise people know the principles of Tao prevail in ecology, society, and individuals.

Bill Devall and George Sessions' description of ecological consciousness also applies to Tao leadership. It is realizing "everything is connected" and "a process of learning to appreciate silence and solitude and rediscovering how to listen. It is learning how to be more receptive, trusting, holistic in perception," cooperative, and nonexploitive.[5]

Tao leaders listen to opponents as well as their friends. Conscious of positive and negative energies, *yin* and *yang,* they learn from both. Turning within, they listen to themselves as well, trusting in their intuition, their inner guidance.

Dag Hammarskjöld, former Secretary General of the United Nations, practiced this lesson of Tao. Thoughtful, contemplative, intensely private amid a busy life of public service, he recognized the importance of listening. As he wrote in his personal journal, *Markings,* "The more faithfully you listen to the voice within you, the better you will hear what is sounding outside."[6]

Because they listen, Tao leaders can understand and solve complex problems. Their patient observation brings greater insight and empathy. Hammarskjöld's colleagues all remarked on his exceptional patience in listening to people, and he wrote that "openness to life grants a lightning-swift insight into the life situation of others."[7]

Hammarskjöld worked eighteen to twenty hour days for weeks on end in times of crisis, maintaining his equanimity. As Secretary General during the tense years of the Cold War, he resolved many international crises, earning the respect of leaders in both the United States and the Soviet Union.

An intensely spiritual man, Hammarskjöld wrote of "the uncarved block," practicing the wisdom of detachment. "Remain at the center, which is yours and that of all humanity," he said. "For those goals which it gives to your life, do the utmost which, at each moment, is possible for you. Also, act without thinking of the consequences, or seeking anything for yourself."[8] A dedicated citizen and civil servant of the world, he affirmed in his life the larger vision, personal discipline, and inner strength of the Tao.

Leading with Courage

The *Tao* tells us:

"A man with outward courage dares to die.
A man with inward courage dares to live."

(TAO 73)[9]

One man who exemplified the courage of Tao was Raoul Wallenberg, a young Swedish diplomat who singlehandedly saved the lives of 100,000 people during World War II.

On a dark night in Budapest in October of 1944, a train was being loaded with Hungarian Jews destined for the gas chambers. Suddenly a tall young man climbed aboard the roof of the train, handing out Swedish documents to the desperate people—their passports to life and freedom.

Daily, Wallenberg risked his life to save people condemned by the Nazis, intercepting the brutal death marches, taking Jews into his protection, moving them to safe houses, and facing the wrath of Adolf Eichmann who publically vowed to kill him. Born to a wealthy Swedish banking family, he gave up a life of ease to follow his heart, doing everything he could to halt the atrocities. He seemed to be everywhere, confronting the Nazis in the streets, appearing when they came in the night to take people away.

Wallenberg had no protection other than his diplomatic status, no staff or official backing from his government. He relied upon his wits, his resourcefulness, and his skill at negotiation. And yet he accomplished miracles with his makeshift documents, his courage, his strength of will. To the Hungarian Jews he came, like an angel in the night, empowered by conscience to save them.

In January of 1945, when the Russians entered Budapest they found this lone Swedish diplomat, who had stayed behind during the allied liberation, determined to protect his people. Unable to comprehend what he'd been doing—why was a Swedish Christian capitalist saving Jews?—they took him into custody, convinced he was a spy.

The Swedish government asked for his release in 1945 and again in 1946. His family grew worried. They were told he'd be released soon, that he'd died in captivity, that he was alive and would soon be released. But Wallenberg never returned. Reports from former Russian prisoners state that a Swedish man, honored by those who knew him, was still alive in some distant prison in the Gulag. He was sighted in 1959, 1963, and as late as 1975. But the Russian government has remained silent.

We're left with the memory of his courage in the face of adversity, the gratitude of the hundred thousand he saved, and the mystery of the life of Raoul Wallenberg. Having liberated so many others, then cruelly, ironically caught in a web of cold war intrigue, his example shines like the light of some distant star against the darkness. A secular saint, with the "inward courage" of Tao, he dared to save the lives of others and affirm at great personal cost the more humane, just, and harmonious world to which we may one day hope to evolve.

The Leader as Facilitator

Tao leaders quietly empower others. Lao Tzu tells us:

"When Tao people lead and the work is accomplished,
The people say, 'We did it ourselves.' "

(TAO 17)

Inspired by this quote from the *Tao*, psychologist Carl Rogers carried it in his wallet as a daily reminder. In his person-centered therapy and peace negotiation, he saw his own role in the Taoist tradition of leader as facilitator.

Creating an atmosphere of trust and cooperation, affirming the larger vision, such leaders work with the team to achieve the good of the whole. They help others grow as individuals, to become more confident, competent, and successful. This is an ongoing process of personal engagement, never a matter of ego, flashy behavior, or personal fame.

Tao leaders are not successful in and of themselves. Their power is not personal but interpersonal. Such a leader is successful when the group works together, when its members excel.

James Treybig, founder of Tandem Computers, follows this path because it also makes good business sense. Since its inception in 1974, Tandem has flourished with a team approach that boosts employee morale, creativity, and productivity.

We read in *Megatrends* that in the traditional top-down authoritarian company, American employees "habitually surrender the most basic rights to free speech and due process . . . when at work each day."[10] Not so at Tandem, which promotes an egalitarian atmosphere of openness and trust. Gone are the old layers of hierarchy and their symbols: executive lunchrooms, washrooms, and walls of intimidation. At Tandem, everyone calls Treybig by his first name, "Jimmy," and knows his door is open. He has an office no bigger than any manager's. When guests visit Tandem, he meets them in the conference room.

Tandem emphasizes openness and communication. The latest in electronic technology—computer mail, a television network—and frequent company newsletters tell employees what's going on. A Creativity Forum rewards people for new ideas. Through stock options, employees become co-owners of the company, keeping informed about Tandem's financial status through quarterly teleconferences. This participation encourages loyalty, greater productivity, and more attention to problem solving.

Many decisions at Tandem are made by consensus. Most departments meet frequently, and often an entire department interviews job candidates to see if they get along well with the team. "Town meetings" are held regularly for employees to discuss new developments.

This team approach is balanced, with respect for individuality.

Employees can choose flexible work hours. Tandem employees tend to work very hard, so the company gives them six-week paid sabbaticals every four years for renewal and personal growth. During the past few years, Tandem employees have done everything from vacationing, remodeling their homes, visiting relatives, studying music, and learning a foreign language to mountain climbing in the Himalayas. One man took a gourmet cooking class at the Cordon Bleu in London. Another spent the time at home with his new baby.

A balanced life is another important principle at Tandem. Employees have a comprehensive health care plan with dental and optical services. They attend free noon seminars on health issues such as stress, cholesterol, diet, and AIDS. Tandem also provides a company swimming pool, weight rooms, tennis courts, and exercise facilities in many locations.

Tandem nurtures the spirit of community and communication among employees in many ways from consensus meetings to weekly "popcorn parties." At 4:00 PM each Friday people gather for popcorn, chips, beer, and soft drinks, sharing ideas and building better working relationships. And these policies pay off. Tandem has one of the lowest employee turnover rates and builds the most reliable computers in the industry.

Recognizing its part in the larger human community, Tandem offers special "service sabbaticals." Employees may take time off with expenses for themselves and their spouses to pursue humanitarian projects. Some have volunteered in local shelters; others have gone to Africa to teach new farming methods or built schools in Appalachia. In this way Tandem supports work for social justice as an integral part of life.

By facilitating teamwork, personal initiative, balance, and social responsibility, Jimmy Treybig applies cooperative values to the workplace, helping people live healthier, more creative lives, while building a successful company that continues to excel.[11]

Leading with the Tao

You needn't be a corporate executive, diplomat, or political figure to lead with the Tao. You can help build a more peaceful world by practicing the principles of Tao in your life and work. Many others have already joined you. In the early 1980s the Stanford Research Institute discovered that over 15 million adult Americans were choosing lives of greater simplicity, cooperation, ecological awareness, and personal growth. [12] The number is constantly increasing, changing the way we live, creating more peaceful cycles in our society.

TAO QUESTION

When we take on leadership roles at home and at work—as parents, teachers, counselors, ministers, managers, business and community leaders—we need to ask ourselves: how can I help create an atmosphere of greater trust and commitment? How can I help others do their best? Work with the cycles? Create greater harmony?

We can learn by listening, watching, observing the cycles of Tao. We can also learn from others. We all know people who exemplify this kind of leadership.

PERSONAL EXERCISE

- Go off by yourself for a few minutes, relax, close your eyes and take a deep breath.
- Now think of someone who has taught you about leading with Tao. See this person in your mind's eye.
- How does this person lead with Tao? What does he or she do? Focus on the details. See them as vividly as possible.
- What can you learn from this?
- How could you apply this lesson to your life?
- See yourself doing this. How would it look? Feel? Experience this in your imagination as vividly as possible. What would you do and say?
- Accept the lesson with gratitude. Say to yourself, "Thank you. I lead with Tao."
- Open your eyes, stretch, and return to your activities, aware that you are a leader, creating new positive cycles in your world.

Leading with Tao is a continuous challenge. How do we create harmony from the conflicting experiences around us? How do we affirm both inner and outer peace?

The answer lies in our conscious, creative use of energy. Aware of the cycles in nature, we develop our vision. We learn when to act, when to withdraw, seeing our place in the larger pattern.

Facing a world of conflict and confusion, we must remember to stay centered, to maintain our inner balance. Centered, we endure. Like an aikido master, we channel tremendous power. Off balance, our enthusiasm can easily become misguided, undermining our health or sweeping us into fanaticism.

We must never let a cause, an organization, a career, a relationship so completely eclipse our lives that we forget who we are. We must flow with the ongoing currents of our world but never become submerged in them.

As much as possible, we must remember to see the larger patterns, to balance our needs with those of the planet, doing no violence to ourselves or others. Respectful of the life process, watchful of our timing, we lead with Tao, creating new possibilities for our world.

Affirmation

I now know my life is peaceful and harmonious.
I lead with Tao.
I listen carefully, aware of the cycles within and around me.
I cooperate with them.
I act with courage and confidence.
I work with my team for the good of the whole.
I respect myself and the process.
I harmonize with nature and all others in my world.
I accept greater peace in my life now.
And so it is.

SECTION
IV

THE
WAY
OF LIFE

CHAPTER 18

KEEPING THE ONE

"The Tao person embraces the one
And lives in peace by its pattern."

(TAO 22)[1]

T HE *Tao* teaches us to embrace the one, to realize that beyond all
apparent change, life is an essential unity. By regularly meditating, observing nature, and listening to that still small voice within,
the Tao person returns to this all pervading oneness. The Chinese call
this practice *shou-yi,* or "keeping the one," which is the theme of all
Taoist art and the lesson of this chapter.[2]

Recognizing the One

Modern discoveries in physics, psychology, and ecology reinforce
the *Tao*'s lesson of oneness. Physics has redefined our view of the
universe. No longer do we see it as a collection of disparate parts but
a unified whole. All life is interconnected by dynamic patterns of
energy.

Jungian psychology echoes this vision of unity, affirming that on
the unconscious level we all participate in a unified awareness, the
collective unconscious, which contains symbols and wisdom common to humankind. Carl Jung taught his followers to develop their
intuition as a means of reaching this collective wisdom. Jungian
analysts see synchronicity, those otherwise inexplicable coincidences
that link our lives, as further evidence of the collective unconscious.[3]
People meet unexpectedly, then realize they have much in common.
Two people say the same thing at the same time. Before you can go to

the phone to call a friend, that person calls you. To Jungians such synchronicity shows we're all part of something larger than ourselves.

Our current ecological problems—pollution, acid rain, and the depletion of the ozone layer—remind us daily that we're not separate entities but part of a complex web of life. Any careless action—an oil spill, the release of noxious chemicals—produces harmful reactions far along the chain of life. During the past few decades, we've ignored our oneness with nature. Mindlessly violating the environment, we've put ourselves and our future at risk.

Our very mistakes confront us with the oneness we've ignored. Industrial pollution and acid rain transcend national boundaries, affirming our underlying unity. The Greenhouse Effect threatens to upset the climate throughout the world because we're covering the earth with concrete, driving cars that spew out massive amounts of carbon dioxide, and destroying tropical rain forests at an alarming rate. The mounting evidence makes it impossible to deny that we and other life forms are part of one collective body know as planet Earth.

This chapter will help you recover the oneness of Tao. You'll practice *shou-yi* (keeping the one) in a guided meditation. You'll learn how to avoid fragmentation, those distractions that keep us from seeing the whole, and you'll discover how oneness with Tao helps make a positive difference in the world.

The sense of oneness with all creation can best be achieved through meditation or contemplation, which awakens our powers of intuition. Our intellect analyzes and separates reality into logical categories, but the Tao transcends reason. Like water, it contains tremendous strength. It nurtures, but cannot be grasped. Yet it *can* be experienced through our right brain faculty of intuition.

PERSONAL EXERCISE: GUIDED MEDITATION

- Go to a quiet place where you won't be disturbed. Relax, loosen your clothing, kick off your shoes, and sit or lie comfortably on the floor.
- Gently rub any parts of your body that feel tense, then relax, close your eyes, and breathe slowly and deeply.
- Imagine yourself standing by the ocean, watching the waves flow slowly in and out. In alternating patterns of *yin* and *yang,* the tide follows the inevitable rhythms of nature.

- Smell the salt air and feel the gentle breeze as it flows off the water. The delicate spray touches your face, uniting you with the ocean, one with nature, one with Tao.
- Look out to the horizon. See the wide expanse of ocean before you, extending as far as the eye can see, more enduring and powerful than the centuries of humanity who've roamed its shores and ridden its waves. This is the enduring power of Tao: fluid, nurturing, the source of all life.
- Hear the crashing waves, the distant cries of seagulls circling overhead, creatures of earth, sea, and sky. Feel your spirit flow with the waves and soar with the gulls, knowing you are one with the wind and waves, one with Tao.
- Placing your hand on your wrist, feel your own pulse alternating in harmony with the rhythms of Tao, the rhythms of the sea. They're your currents, your life force, sharing the same salinity, one with the sea.
- Know that wherever you go, whatever you do, you're one with the ocean and all it touches: the rivers that flow from the mountains to the sea, the life that lives within and around it, the seabirds, fish, and coral, the tiny crustaceons, giant whales, and the people who stand on its distant shores.
- Feel yourself one with the ocean as it embraces this planet, extending across the Atlantic from Europe and Africa, reaching north to the Arctic and south through the straits of Magellan to the Pacific. Then the waters flow down to the Antarctic and over again to the Atlantic, uniting all life in an azure embrace, encircling the small blue planet we call home. Know that you are one with the planet, one with Tao.
- When you're ready, slowly open your eyes and stretch, feeling relaxed and at peace, filled with new energy and inspiration.

Whether we meditate on the ocean in our imagination or contemplate it in actual experience, we unite with the infinite power and presence of Tao. One with Tao, we live from our deepest center, our actions informed by enduring wisdom and power.

Practical Mysticism: Taking Positive Action

Taoists are known for their practical mysticism, their union of spirituality with social action. While Christian or Mohammedan mystics seek union with God, Taoists seek unity with God in nature.[4] Being one with nature means acting *in* nature, harmonizing with the natural cycles of the world. Following the Tao leads people naturally from contemplation into action.

American naturalist John Muir wrote that "most people are *on* the world, not in it—have no conscious sympathy or relationship to anything about them—undiffused, separate, and rigidly alone like marbles of polished stone, touching but separate."[5]

Muir's own sense of oneness led him to write *The Mountains of California,* found the Sierra Club, campaign in Congress to preserve our natural wilderness, and establish Yosemite National Park. A Tao person deeply rooted in nature, Muir's sense of oneness led to positive action.

Following the Tao, we develop greater peace within and promote peace around us because we know that individuals, society, and nature are all united. Like the Buddhist masters or Bodhisattvas, Tao people cannot find true peace by themselves, for nothing lives in separation. Like Gandhi, a Tao person knows that outward effort is successful only when it flows from a profound inner awareness, that inner peace is incomplete without the corresponding action for peace in our world.[6]

Ecologist Tom Moss also took positive action. From his studies of the northern Pacific Coast, he realized that native birds and wildlife were dwindling because they were losing their natural habitat. In January 1988, he began his personal campaign to rebuild the native ecology of the area by replacing the missing piece in the pattern, restoring the natural landscape of Asilomar State Park.

For years, the sand dunes overlooking the blue Pacific had been invaded by grass and iceplant, planted by well-meaning people to prevent erosion. These plants had driven out the local grasses and wildflowers, depriving local birds and insects of their habitat. Removing the invasive grass and iceplant, Tom began planting seeds in his greenhouse and setting out small native seedlings on the dunes— feathery green sagewort, native lizard tail with its bright orange flowers, small spade-leafed sand verbena, and the yellow menzies wildflower, an endangered species protected by law. He covered the small plants with protective chicken wire cages, marking them with colored ribbons, and watching carefully to see they took hold. Constructing new paths for park visitors, he posted signs: "fragile area.

Stay on boardwalk." He set up an exhibit to explain what he was doing and planted more seedlings, thousands of them a year.

Now the sand dunes are returning to life, a landscape of gentle pastels along the shores of the Pacific. Varying shades of green add subtle colors to the pale golden sands: blue green sagewort, soft green verbena, the bright green foliage of California poppies, subtle shades of green and tan accentuated by tiny orange and yellow flowers. Birds circle overhead and monarch butterflies fly in and out among the flowers. The entire scene is one of wholeness and peace.

With his signs and exhibits, Tom reaches out to others in this coastal habitat. Many people have become more aware of the fragile beauty of the environment, more conscious of their oneness with nature. On my last trip to Asilomar, I met a local woman volunteer in the greenhouse. "You have to do something to help preserve the environment," she said, admitting that she sees it as an extension of herself. "It's a lasting contribution, and it's going to be here a lot longer than I am."

Affirming Oneness in Our World

The dune restoration project is only one example of how our vision of wholeness leads to positive action. There are more examples in *your* community and further opportunities in *your own* life. How can you actively "keep the one" in your experience? Find out in this exercise.

PERSONAL EXERCISE

- Find a quiet space, close your eyes, relax, and take three deep breaths.
- Now ask yourself, "How can I better keep the one in my life? Is there something I can do to affirm greater health and wholeness in my world?" As you ask yourself the following questions, an opportunity for action will present itself.
- "*In my environment:* what can I do to promote greater unity? How can I cooperate with the native plants and animals in my area? What do they really need right now? How can I help?"
- "*In my work:* what can I do to promote greater unity? What is my vision of the whole? Have I been leaving something or someone out? How can I promote greater cooperation and understanding? Can I

communicate more clearly? Share my ideas with someone? Include a new person on a project?"

- "*In my relationships:* what can I do to promote greater unity? with my friends? my family? my community? my neighbors on the planet? Can I communicate more clearly? Share more of my time and energies? Devote more time to personal renewal? Expand my circle to include others?

- When you come up with your opportunity for positive action, see yourself doing what you choose to do. See the action completed. Feel the healing energies and experience a greater vision of the one.

- Now open your eyes and commit yourself to this personal action. Know that as you do, you release new healing energies into the world and become more strongly and consciously a person of Tao.

Avoiding Fragmentation

The *Tao* tells us that:

"All things return to Tao
As the rivers flow down to the sea."

(TAO 32)

We're all part of the one, but sometimes we get distracted by details. Caught up in one of the rivers, we lose our vision of the ocean. In modern life, this can happen all too often.

One hazard is overspecialization. Buckminster Fuller once made a remarkable discovery while attending a conference of the American Association for the Advancement of Science. Reading through the program he noticed two papers in completely different fields, each discussing the phenomenon of extinction. Unaware of each other's work, a biologist had studied extinction among species and an anthropologist had studied extinction among human tribes. Both had arrived at the same conclusion: the cause was overspecialization, which limits our options and weakens our ability to respond to challenges.[7]

How can we avoid overspecialization? By striving to remain balanced. We must resist the cultural pressures which would reduce us to an occupational or social role. To affirm our wholeness, we need to make time for meditation, exercise, creative hobbies, and remember to follow our own rhythms.

Another hazard to "keeping the one" is a shortsighted preoccupation with our own local group or issue to the exclusion of everything else. An example of this occurred in the Italian city states. Florence, Genoa, and Venice became world trade centers and inaugurated the flowering of the Renaissance. However, when England, Spain, and France became unified nations, Italy's strength became its greatest weakness, delaying Italian nationalism for centuries. So strong were its parts that Italy couldn't come together as a country for centuries. Even today, regionalism and factionalism dominate Italian politics.

Politically and personally, some individuals identify so strongly with a group that they fail to see the larger whole. Emotional commitment to a relationship, family, church, or career is admirable, but not when it blocks our vision of the larger community.

For far too long, extreme nationalism has kept us from developing a global vision. We may not agree with other governments. We may not even like each other. But the fact remains that we are all neighbors on this planet. We drink the same water and breathe the same air as the other lives that inhabit planet Earth. Anything less than this realization is a repudiation of the one, a denial of Tao.

Living the One

The Tao's lesson of oneness leads us to seek peace not in fragmentation or narcissistic isolation from the world but wholehearted participation in it. As Mark Satin said in *New Age Politics,* "Healing one's self leads almost inevitably to a sense of oneness with other beings and to a desire to heal society."[8] Following the Tao, our quest for balance and wholeness extends outward, informing our every action.

Healing the planet through a recognition of oneness is the mission of John Randolph Price, Texas business leader and author of *The Planetary Commission.* In 1984, Price decided that if enough people gathered together in meditation they could "change the collective consciousness of humanity." He made a plan, that at noon Greenwich time on December 31, 1986, people from all over the world would meditate for peace.

In a groundswell grassroots movement, Price and his wife Jan spread the word by speaking at churches. There was no official fundraising or publicity, yet by December 1986 the story hit the newspapers and over five hundred million people in seventy-seven countries responded, meeting in meditation to help heal the planet.

Since then, the world has witnessed a growing desire for peace, breakthroughs in international cooperation, and improved relations between the United States and Soviet Union. Coincidences? Price doesn't think so. "When so many millions of people come together at once with a sense of peace and with a spiritual ideal in their hearts," he said, it must "have consequences."

World Healing Meditations are now held annually at noon Greenwich time on December 31 and Price's goal is to reach two billion people, spreading the message of peace through a growing recognition of our oneness.[9]

Like John Randolph Price, we can achieve amazing results by drawing upon the oneness of Tao. In our lives, in moments of meditation, recognition, or conscious action, we become part of this powerful oneness.

Seeing beneath the ebb and flow of daily life into the ocean of oneness that flows within and around us, we, too, can begin to heal our world. As a seed grows outward from the tiny germ at its center, so peace grows outward from our innermost being. By living the oneness of Tao, each in our own way, we can act with wisdom and grace, bringing greater harmony to the planet.

Affirmation

I now know my life is peaceful and harmonious.
I keep the one in my life.
I am one with all the life on this planet.
I avoid fragmentation and affirm oneness
    through positive action.
I respect myself and the process.
I harmonize with nature and all others in my world.
I accept greater peace in my life now.
And so it is.

CHAPTER 19

THE WAY OF LOVE

"I hold three treasures
Close to my heart.
The first is love;
The next, simplicity;
The third, overcoming ego."

(TAO 67)

THE Tao is the Way of Love, a path of compassion that enables us to see beneath apparent discord into the underlying unity of all creation. Compassion for ourselves and others breaks down illusions of separation, bringing greater harmony to our world. We can better understand the Way of Love by referring to the Chinese characters used to portray it.

The Chinese term for compassion, *tz'u,* combines two characters. *Hsin* means both heart and mind, the source of all thought, feeling, and motivation. The character *tzu* (abundant vegetation) placed above *hsin* indicates an open and compassionate heart. Taoist compassion unites the individual with all creation.[1] As there's no inner division in Chinese between head and heart, with compassion there's no outer division between ourselves and our world. The Way of Love overcomes apathy, fear, defensiveness, and aggression.

This chapter will explain love's unifying properties, its ability to transcend ego. It will show us how to follow this path by 1) loving ourselves, 2) avoiding divisive criticism, 3) transcending the anger habit, and 4) reaching out to the world in loving service.

The Unifying Power of Love

The power of love has united human beings for centuries. It has inspired masterpieces in poetry, music, and the visual arts, yet still transcends our ability to explain. As mysterious as the Tao itself, love is more than the sum of its parts, connecting our souls ineffably, unforgettably, forever. It takes us beyond our personal limits, expands the scope of individual consciousness. Illuminating a lonely and confusing world with the light of new awareness, love takes us in a quantum leap to a world beyond ego, a new way of knowing.

Plato described love as the union of two souls with divinity itself, Dante's love for Beatrice led him to the gates of paradise where he sang of "the love that moves the sun and the other stars." The ancient Taoist Chuang-Tzu taught that through love we experience the inherent connections between ourselves and others, seeing all creation as one.[2]

Love Is an Active Process

Everyone wants love. According to psychologists, we all *need* love. Abraham Maslow placed the need for love directly above our need for air, water, food, and shelter. But for many, the search for love is frustrating and misdirected. Erich Fromm explained that "most people see the problem of love primarily as that of being loved rather than that of loving." We spend our time trying to make ourselves "lovable" with the right clothes, cosmetics, and conversation, then wait for the right person to come along and love us.[3]

Our frustration comes from defining love as a product, not a process, waiting for fulfillment instead of actively extending ourselves. Love requires us to *do* something: to reach out, to act, speak, give of ourselves. In so doing, we become active expressions of love.

A tall, attractive blonde in her mid-thirties, Phyllis was anxious and unsure of herself, searching for love and fulfillment. After still another abusive relationship, she entered group therapy.

In the first session, she sat huddled in her chair. Her eyes cast down, her voice quavering, she asked, "What can I do to meet the right man?"

But instead of answering her question, the therapist asked, "What do you really *like* to do?"

"What?" she answered, wide-eyed and incredulous. "What do *I* like to do? . . . Cook. I love to cook."

"Well then, sign up for a gourmet cooking class," the therapist said.

"Cooking class! How can I meet men in a cooking class?" she said, shaking her head in disbelief.

The point was for her to stop waiting around like some fairytale princess and get on with her life. By following her own interests, she could become the person she was meant to be.

The last time I saw Phyllis was at her bon voyage party. Radiant and self-assured, she looked like another woman. Gone was the hesitant, needy person I'd first known. The new Phyllis was surrounded by friends—from her work, apartment building, and gourmet club, who'd arranged this festive pot luck. She was happily making plans to start a new life in Colorado, inviting us all to visit when she got settled.

During the past eight months, Phyllis improved her cooking skills, met new friends, got a big promotion at work, and created a joyful life—because she stopped waiting to be loved and started loving her own life. In her next relationship she won't lean on some man out of loneliness, but reach out to share the dynamic, loving person she is.

The Way Beyond Ego

Expressing love takes us out of our limited egos. We soar above earthbound individuality, perceiving our part in the larger pattern. Like an aerial view of our favorite city, love lifts us up to discover a wondrous symmetry. New patterns of harmony emerge as we see how all life connects.

The Way of Love is not the egotistical possessiveness which masquerades as love in too many relationships. *Tz'u* expresses itself by sharing joyously with no thought of return. Transcending our limited egos, it unites us with the good of all.

For Taoists, *tz'u* is the natural expression of a balanced soul. If our energies are harmonious, we naturally reach out in benevolence toward all creation, creating harmonious new cycles.[4]

A longtime student of Taoism, Carl Jung recognized the power of love to expand our consciousness, bringing us into "a reunion with the laws of life."[5] His description of psychological maturity (individuation) echoes Taoist descriptions in which our self expands to include the world around us, all apparent discord and duality resolving into greater harmony.

Love dispels the shadows of conflict. Dualistic illusions of "self" and "other," fade in the light of new awareness. As the *Tao* tells us:

"The earth is everlasting
Because it does not live for self alone
But exists as one with life.
The people of Tao transcend self
Through loving compassion
And find themselves
In a higher sense.
Through loving service
They attain fulfillment."

(TAO 7)

The Way of Love unites us with Tao. Those unitive moments when we reach out lovingly in consciousness or service bring us the purest joy we can know. We've all been blessed with such moments, but they usually occur unexpectedly, sweeping us into brief but beautiful communion. As Tao people, we can expand this vision to encompass all we do.

The Way of Self-Acceptance

While the ego builds walls, love builds bridges, leading us beyond defensiveness to trust, wholeness, and peace. The *Tao* tells us that:

"Tao people know themselves,
And make no display,
Accept themselves
And are not arrogant."

(TAO 72)

Self-blame and self-doubt only perpetuate conflict. Self-acceptance brings greater peace to ourselves and our world.

Tina Clare, who teaches classes in meditation and personal growth in northern California, sees self-acceptance as the first step on the spiritual path. I spoke with her one afternoon at her meditation center, nestled beneath a spreading oak tree in Los Altos Hills. "We built the center honoring the space of this 150-year-old tree," she told me. The tree, she added, is a wonderful teacher with its lessons of perseverance and cyclical renewal.

Crafted of wood beams, cedar paneling, and glass, Tina's Center of Light sits high on a hill open to the trees and sky. Its circular space is furnished simply in colors of sand, rose, and beige, accented by a few seashells.

The day was stormy; the stress of two jobs and the change of seasons had given me a sinus headache, but when I walked inside, my head suddenly cleared. Could years of meditation have refined the energies here, creating a healing space?

"I try to create a space where people can very naturally drop their masks and share from the heart," Tina told me with a smile. She begins her private counseling sessions, classes, and workshops by establishing a safe place where people feel at ease.

By honoring the person and the process, she helps nurture self-acceptance. She listens thoughtfully, her blue eyes sparkling like the turquoise and silver jewelry she wears, a momento of her travels in Peru. By listening carefully, she helps people learn to listen to themselves.

After studying Native American and Eastern religions for over twenty years, she sees the major spiritual streams converging in a few simple truths: the oneness of all life, honoring ourselves and one another, harmonizing with nature, and accepting our own internal authority. Using guided meditation, soft music, Tibetan chimes, and natural images, she helps people rediscover their inner space, become aware of their purpose.

Tina sees a direct connection between inner and outer peace. "We can't nourish others any more than we've been nourished, so our first responsibility is to nourish ourselves," she explained. By listening to ourselves, we learn when to reach out in new directions, when to withdraw from depleting situations, when to go within for personal renewal.

PERSONAL EXERCISE

What do you need now at this point on the path? By listening to yourself, you will surely know. Treat yourself to this gentle shell meditation, inspired by Tina Clare:

- Go off by yourself in a peaceful place where you won't be disturbed. If possible, take a walk, sit under a tree, get back in touch with nature.
- Relax, sit comfortably, loosen your belt and kick off your shoes. Wiggle your toes, stretch and unkink your body.
- Now close your eyes and breath slowly and deeply, focusing on the rhythm of your breathing. With each breath let go of the outer world, becoming more and more relaxed.
- As you listen to your inner rhythms, feel yourself surrounded by the soothing sounds of the ocean. Now see yourself walking along the shore. Feel the wet sand crunching beneath your feet and the soft ocean breeze caressing your body. Smell the fresh salt air.
- As you walk along the beach you see a beautiful shell in front of you. Bending down, observe the shell, running your hand along its curved surface.
- As you watch, the shell begins to expand. Gradually it becomes as large as you are, even larger, large enough for you to enter.
- A gentle light flows out from the shell, inviting you inside. Slowly, gradually, walk into the shell, down the curving hallway, into the deep healing space within.
- Surrounded by the gentle, soothing energies, let go of anything from the past that you wish to release. Take a deep breath. Release it. It's gone.
- Now ask yourself a question: "What will solve my current problem?" "What direction shall I take?" or simply "What do I need to

know?" Relax and know that the answer will come—perhaps now, perhaps later as you go about your other activities. Take another deep breath and release it.

- When you're ready, you can leave this healing space, walking back out the curving hallway into the fresh salt air.
- Standing back on the beach once more, watch the shell gradually return to its original size.
- As you return to normal consciousness, know that you take these healing energies with you. Gradually open your eyes, stretching, returning to your other activities, deeply refreshed and aware of the inner truth of who you are.[6]

Tina Clare works with gentle meditations, natural harmonics, and movement. She doesn't believe in aggressive encounter groups. "Nature never forces growth," she says, "but allows it." We each unfold from our own center of self-acceptance, according to our own rhythms. When we ask a question in meditation, the answer comes in its own time.

Transcending Judgment

Recognizing our inner rhythms is a major part of self-acceptance and an important lesson of Tao. As each plant has its own cycles, so do we. Judging ourselves in comparison to others is unnatural and unjust. Daffodils bloom in early spring while chrysanthemums grace the gardens of autumn. A wildflower blossoms for only one season, an oak tree may live for hundreds of years, and California's giant sequoias have endured for thousands. Like the trees and flowers, we each have our own rhythms, our own time of fruition. Who is to say what pattern is right for us? Only we can know.

We practice tz'u or loving compassion when we stop judging ourselves and others. For if we're all unique beings with individual life patterns, how can we judge another? The Tao asks us only to follow our own path with heart.

In the western world, our habit of analyzing and judging has led to an age of technological wonders, but it's also alienated us from ourselves and one another. Focusing on differences instead of similarities, we've created walls of separation between individuals, groups, and nations.

Too often criticism blocks compassion, separating us into po-larized factions. Dr. Gerald Jampolsky says that even constructive criticism is often a veiled attack, an attempt to prove we're right because someone else is wrong.[7] The *Tao* tells us simply:

"A good person does not argue
Who does so is not one with Tao."

(TAO 81)

A judgmental attitude helps neither ourselves nor others. Arguing or preaching rarely changes other people. Even if our opinions are justified, criticizing others usually makes them wary and defensive. And it takes our attention away from our own lives, which we *can* change.

Watch your thoughts and conversations. Self-righteous criticism and arguments only massage the ego, perpetuating separation, increasing personal and planetary conflict. The *Tao* tells us:

"Though some people seem bad,
Do not reject them."

(TAO 62)

The *Tao* counsels tolerance, not out of weakness but to preserve our power. Condemnation fragments us as groups and individuals. By choosing separation we lose our oneness in Tao; in tolerance we regain it. Lao Tzu tells us:

"To follow Tao brings compassion.
Compassion brings tolerance.
Tolerance brings strength.
Strength means harmony with nature;
Harmony with nature means oneness with Tao.

One with Tao, you are empowered
And your life will be free from harm."

(TAO 16)

TAO QUESTION

As we seek to live more peacefully, let's ask ourselves: Does this (thought, action) produce greater separation or greater peace? Let's develop the healing power of *tz'u* by focusing on the growing potential for *good* in ourselves and others.

Transcending Anger

As we follow Tao, we recognize the destructive power of anger. Expressed outwardly, it has filled our world for centuries with violent conflict, crimes of passion, and all manner of suffering. Repressed and kept within, it undermines our health, poisoning our minds and bodies.

One of our most important lessons is how to deal wisely with anger. Until we do, we'll continue to perpetrate violence upon ourselves and others.

The *Tao* teaches that everything in life is comprised of energy. Anger is very powerful energy. We cannot ignore it, for it ultimately expresses itself, injuring ourselves and others. Peace Pilgrim, a woman who walked over 25,000 miles on a pilgrimage for peace, taught people to transform their "anger energy" into constructive action, channeling it into aerobic exercise or using it to complete a necessary task.[8]

Plagued by post-Vietnam stress syndrome and a painful divorce, Steve had to do something to release his violent anger. Whenever his ex-wife called with another screaming tirade, became hysterical, or threatened to take the children and go back to Italy, Steve would run down the street as fast as he could. The scenes flew by him in a blur as he covered the two miles between his house and the municipal rose garden. He'd often throw himself down on the grass to catch his breath. Then, exhausted but centered, he'd walk around and smell the roses before going home to face the problem. Releasing his anger this way expelled Steve's violent emotions and cleared his mind, as well as providing healthy aerobic exercise.

The next time you feel angry, take this powerful energy and transform it. Direct it into useful work or exercise: run around the block, pull weeds in the back yard, go for a brisk walk to clear your head— use your body to express the energy. Do *not* spew out anger in violent words and actions, reckless driving, or acts of retaliation and revenge. The world has suffered too long from such misdirected anger. Release this powerful energy in a constructive direction, then return to a space of love to handle the problem.

Our anger is real. We cannot deny it. But neither must we allow it to dominate or victimize us, perpetuating a hostile world. Learning to channel the anger energy contributes immeasurably to the harmony around us and is a crucial step on the path of peace.

Living in the Present

The power of love brings our lives dramatic immediacy. With no time to dwell on the past or worry about the future, we're here completely, one with the moment, without separation in time or space.

When our personal relationships slide from the magical to the mundane, they become heavily laden with accretions of the past and demands for the future. We look at our loved one and think to ourselves, "You didn't . . ." "You shouldn't have," "You should." All those silent grudges and demands cement themselves into a wall between our two souls, making it harder to meet in love and trust.

Perhaps that's why new relationships, new friendships, are so exhilarating. Then we have no history, no expectations to drag us down. We can express ourselves freely, sharing our highest potential. Can't we bring that vibrant quality to *all* our relationships by releasing the past, refusing to nurse old grievances?

PERSONAL EXERCISE

Is there someone in your life you resent for old injuries and disappointments? This exercise will remove grudges against anyone, living or dead.

- Find a quiet space where you won't be disturbed. Relax, release any tension in your body, and sit comfortably with your spine straight.
- Close your eyes and visualize that person seated before you. Take a deep breath and release it.
- Now say out loud three times: "I forgive you and I forgive myself."
- Take another deep breath, let it out and feel any remaining tension leave your body.
- Now open your eyes. Renewed and refreshed, return to your usual activities.

Repeat this exercise whenever you think of this person until your emotions are cleansed and your heart is at peace.

Living in the present frees us from bondage to old hurts and resentments. Imagine how much freer your relationships would be if you lived more fully in the present. Imagine how the nations of this world would relate if they released the centuries of conflict, prejudice, and suspicion that divide them. Focusing on the present, they could work together to solve our global problems of hunger and pollution. Eliminating the blaming and posturing, they could get down to constructive action, building bridges of peace instead of walls of hostility.

The Way of Loving Service

As the waters of a pure mountain spring slowly cleanse a stagnant pond, so by circulating loving energies we can gradually heal our world. Tina Clare asks us to expand our definition of service. It doesn't always mean arduous work or self-sacrifice. A simple compliment can change the energies around us. A kind word can begin a positive new cycle, influencing dozens of other interactions.

Tao people like Tina are aware of the energy around them. They know when to give a compliment, when to express gratitude, when to remain silent. When she goes out into the world each day, she asks what contribution she can make.

Recently, she was having some brochures prepared at a busy print shop. With the phone ringing, two machines cranking out copies, and patrons asking to be helped, one harried clerk was trying to do everything. When Tina came in, she looked compassionately at the young woman behind the counter and said "It's OK to breathe." The woman looked back at Tina, took a deep breath, smiled and said, "Thank you." That was all.

Determined to apply this lesson, I found myself yesterday plough-ing through San Jose rush hour traffic at 5 P.M., with one errand to complete before coming home. As I pulled into the frozen yogurt shop to pick up a quart for Gwilym, I noticed with dismay that the shop was filled with over a dozen pre-teens in bright green shirts, all lined up to get frozen yogurt cones. Parents and coaches stood by, trying to organize things. Realizing I could either succumb to impa-tience or enjoy the show, I chose the latter. I talked to one young girl about the flavors and then turned to the adults, who looked tired and done in. "What kind of team is this?" I asked.

"We're the Price School volleyball team," one of the coaches said with obvious pride.

"What a wonderful thing for young people to be part of a team," I said. The two mothers smiled and suddenly didn't look so tired.

There's a hidden advantage to service, I found. It's so much fun that it energizes both giver and receiver. In fact, I'm not quite sure who was the real recipient of my *tz'u* experiment. We all seemed happier and more energetic. Then another customer came in and asked if I was part of the team. I said no. But perhaps in another sense I am. For as the Tao says, we are all one.

Affirmation

I now know my life is peaceful and harmonious.
I live with compassion.
I love and nurture myself.
I do not criticize myself or others.
I channel my anger into constructive outlets.
I live in the present, releasing the past.
I reach out in loving service.
I respect myself and the process.
I harmonize with nature and all others in my world.
I accept greater peace in my life now.
And so it is.

CHAPTER 20

HARMONIOUS ACTION: WU WEI

"The way to greater light leads through the darkness.
Going ahead feels like falling back.
The even path seems rugged and hilly,
The highest power a yielding valley."

(TAO 41)

THE *Tao* is filled with paradox. It's often irrational, illogical: "Going ahead feels like falling back . . . . The highest power a yielding valley." Nowhere is this more apparent than in the concept of *wu wei*.

Wu wei is harmonious action, but it often looks like *inaction* because it's not what we expect. Instead of the dominating, forceful way of ego, *wu wei* is an action of *consciousness* in union with Tao. Sometimes it means waiting for the right moment, sometimes acting spontaneously, intuitively. As Thomas Merton explained, *wu wei* is "not a violent manipulation of exterior reality and 'attack' on the outside world, bending it to [our] conquering will," but action "in harmony with the hidden power that drives the planet and the cosmos."[1] *Wu wei* transcends the immature patterns of willful selfishness that so often divide our world and violate the natural order. Following *wu wei*, we cooperate with nature to restore harmony.

This chapter will give us a deeper understanding of *wu wei* by describing its three attributes: 1) harmonious action, 2) nonviolent attitude, and 3) attention to process.

Harmonious Action

Wu wei flows naturally from the holistic vision of Tao. When we see ourselves as part of the larger whole, we cooperate with the rhythms of life. For Taoists, such cooperation was the original state of the world. Chuang Tzu tells us:

> "In the age of perfect virtue, men lived in common with birds and beasts, and were on terms of equality with all creatures, as forming one family."[2]

With such a vision, we naturally reach out to protect the life on this planet. Taking action leads in turn to a deeper recognition of our oneness with life, expanding our vision, courage, and commitment.

On their whale rescue missions, Greenpeace members have experienced uncanny, almost mystical communions. Robert Hunter describes one such incident. Placing themselves in the water between whales and their attackers, Greenpeace members had just saved five whales from a Russian whaler. The next morning one member celebrated by singing a song on deck. The music flowed out over the speakers across the churning waves.

Suddenly, five whales appeared on the horizon and approached the Greenpeace boat. Closer they came, breaching and blowing, moving in time with the music. They encircled the boat for nearly an hour. Then they pulled ahead, stopped, and lifted their massive heads out of the water, their large eyes level with the boat as it passed.

The crew stood silently on deck. "It was as though the whales were saluting us," Robert Hunter said. "The whales *were* saluting us. It was a conscious and deliberate action on their part."

Then the whales sounded and vanished beneath the sea, surfacing again far off on the horizon. As the crew stood watching, a brief shower passed and a rainbow appeared above the whales.[3]

A surprising synchronicity of rainbow, music, and whales affirmed something that logic cannot explain. Why had the whales come so close to a boat so similar to the dreaded whaling vessels? It was as if they knew—and acknowledged—those who helped them, as if the work of Greenpeace were blessed by the whales, the rainbow, and the oneness of life.

Ancient religions have always taught reverence for life and respect for the natural cycles: the ebb and flow, winter and spring, *yin* and *yang* that comprise all existence. Egyptian mystery cults equated the cycles of life with the myth of Isis and Osiris and the annual fluctuations of the Nile. The Druids celebrated the changing seasons, lighting bonfires in the darkness of winter, and affirming the return of spring with the fires of Beltane. Native Americans had ritual celebrations of the seasons and held hunting grounds sacred, offering prayers before taking any animal life.

The *Old Testament* enjoins Jews and Christians to be good stewards of nature, to "dress and keep" the Garden of Eden, our earthly home (Genesis 2:15). The Buddhists teach reverence for life and natural systems. If we affirmed what E. F. Schumacher called "Buddhist economics," we would regard nature with wisdom and care, not wanton exploitation. What is now common practice—mindless pollution and excessive use of nonrenewable resources—would be seen as "act[s] of violence."[4] We would practice *wu wei*—nonviolence and respect for nature—in every aspect of our lives.

Hindus, too, advocate nonviolence, upholding the principle of *ahimsa* which inspired Mahatma Gandhi. Ahimsa means consciously living so as not to harm other life forms: individuals, animals, and the environment. Gandhi was a strict vegetarian and lived as simply as possible, practicing his beliefs in the smallest rituals of daily life.

Wu wei teaches us to work *with,* rather than against natural laws. Taoists see nature as a balanced, self-perpetuating system. If catastrophes occur, they believe it's because people have upset the balance.[5]

Recently, scientists have recognized this lesson of Tao in the fields of energy and ecology. The First Law of Thermodynamics tells us that "energy is neither created nor destroyed. It merely changes from one form to another."[6] With this insight, we recognize the folly of wasting valuable energy sources. By recycling, cooperating with the cycles of nature, we can use glass, tin, and paper products again and again without depleting or polluting our environment.

In a balanced ecosystem, plants and animals live together in what Fritjof Capra has called "a combination of competition and mutual dependency."[7] Predators keep other species in check, maintaining the balance. When any species exceeds its limits, famine and devastation follow. Each system has its limit or "carrying capacity."[8] One land area can support only so much life. Too many of one species and the entire system collapses.

This lesson is clear to anyone who's ever raised tropical fish. A fishtank is a tiny ecosystem where balance is crucial. When I first set up my aquarium I couldn't understand why the fish were dying. The water was clean, the fish seemed healthy, and we certainly fed them enough. But since the tank was new, the water was *too* clean. A "seasoned" tank gradually develops enough beneficial bacteria to break down the fishes' waste products. Ours had not. Then there was the food. Without enough food, the fish will starve. But too much food falls to the bottom and pollutes the tank.

Once we got the bacteria and the food figured out, our tank seemed stabilized, so we bought more fish. Wrong again. A harmonious community requires the right number and right kind of fish. The carrying capacity of any tank is one inch of fish per gallon of water: in our case eight small fish was the maximum. Exceeding that causes imbalance, pollution, and disease. Our final error was putting the wrong kinds of fish together. Some fish are just not good neighbors. Our two white angel fish looked beautiful but were quite vicious, attacking and killing the peaceful guppies. We finally removed them from the tank and took them back to the pet store.

Our tank is now stabilized: red-tailed guppies and blue and red striped neons swim about in colorful patterns, and two white catfish eat the debris from the bottom of the tank. One catfish was listless and lonely, so we got another to keep him company. Now everyone seems happy, but balancing all the systems was not easy.

After my fishtank experience, I began wondering about the carrying capacity of my community. Every day, it seems, more houses and office buildings go up, more open space disappears, more people move in. Developers are busily arranging deals, business is rapidly expanding, but has anyone stopped to consider how many residents this area can handle before we, too, begin destroying ourselves by polluting our tank?

On a global scale, we all need to respect our fragile ecosystem, recognize Earth's limited carrying capacity, and work for responsible population control. The world population has more than doubled in my lifetime, increasing from 2.5 billion in 1951 to 5 billion in 1987, and if current trends continue it will reach 8.4 billion by 2025.[9] Surely, our right to life on this planet will endure only so long as we practice the wisdom of *wu wei,* respecting other life forms and recognizing our place in the complex web of life.

Nonviolent Attitude

Water has long been a symbol for the action of *wu wei*. It flows naturally, conforms to its environment, yet possesses tremendous strength. As the *Tao* explains:

"Nothing on earth
Is more gentle and yielding than water,
Yet nothing is stronger.
When it confronts a wall of stone
Gentleness overcomes hardness;
The power of water prevails."

(TAO 78)

Have you ever seen the Grand Canyon, carved by the Colorado River through miles of solid rock? How about Carlsbad Caverns or Mammoth Caves with their amazing stalagmites and stalagtites created as water deposited minerals drop by drop over the centuries? These are nature's monuments to the power and persistence of water.

Like water, the nonviolent attitude of *wu wei* is the gentleness that overcomes the hardness of stone. The force of love and compassion can surmount incredible obstacles.

Have you ever disarmed anyone with an unexpected act of compassion? At age sixteen, Gary began dating Maureen, who was two years older. He knew she'd been seeing Hank, a young Marine away on active duty, but didn't know they were engaged.

When Hank came home and learned his fiancée was seeing someone else, he was furious. He tracked Gary down, planning to beat him up. When he found him, he bellowed, "Do you know who I am? I'm Hank Stevens!"

Hank certainly looked upset about something, Gary thought, so he reached out and shook his hand. "I'm pleased to meet you," he said. "I've heard so much about you."

Hank stood there, dumbfounded. All the hate drained out of him. He slowly turned and walked away.

The next year Hank married Maureen. Gary went away to college and later became a successful diplomat, applying the power of *wu wei* to political confrontations.

We'll consider the political use of *wu wei* in the next chapter, but first let's discover how it operates on the personal level.

Wu wei transcends ego. Aware of the natural cycles, a Tao person doesn't force his will upon events; he empathizes and cooperates, working with the natural cycles. Gary's empathy for Hank broke through the walls of anger and deception, defending himself by disarming his opponent.

Using *wu wei*, an aikido master responds to the energies of his opponent, neutralizing them with a spontaneous block or turn. Like martial arts masters, Tao people respond wisely to the energies around them. They do not willfully oppose them, but seek their larger possibilities.

The Power of Trust

The *Tao* says:

"If you do not trust others,
Others will never trust you."

(TAO 17)

As water carves through the hardest stones, trust wears down the rigidity of defenses, building greater openness between people. Building peaceful valleys in the hearts of men and women, trust unites them in a bond of peace.

The Tao person affirms this power of trust, sometimes in the most hostile circumstances. For the *Tao* tells us to:

"Be good to those who are good,
And to those who are not.
For goodness increases goodness.

Have faith in those who are faithful
And in those who are not.
For faith brings greater faith;
And goodness and faith build peace."

(TAO 49)

Years ago, Sally's faith in others was badly shaken. After her divorce from an abusive alcoholic, she moved to Seattle to begin a new life. But Henry's creditors followed, confronting her with bills he'd run up before the divorce. So for over a year, a third of her salary went to pay off his debts.

Finally, the debt was paid, but Sally remained angry and resentful. She threw herself into her job as a college counselor, trying to forget the pain. Becoming friends with a congenial group of students, she began to regain her faith in others, but one night this faith was tested.

A young art student named Pete had rebelled against problems at home and stress at school by going on a binge. When he was jailed as drunk and disorderly, his friends came to see Sally. Only college students, they couldn't raise the bail money. Could she do anything to help?

Sally was the only one with a full-time job. The officials said if she'd guarantee Pete's good behavior against her wages, they'd let him out. But the sum was a staggering $2000. Swallowing her doubts, she signed the papers and Pete was released. Quietly Sally told him, "I'm placing my trust in you. I know you can get your life together."

This time her faith was not misplaced. Pete stayed sober, worked hard, and produced some fine artwork. Two years later he graduated from college and went on to a promising career. At graduation, Sally felt a new sense of lightness, her resentment replaced by trust in others and faith in the goodness of life.

Not only trust but sincerity is essential to *wu wei*. Nonviolent action works only when we mean what we say, when our actions come from the heart. It can neutralize aggression only when our attitude is consistent with our act. As one longtime student of *Tao* explains, the Tao person "knows that even to be non-aggressive can be aggression, if by one's non-aggressiveness one makes others feel inferior."[10]

The right attitude is essential because *wu wei* works with the subliminal energies within and around us. Though barely discernible, a note of insincerity or condescension is picked up by our unconscious. A half-hearted attempt at *wu wei* becomes a hollow gesture that doesn't work. It may even increase the cycles of hostility.

Why is it that Mildred's effusive attempts at friendship always ring false? She gives her coworkers presents, greets them with elaborate words of praise, yet many feel they can't trust her. "What does she want now?" they wonder when they see her coming down the hall. Although Mildred's words are ever so kind, her secretary resents her condescending tone. Beneath all the amicable gestures, people sense she's not being honest with them.

I've learned through years of counseling, teaching, and problem solving that my actions work only when I believe in them. If I cannot do something in good faith, it's better not to do it at all. This lesson is essential in the practice of *wu wei*.

Attention to Process

The final aspect of *wu wei* is attention to process. Guided by a vision of the whole, Tao people do not act for themselves alone because they see beyond the illusion of separation. *Yu wei* or willful, egocentric action, naturally gives way to *wu wei* when we recognize our part in the larger whole.

The *Tao* tells us:

"The wisest person
Trusts the process
Without seeking to control."

(TAO 2)

Seeing our part in the larger process, we act naturally, spontaneously, following the way of *tzu-jan,* which in Chinese means both "nature" and "to act naturally." Tao people follow their intuition.

One with nature, one with Tao, they naturally take the right action at the right time.

Trusting the process, Tao people also practice the wisdom of timing. They know when to take action to prevent or neutralize negative cycles. The *Tao* tells us:

"Peace is maintained with the wisdom of Tao,
Problems prevented before they begin.
For what is rigid is easily broken;
What is small, easily scattered.
Tao people deal with trouble before it begins.
Affirming order, they prevent confusion."

(TAO 64)

The wisdom of *Tao*, like that of *Ecclesiastes*, affirms that there is "a time for every purpose under heaven." To follow the Tao is to recognize the cycles and harmonize with them.

Non-Tao people like Esther are always overwhelmed with crises. Deadlines sneak up on her at work and she runs around breathlessly trying to unload her work on colleagues. Because she forgot to plan a board meeting until the last minute, the graphics and reports were unceremoniously dumped on employees in two departments, fouling up their schedules and their tempers. Whenever anyone sees Esther in the cafeteria, they turn and walk away, afraid she'll try to pressure them into doing more of her work.

Although she always seems terribly busy, Esther doesn't have any more work than the other managers. But she's so disorganized she can't see the cycles, the waves of events around her. Life for her is a constant struggle. Instead of riding the waves like a Tao person, she's tossed about in their wake.

The change from struggle to serenity is as close as a change in attitude, a move to the wisdom of *wu wei*. Recognizing our oneness with Tao, acting in harmony with the changing cycles, we too can bring greater peace to our world.

Affirmation

I now know my life is peaceful and harmonious.
I affirm the wisdom of *wu wei*.
I practice harmonious action, nonviolent attitude,
    and attention to process.
I am careful with my timing.
I respect myself and the process.
I harmonize with nature and all others in my world.
I accept greater peace in my life now.
And so it is.

安平太

SECTION
V

THE
WAY
OF PEACE

CHAPTER 21

RESOLVING CONFLICT

"Practice *wu wei*,
Work without contending.
Enjoy the mild and subtle tastes.
Watch the actions,
Great and small.
And always
Meet conflict
With compassion."

(TAO 63)

FOR centuries the most common response to conflict has been violence: emotional, physical, interpersonal, and international, culminating in the ritualized murder we call war. Many people equate conflict with war and seek peace by designing the "perfect" society, repressing our individuality in an attempt to eliminate conflict from our lives. But the *Tao* teaches that peace cannot be found in utopian ideals which violate our nature. The more we deny or repress conflict, the more we wrestle with our shadows, the further we wander from Tao.

It is not conflict itself but how we respond to it that produces violence. The *Tao* teaches that conflicting values, conflicting interests are inevitable, intrinsic to life. The polarities *yin* and *yang* are everywhere present. Opposition is not something to be feared. *Yin* and *yang* originally meant the sunny and shady sides of a mountain, contrasting polarities combined in the wholeness of life. The *Tao* says that:

"Long and short complete one another.
High and low rely on each other.
Pitch and tone make harmony together.
Beginning and ending follow each other."

(TAO 2)

When seen in this context, conflict is normal: between people, between groups, even within individuals. Each of us has conflicting needs and desires. We experience conflict between desire and conscience—or as Freud put it, id and superego—and reality often conflicts with our expectations.

Facing conflict is how we learn. According to developmental psychologists, it's the basis of all thinking, problem solving, creativity, and personal development.[1] Through cognitive dissonance—when external reality conflicts with our belief system—we gain new ideas and insights.

Old beliefs are always challenged by new discoveries. When this happens at a societal level, we have a paradigm shift. In the Renaissance when Gallileo challenged the old geocentric view of Earth as the center of the universe, western humanity gradually discovered a solar system that changed forever our view of the cosmos and ourselves. Through conflict we often learn to see more clearly.

Avoiding Dualism

The *Tao* teaches that conflict is part of the evolving cycles of life. But when we polarize opposition into "us against them," perceiving ourselves as "good" and our adversaries as "evil," we fall into the logical fallacy of the false dilemma, losing the wholeness of Tao.

When we're caught up in dualism, conflict invariably turns into combat. Fearful and defensive, we project our negative shadows upon our opponent, whom we see as the *cause* of all our problems. We define conflict resolution as a matter of either "winning" or "losing," defeating our opponent or being defeated. All other options vanish, and instead of using our energies to solve the problem, we turn in fury upon our perceived "enemy."

Dualism has affected our justice system, dating back to the medieval "trial by combat," which resolved conflicts by a fight to the death between opponents. The clash of competing polarities endures in the adversary system of justice, which pits plaintiff against defendant. Complex issues are reduced to false dilemmas, with decisions of "innocent" for one party, "guilty" for the other. Instead of blood, this ritualized combat spills billions of dollars annually, most of it into the pockets of competing lawyers.

The old dualism escalates into argument and accusation. As Chuang Tzu explains:

"Granting that you and I argue.
If you get the better of me, and not I of you,
Are you necessarily right and I wrong?
Or if I get the better of you and not you of me,
Am I necessarily right and you wrong?
Or are we both partly right and partly wrong?
Or are both wholly right and wholly wrong?
Since you and I cannot know,
We all live in darkness."[2]

Resolving conflict through combat leaves us groping in darkness. It is not the way of Tao.

PERSONAL EXERCISE: HOW TO STOP THE BLAMING GAME

The next time you find yourself blaming someone instead of trying to solve a problem, stop and ask yourself: "Is this my shadow?"

Whatever you fear or dislike in others ultimately points back to yourself. Take time to center, examine your thoughts and feelings. What do you really fear or dislike? Work to improve these traits in yourself and you'll become more centered, less judgmental, able to face conflicts with wisdom and detachment.

As people realize combat cannot solve problems, they seek healthier alternatives. Some forward looking attorneys are using arbitration and mediation to resolve legal disputes. Progressive corporations and universities are adopting the Swedish concept of an ombudsman, an individual hired to resolve internal conflict.

How to Stop Making Enemies

The old perception of conflict as combat only narrows our vision, limits our choices, pulls us into endless struggles between competing polarities. The *Tao* tells us:

"There is no greater disaster
Than enemy-making
For then you lose your treasure,
Your peace.
When conflict arises,
Compassion always prevails."

(TAO 69)

Making enemies gives away our power, keeps us from taking responsibility for our lives. Instead of resolving conflict, we focus our attention on fearing, hating, and lashing out at perceived "enemies."

Enemy-making happens on all levels from the interpersonal to the international. Just last week my friend Penny was involved in a conflict with a dog breeder over the contract on her collie, North Star. She'd bought her puppy over six months ago and still hadn't received the contract from Zack Edwards, who raises collies on his ranch in Colorado. When the contract finally came it stated that Edwards reserved the right to use her dog as stud.

Penny felt betrayed and violated, afraid that Zack could come in his truck at any time and take away her dog. When she couldn't reach him by phone, she called all the dog breeders in town. One woman told her that she'd better get a lawyer; another said if she didn't sign the contract, Zack could repossess her dog.

Finally Penny called me. Did I know a good lawyer, she wondered. She'd already called two who said she had a case. She could sue the breeder for breech of oral contract. But she didn't want to go to court. She just wanted her dog.

"Are you sure Zack Edwards really wants that clause in the contract?" I asked. "Have you talked to him?"

"No," she answered. "He's supposed to call me back but hasn't yet."

"Well, before you start suing him, you really ought to find out the facts. Before they're signed, contracts are negotiable documents. You need to talk." I told her. "And try not to see him as an enemy. The whole thing might be a miscommunication."

Sure enough, two days later, Zack called and apologized. He'd sent her the wrong contract, the one meant for other breeders. He said to delete the troublesome clause. The dog was hers.

As Penny learned, resolving conflict often means looking beyond our fears to search for the facts. Taking time to find out the truth prevents many conflicts from turning into combat.

Our response to conflict determines the shape of our future. If we define conflict as combat, we produce violence. If we react with fear, we paralyze ourselves or retreat into rigidity and defensiveness. Our challenge is to see conflict without narrowing our vision, to remain flexible, open to many options. The *Tao* reminds us that:

"All green plants are tender and yielding.
At death they are brittle and dry.
When hard and rigid,
We consort with death.
When soft and flexible,
We affirm greater life."

(TAO 76)

How can we respond to conflict like the Tao itself, combining all elements into creative patterns of renewal? That is our quest in this chapter as we learn to 1) affirm *Te,* 2) seek greater clarity, and 3) practice the politics of nonviolence.

Affirming Te

Centered and one with Tao, we respond with wisdom and detachment. As we learned earlier, *Te* is the power of Tao, the wisdom beyond ego that guides us to right action. When we act with *Te* we remain calm and focused. We work with the cycles of life instead of against them, seeing beyond the patterns of fear and confusion, defensiveness and aggression. But to affirm *Te* we must detach from the conflict long enough to get centered, returning to the infinite wisdom of Tao.[3]

PERSONAL EXERCISE: CENTERING

The next time you're caught up in conflict, do this centering exercise:

- Go off by yourself for a few minutes. Detach from the conflict long enough to refocus your energies.
- Stand with your knees slightly bent and your arms relaxed, held out in front of you at waist level.
- Focusing your attention on your *hara,* two inches below your navel, take a deep breath.
- Now release it, letting go of all tension and anxiety.
- Breathe in once more, focusing on the *hara,* slowly taking in new energy.
- Now release it, feeling centered, relaxed, at peace.

After a while, you'll be able to center by merely focusing on the *hara* while taking a deep breath. Swiftly, effortlessly, you can center yourself in any situation.

Achieving Clarity

With *Te* comes clarity, the ability to see through problems to solutions. When we're centered, our fears no longer magnify our problems, making us see other people as enemies. Penny reached clarity by talking to me. I've often achieved it by doing the breathing exercise, talking to a centered person, meditating, writing in my journal, or working in my garden—anything that takes me away from the immediate conflict and brings me back to center, back to Tao. With clarity, we see new possibilities, new solutions.

The Politics of Nonviolence

Personally and politically, the *Tao* teaches the way of nonviolence, resolving conflict through nonresistance. A Tao person knows that aggressive action only perpetuates the violence in our world:

"The wise leader
Does not choose aggression
To conquer by force
For this brings only resistance.
He knows that where armies march
Thorns and brambles grow
And years of want will follow.

The wise leader stops
When he achieves his goal,
Does not glory in conquest
Or gloat in victory.
He works with natural cycles
And does not use violence.

Aggression results in loss of strength
And violates Tao.
Whatever violates Tao
Will not endure."

(TAO 30)

The Tao leader neutralizes negative cycles by practicing the politics of *wu wei*. Throughout the years many have walked this path from Thoreau to Gandhi to Martin Luther King, affirming oneness and compassion. Their actions fall into two categories: 1) bearing witness for truth and 2) taking nonviolent action.

Bearing Witness for Truth

Bearing witness affirms the Taoist principle of oneness. The Quakers, who have a long tradition of witnessing, believe that once we recognize an injustice in our world, that knowledge becomes part of us. We can no longer turn away in ignorance.

Witnessing takes many forms. It can mean participating in demonstrations or writing letters to support your cause. During the 1970s and 80s a growing number of ecological groups bore witness to preserve our environment. People demonstrated against nuclear weapons, tied themselves to trees to prevent the destruction of forests, circulated petitions, and conducted letter-writing campaigns. Organizations like Greenpeace dramatized the plight of whales, seals, and other endangered animals.

The point of such actions is to raise people's consciousness, to promote greater clarity. Witnessing is the first step in solving any large problem, for we must know and understand before we can act effectively.

As the mass media transforms the planet into a global village, witnessing becomes a powerful force for change. Newspapers, radio, and television connect us all in a planetary network, an interlocking web of consciousness. An event on the other side of the globe is regularly broadcast into billions of living rooms, making the oneness of life an everyday experience.

Greenpeace uses the power of media, believing that "awareness itself is the cure. If a mass awareness developed about the seal problem, the problem would be solved." Founding member Robert Hunter said that "if crazy stunts were required in order to draw the focus of the cameras that led back into millions and millions of brains, then crazy stunts were what we would do. For in the moment of drawing the mass camera's fire, vital new perceptions would pass into the minds out there that we wanted to reach. Mass media is a way of making millions bear witness at a time."[4]

Amnesty International bears witness to the plight of political prisoners worldwide. Every two months Amnesty sends a list of prisoners of conscience to members who write letters to political leaders in the countries involved. Over the years hundreds of people imprisoned for religious or political beliefs have been released. Their conditions improved after authorities received the letters, for they realized all over the world people were watching.[5]

In America, the Quakers conduct an active letter-writing campaign to promote more humane politics. Realizing that elected officials must be responsible to constituents, Quakers appeal not only to conscience but political pragmatism. They recommend building long-term relationships with elected representatives and thanking them for important votes.

My friend Barbara takes her witnessing very seriously. She keeps up on important issues and writes letters—often as many as six a day—to government officials. With a smile she says that "being a Quaker is a real responsibility." I'll find notes from her in my mailbox at work, asking me to contact my state or federal representative when an important vote is coming up. Sometimes she leaves information on consumer boycotts or social justice work.

Barbara's witnessing gets results. Recently, she mobilized all her friends to call Assemblyman Chuck Quackenbush, who cast the important swing vote to ban semi-automatic rifles in California. But equally important is the power of personal example. Because of Barbara, I now subscribe to the *Friends' Washington Newsletter*, staying informed and writing letters on important issues. Because of Barbara, another colleague has become concerned about the homeless, and several students are working in local shelters and soup kitchens. With her friendly disposition and generous spirit, Barbara has become the conscience of our department, gently helping us all to become more socially responsible, more concerned about the world we live in.

PERSONAL EXERCISE: WRITING POLITICAL LETTERS

Writing government officials is a simple way to witness for a cause you believe in. These pointers will get you started:

- Choose one or two issues. Study them in depth and find out how your elected representatives stand on them.
- Develop a plan of action. Tell friends what you're doing and encourage them to join you.
- Write short, timely letters to your representatives, focusing on one

subject at a time. Remember: personal letters carry much more weight than form letters.

- Follow your representatives' votes and thank them for taking positive action or continue to register concern.
- Meet with your representatives when they're in your district. Take other concerned people along to discuss your issue, preparing for the meeting in advance.
- Keep learning and keep communicating. Your voice does make a difference.[6]

Nonviolent Action

Courageous people over the years have practiced nonviolent action, using compassion and concern for truth to neutralize the cycles of violence and social injustice.

Nonviolent political action takes many forms: from mild symbolic protests, vigils, and peaceful demonstrations, to direct action like boycotts, strikes, and campaigns of noncooperation which immobilize the opposition. One dramatic example of the latter is civil disobedience: deliberately breaking an unjust law to affirm a higher moral principle.

Those who practice civil disobedience have been arrested and imprisoned, but their example has moved the conscience of nations. Henry David Thoreau wrote, "Under a government which imprisons any unjustly, the true place for any just man is also a prison."[7] Thoreau was jailed briefly for refusing to pay taxes which supported slavery and the Mexican War. Martin Luther King, Jr. wrote in his letter from Birmingham jail that "one has not only a legal but a moral responsibility to obey just laws. Conversely, one has a moral responsibility to disobey unjust laws," calling unjust law "no law at all." In an affirmation of oneness, he said that "injustice anywhere is a threat to justice everywhere. We are caught in an inescapable network of mutuality, tied in a single garment of destiny. Whatever affects one directly, affects all indirectly."[8]

Protesting against unjust laws, affirming the oneness of all human experience, those who practice the politics of *wu wei* demonstrate three important lessons of Tao: 1) clarity, 2) compassion, and 3) a vision of oneness. The results of their actions affirm the power of moral leadership.

Promoting Clarity

Before taking action, moral leaders such as King and Gandhi asked their followers to investigate the facts, negotiate with opponents, and prepare themselves to act in the spirit of nonviolence.

We recognize here the steps of clarity and centering discussed earlier. For one must know the truth and be at peace within to practice the politics of *wu wei*. King and his followers held workshops on nonviolence, undergoing "a process of self-purification." They asked one another "Are you able to accept blows without retaliation?" "Are you able to endure the ordeal of jail?"[9] Gandhi taught people to practice *ahimsa*, or loving compassion, to treat opponents with respect and concern, looking beneath the cause that divided them to their common humanity.

Gandhi and King also told the general public about their goals and why they were taking nonviolent action. Thus, they included concerned onlookers as witnesses to their cause, increasing the pressure upon authorities to change the situation.

Affirming Compassion

On the surface, the politics of *wu wei* resembles many strikes and work slow downs, nonviolent demonstrations and protests. But there's one essential difference: the attitude of the participants. Many have marched and demanded their rights with anger in their hearts, bitterly, self-righteously accusing their opponents. This is not *wu wei* but enemy-making, maintaining the dualism of "us against them." Such an adversarial relationship can only win temporary battles: it cannot lead to peace. For the *Tao* tells us:

"People of Tao
Act with compassion
And do not contend."

     (TAO 81)

Affirming compassion, Gandhi treated all human beings with equal respect, including the soldiers and government officials who opposed him. He condemned noncooperation when it was used as an expression of anti-British sentiments, believing that "for a non-violent person the whole world is one family. He will thus fear none, nor will others fear him."[10] Practicing this philosophy, he astonished many of his followers by inviting British opponents to tea, transcending political differences by meeting with them on a personal level. What some rabid Indian nationalists saw as "selling out" was only another step in the politics of *wu wei*, or in Gandhi's terms, *satyagraha*, the "truth force" that led to eventual victory over British oppression.

Former U.N. Secretary General Dag Hammarskjöld recognized the power of compassion in resolving disputes. "You can only hope to find a lasting solution to a conflict," he said, "if you have learned to see the other objectively, but, at the same time, to experience his difficulties subjectively."[11]

Clarity and compassion resolve disputes at a higher level, creating a new understanding between opponents that builds the foundation for a lasting peace. The politics of *wu wei* transforms conflict from combat into an opportunity for cooperation, breaking through the cycles of violence to build a new pattern of harmony. As Thomas Merton realized, "The only real liberation is that which liberates both the oppressor and the oppressed" from what he called the "tyrannical automatism of the violent process."[12]

Knowing that the Tao works in cycles of energy, we recognize the politics of *wu wei* not as weakness in the face of adversity but an attempt to transform the very dynamics of adversity into a new synthesis, a new cycle of peace. With a message very much like the Christian *caritas* which guided Martin Luther King, the *Tao* teaches its followers to:

"Be good to those who are good
And to those who are not.
For goodness increases goodness.
Have faith in those who are faithful
And in those who are not.
For faith brings greater faith
And goodness and faith build peace."

(TAO 49)

Affirming Oneness

Affirming the principle of oneness, the politics of *wu wei* transforms the relationship between opponents by transforming their perceptions. To quote two modern political theorists, the conflict becomes no longer a subject for dispute but "a problem which they face in common." They become "not contenders but partners and their oneness in this respect constitutes the possible foundation for transcending the conflict."[13] Free from the tyranny of hate and fear, people can work to solve the problem, affirming a new sense of cooperation.

To achieve this oneness, people have been willing to face danger, brutality, even death. The campaign of *wu wei* is not without casualties. Civil rights workers were brutally beaten in the American South, Gandhi's followers were kicked, beaten, even shot by their oppressors. Practicing *wu wei* requires the courage of any soldier even more, for when facing danger one must neither fight nor run away but stand courageously, compassionately, for the common good.

In the politics of *wu wei*, the path and destination are the same. A relationship of truth and compassion is the goal, truth and compassion the only means to that goal. Tao people live that relationship every step of the way, facing violence, even death as part of the process of change to which they would even sacrifice their lives. Violence used upon them operates in what Gene Sharp has called "political jujitsu." Violent oppression undermines support for the oppressor, ultimately bringing the cycles of violence to a halt.[14]

The Power of Wu Wei

The *Tao* tells us that:

When it confronts a wall of stone,
Gentleness overcomes rigidity;
The power of water prevails."

(TAO 78)

Those who practice the politics of *wu wei* draw upon this paradoxical power: by yielding, overcoming great obstacles. Gandhi led India to independence without modern technology, weapons, or economic support. In his campaign of *satyagraha* he mobilized the only resource he had: a country of 300 million people with strong spiritual values. Slowly, patiently, Gandhi's *satyagrahis* touched the hearts of their British oppressors until they withdrew, liberating India and themselves from continued injustice.

During the civil rights campaign in America, people learned that segregation was wrong, a contradiction of their very democracy. With marchers and freedom riders dramatizing the injustice, the laws began to change, liberating the souls of many blacks and whites alike from the chains of fear and discrimination.

Some skeptics argue that nonviolence can prevail only in select instances, that it has no power against the ruthlessness of a Hitler. However, history proves them wrong with successful campaigns of *wu wei* practiced against the Nazis during World War II.

The Danes protested against the Nazi occupation of their country in 1940 with social, political, and economic noncooperation, resisting attempts to incorporate them into Hitler's New Order. They engaged in work slowdowns, boycotted German concerts in favor of community songfests with traditional Danish music. When the Nazis ordered all Danish Jews to wear the star of David, scores of other Danes, beginning with the King himself, appeared wearing the star. They refused to carry out Nazi orders for repressive measures against the Jews, helping over 7000 escape to Sweden, and in August 1943 went on strike against the occupation government.[15]

Noncooperation with Nazi orders occurred even among German ranks. In occupied France a young Nazi guard let an American Quaker relief worker through a checkpoint without a pass. Years before, at the end of World War I, American Quakers had sent food to his family and the young German felt a continuing bond of goodwill toward these people, now supposedly the "enemies" of the Reich.

German noncooperation operated on an even larger scale in Norway, which had sheltered hundreds of German children to save them from starvation at the end of World War I. Hitler's Reich send two battleships filled with young Nazi soldiers who'd lived among the Norwegians to invade their former host country. But the bonds of compassion were stronger than the power of war and the German High Command. The young soldiers returned to their ships, refusing to fight against the people of Norway who had treated them like members of their families. This took great courage, for the soldiers could have been shot for disobeying orders. But the High Command respected their wishes and shipped them off to other assignments.[16]

Repeatedly, we see how compassion overcomes the cycles of violence. While violent reactions produce only more violence, the politics of *wu wei* creates a new cycle of peace and understanding. Personally and politically, the *Tao* tells us to build peace by resolving conflict wisely, for:

"When conflict is settled
And resentment remains
Surely other conflicts
Will follow.
Tao people negotiate wisely
And work for agreement.
Wise people seek solutions;
The ignorant only cast blame.
The Tao forever favors
The compassionate and wise.

(TAO 79)

Affirmation

I now know my life is peaceful and harmonious.
I resolve conflict with compassion.
I center myself.
I seek clarity.
I affirm oneness and work with the larger patterns.

I act nonviolently, treating everyone with love and respect.
I respect myself and the process.
I harmonize with nature and all others in my world.
I accept greater peace in my life now.
And so it is.

CHAPTER 22

BUILDING COOPERATION

"Cooperate, and there will be no harm,
Only happiness, order, and peace."

(TAO 35)

COOPERATION forms the very foundation of life as we know it: creating all matter from subatomic energy waves, combining the millions of cells that comprise our bodies, shaping all nature, art, and human society.

Lao Tzu teaches that cooperation is natural to life. Fear and aggression arise when people forget the oneness of Tao. Riane Eisler's research provides archaeological evidence for Lao Tzu's cooperative paradigm. In her book, *The Chalice and the Blade*, she refutes the claim that humans are naturally aggressive. Tracing our history back five thousand years to a time without warfare, Eisler describes flourishing partnership societies where power was perceived as the ability not to destroy but to nurture and sustain life. Ancient Minoan and Old European art emphasized the cooperation of men and women and a deep reverence for the cycles of nature, revealing values far different from those later imposed by warrior hordes who stormed throughout Europe. These invaders brought their warrior gods to a once peaceful people, along with violence, patriarchal order, the oppression of women, and a competitive world view.[1]

Many societies, East and West, tell of a mythical "golden age" of peaceful cooperation buried deep in the mists of time. This cooperative paradigm remains embedded in our cultural memory, acknowledged by political leaders, even today. When Anthony Donovan interviewed diplomats at the United Nations in 1983, most of them defined peace as cooperation.[2]

241

Peace occurs when "cooperation overcomes conflict" according to political scientists. In a process known as functionalism, two or more parties cooperate when a common good transcends their competing interests. One example of this is the European Economic Community. After centuries of war, Western European countries are learning to cooperate economically, forging the pattern for a united Europe through the bonds of international trade.[3]

Developmental psychologists see cooperation as an important indicator of adulthood. Individuals grow from childhood dependence through the independence of adolescence to a recognition of our interrelatedness. On the international level, many countries have been arrested in adolescence. Yet as current ecological problems witness, we breathe the same air, drink the same water, share the same sunlight and rain. The *Tao* reminds us:

"The earth and sky cooperate
And the soft rain falls
Equally upon all,
Not by man's laws
But by natural harmony."

(TAO 32)

What keeps us from seeing this harmony, from recognizing our interdependence? Fear. Whenever we feel our security is threatened, we become defensive, hostile, and aggressive. This is true for individuals and true for nations. To cooperate, we must overcome our fears by building trust, developing a deeper understanding of ourselves and one another. This chapter shows how we can do this by 1) identifying common goals, 2) communicating more effectively, and 3) seeing ourselves as part of nature, affirming the Taoist principle of oneness through cooperative political action.

Common Goals

Common goals are great unifiers. A crisis can draw out the best in human beings as we work for the common good. In the 1985 Mexico City earthquake, rescue teams from all over the world arrived to help victims buried alive in the rubble. Following the 1986 nuclear accident in Chernobyl, American and Russian medical specialists worked together to help the hundreds of people injured by deadly radiation. The disasters were enormous, but the response was a hopeful sign of our capacity for cooperation.

Yet often a common goal is not enough to sustain cooperation. Laurel Robertson, author of *Laurel's Kitchen*, tells how she worked on an anti-Vietnam War newspaper in 1967 but the project fell apart because people couldn't get along. "It was devastating," she said, asking "If a great cause can't bind people together, what can?" She found her answer in meditation, realizing that peace must be a balanced effort of hands and heart, right attitude and active work.[4] The *Tao* affirms the importance of attitude:

"People of Tao
Act with compassion
And do not contend."

(TAO 81)

Taoist Communication

We can develop greater compassion through honest communication. Taking time to center ourselves, we can listen carefully to others. The Chinese word for a wise person, *sheng jen* means literally "one who listens." International mediators Arnold Gerstein and James Reagan stress the importance of listening in their book, *Win-Win*. Peace activist Joanna Rogers Macy has called listening "the most powerful tool in peacemaking and any other kind of social change work."[5]

Listening to Ourselves

In order to communicate clearly with others, we must listen carefully to ourselves, recognizing our own attitudes and emotions. The dangers of repression and shadow projections were explained in earlier chapters. Unless we understand our feelings, we complicate communications with hidden agendas and seething resentments.

Feelings convey important messages which we ignore at our own peril. It's not easy to respect our feelings in a society which regards them as an admission of weakness, prizing a cold rationality. Yet getting in touch with what the Chinese call *hsin*, our heart-mind, is an important step in communicating honestly.

PERSONAL EXERCISE

No matter how busy we are, we all need time to listen to ourselves every day. Some people do this the first thing in the morning; others prefer the end of the day. Some take time out to listen whenever they feel off balance. Here are some ways to stay in touch with yourself:

- Keep a journal, recording your goals, your thoughts and feelings in it each day.
- Write down your dreams when you wake up. Do you see any recurrent patterns? What do they say about you?
- Spend a few moments in daily meditation. Ask yourself, "What am I feeling? What am I here to learn?"
- Take regular walks or jogs. Listen to your own mantram: the sound of your breathing, the feel of your heartbeat. Notice the thoughts that come up for you.
- When you're anxious or upset, take a few minutes off by yourself. Ask, "What am I feeling now?" and just listen.

Communicating Honestly

The more we listen to ourselves at a deeper level, the more open we can be to others. Humanistic psychologist Carl Rogers emphasized the importance of openness in maintaining relationships. We've all felt the need for white lies and kind alibis when the truth seemed less than perfect, but often these deceptions create further problems.

Can you recall the last time you were caught up in a jumble of complications resulting from a single lie? How did you feel? Clinical psychologist Lewis Andrews says that lies undermine our integrity, our sense of self.[6] Even well-meaning lies can throw us off balance.

The Tao teaches a reverence for truth. Dishonesty divides us from ourselves and one another, violating the principle of oneness.

We can't cooperate if we don't understand each other. For individuals and groups, withholding information or suppressing negative feelings buys a temporary truce at the cost of real understanding. It cannot build a lasting peace.

During the 70s and 80s, many people went to the other extreme, assaulting others with brutal negativity in the guise of "sharing" and "being upfront" with them. Such brutal honesty is not the way of Tao. Our challenge is to combine openness with compassion in all our interactions.

Listening to Others

The *Tao* teaches not only truthful speech but careful listening, telling us to beware of empty rhetoric, for:

"The truth is not told by flashy words.
Flashy words are not true."

(TAO 81)

Seeking the truth when our world surrounds us with smokescreens of words and images isn't easy. Tao people observe, listen, look beyond words to the nonverbal language of action and gesture.

Carl Rogers saw the therapist's role as that of a listener. For individuals, groups, and nations, he believed that active listening and open communication could build an atmosphere of trust and understanding. In the last years of his life, Rogers founded the Carl Rogers Institute for Peace in La Jolla, California. There he gave workshops and taught interpersonal communication. Together with his dedicated staff he traveled throughout the world, meeting with hostile groups from Central America, Europe, and the Middle East, helping them achieve greater understanding and cooperation, building peace by practicing the principles of Tao.[7]

PERSONAL EXERCISE: ACTIVE LISTENING

Active listening makes us all better peacemakers in our personal and public lives. But it takes practice. Sit down sometime soon with a friend or family member and listen, following these guidelines:

- Sit facing the person without any external barriers (tables or desks) between you.
- Relax, center yourself, and look into the person's eyes.
- Ask an opening question: "So, what's been happening for you lately?" "How's it going?"
- Listen attentively. Don't let your mind wander. Don't talk about yourself.
- Look at the other person. Focus on what s/he is communicating in words, gestures, body language, tone of voice. What emotions are you picking up? Is the person nervous, excited, happy, relaxed, hostile?
- Without seeming mechanical, echo back what you hear, as in: "It sounds like you're excited about your new job," or "This new assignment really has you worried." If the emotions you hear conflict with the words, echo back the feelings: "You sound anxious," "frustrated," "tense," or whatever you hear.
- Then listen again. If you've reflected clearly, the person will agree with you and continue. If not, s/he will clarify the message. Either way you can check your understanding.
- Resist the temptation to talk, to share stories with the other person. Remember, your role is to listen.
- Keep listening, watching for body language, and respond when appropriate.
- When the process seems complete—when the person has reached a new insight, decided to take action, or thanked you for your concern—conclude your listening. You may want to end the session with a hug.

Your careful listening will create a stronger bond between you and your friend.

Authentic communication builds trust, which nurtures cooperation. The more we learn to trust one another, the less we succumb to fear and aggression. Anthropologist David Barash observed that "both human and nonhuman animals tend to reserve their more ferocious aggression [for] strangers."[8] The better we know one another, the less the likelihood of war.

People all over the planet have begun to recognize the importance of communication, building new bridges of understanding through citizen diplomacy and cultural exchange. High school teacher Barbara Warner traveled to the Soviet Union in 1983 on a visit organized by the Presbyterian National Council of Churches. Their mission, she says, "was to explore from a faith perspective how we can build community between the two nations." Gertrude Welch, a longtime peace activist, has visited Nicaragua as well as the Soviet Union. She emphasizes "our responsibility to build bridges between people, to put a face on the people our government calls 'the enemy.'"

Political science professor Jane Curry organized an educational exchange in 1989 between Santa Clara University in California and universities in Poland and the Soviet Union. The same year an elementary school in Los Gatos, California shared drawings and hopes for the future with school children in Lithuania. In pictures and letters, the children expressed their desire for peace, their concern for the environment. If we had peace, said one twelve year old, "maybe we wouldn't have so many problems with environmental pollution."

College student and ballerina Linda Filley, 21, traveled with a dance troupe through Poland and the Soviet Union in the summer of 1988. She helped link our countries, communicating in the universal language of music and dance. Her blue eyes shining, Linda speaks of the love she felt reflected back to her on stage and the friends she made in both countries.[9]

As we learn more about one another, recognizing our common bond, we follow the Tao of peace. As Lao Tzu reminds us:

"The Tao person embraces the one
And lives in peace by its pattern."[10]

(TAO 22)

Building Consensus

Consensus decision making builds peace by working with the energies in a group, allowing the natural patterns of order to emerge. Consensus is a dynamic example of cooperation among equals. Like

Carl Rogers' active listening, it's based on a strong faith in process. The Tao person listens respectfully, realizing that no one person has all the answers, that truth emerges from the process itself.

Consensus avoids the short-sighted solutions imposed by strong personalities or majority rule. It respects minority objections and explores the questions they raise. Differences of opinion—conflicts— are seen as valuable information for the group. In a noncombative atmosphere members work together rather than defending their egos. They carefully examine their own attitudes, listen to others, and remain open to change.

Consensus is supported by:

1. shared goals and purpose,
2. freedom from outside pressures or agendas,
3. democratic sharing of power,
4. a safe, trusting atmosphere,
5. enough time to communicate and reach agreement,
6. awareness of our own and others' feelings,
7. honest communication and Rogerian facilitation,
8. commitment to the process and the greater good of the group.[11]

Consensus takes time: time to listen, time to explain, time to learn. Group members see their own feelings and ideas as part of a larger process and trust that process, even when disagreement keeps them from reaching quick solutions. One dissenting voice in a majority vote would be quickly overruled; one dissenting voice in a consensus group is heard with respect. The *Tao* tells us to:

"Take heed of details
And develop great insight.
Yielding in small ways
Can make you strong.
Take heed of the light
Within and without,
Avoiding misfortune
By seeking the truth."

(TAO 52)

Consensus leads to clearsightedness and solutions that none of us can find alone. I began using consensus out of desperation, when assigned to do something I'd never done before. A few years ago, I directed a summer workshop for high school English teachers. The subject—adolescent crises in literature and life—excited me. But I had only a layman's knowledge of adolescent problems, and I'd never taught high school. So I assembled a group of friends: a counselor and former high school teacher, writing and drama professors, and a specialist in teacher education. Our pre-workshop meetings employed consensus, combining our different insights into a coherent plan.

When the twenty high school teachers arrived for the workshop, our consensus expanded. These committed teachers became valuable resources, making our workshop more relevant with their practical knowledge and advice. In an atmosphere of growing excitement, we shared ideas. A strong sense of community developed as everyone began bringing in books, tapes, and class materials to share. We baked coffee cakes and muffins for the lively breaks when we discussed everything from workshop planning, to teaching strategies, to personal goals.

The result was a workshop described by the official evaluator as a cooperative model for workshops in teacher education. The teachers' active participation not only shaped the initial plan into a successful workshop but created an enduring collegial network. Years later we're still in touch, sharing letters, phone calls, information, and—most of all—friendship and support.

Consensus builds enduring bonds. Democracy in action, it challenges people to get involved rather than rely on "experts" and "authorities" to make their decisions for them. From New Age communities to progressive political groups, consensus is the new model for decision making and grassroots political action. Peter Caddy, co-founder of the Findhorn Community in northern Scotland, says the group makes all important decisions by consensus. Bob Pickford, of the Federation of Ohio River Co-Ops, praises consensus for building unity.[12] Consensus uses collective wisdom and group process to come up with new solutions, joining people in a common bond as peacemakers and problem solvers.

Cooperating with Nature

Like cooperation with one another, cooperation with nature is essential to an enduring peace. This vision inspires many modern poets. Gary Snyder, a longtime student of Eastern philosophy, says "to live lightly on the earth, to be aware and alive, to be free of egotism," to recognize that all life is interdependent. Cory Wade writes of the plight of animals, reminding us to respect the other lives that share our world. [13]

For far too long, the attitude of industrialized countries toward nature has been one of dominance and destruction—of our habitat, our nonhuman neighbors, and ultimately ourselves. It's time we respected the natural laws within and around us, the enduring principles of Tao.

The ancient wisdom of all cultures affirms our oneness with nature. Yet often our technology obscures this essential truth. The words of Chief Seattle in 1854 echo both the wisdom of Lao Tzu and the growing ecological awareness of today:

> "This we know. The earth does not belong to man; man belongs to the earth. This we know. All things are connected like the blood which unites one family. All things are connected.
> Whatever befalls the earth befalls the sons of the earth. Man did not weave the web of life; he is merely a strand in it. Whatever he does to the web, he does to himself." [14]

The awareness that whatever we do to the web of life we do to ourselves grew in the late 1980s as a public outcry against the dangers of chemical pesticides led to an increasing demand for safe, organic produce. In 1989 organic farm certification doubled in California and similar programs have spread throughout Europe, Peru, Mexico, Canada, Japan, and Australia.

Before the advent of synthetic fertilizers and pesticides, all farming was organic, working in harmony with the earth. It has taken decades for us to realize that the poisons we spray on our plants get into the fruits and vegetables we eat. The ancient wisdom newly discovered teaches that what we give out comes back to us; all life is connected, one in Tao.

Building Cooperative Politics

The Tao asks us to expand our usual definition of politics as we see the implications of all actions, large and small, in relation to the whole.

One morning I awakened to an ominous sound as buzz saws relentlessly destroyed three trees next door. Running out to the street, I saw one beautiful sweet gum tree under attack by grim reapers from the department of public works, while another lay dead and dismembered on the ground nearby. The venerable cherry tree next door was also marked for destruction. The work was official, approved by permits because tree roots had cracked the public sidewalks. Sadly, I thought of my years in Germany, where trees are regarded as public treasures, more important than layers of concrete. There a homeowner has to get government approval to chop down a tree, even in his own yard.

Who can say what damage was done to our ecosystem that day, what habitats were destroyed, what disturbance to the fragile balance of oxygen and carbon dioxide in the air we breathe? I vowed to fight further tree removal in my neighborhood and plant more trees in my yard to help restore the balance. So far, a tiny peach tree sits on my porch, awaiting transplanting. But it will be years, perhaps a lifetime, before the damage can be undone. How quickly, how unconsciously, we undermine our habitat.

In recent years, some groups have formed to reverse this destructive trend, bringing the principle of oneness and the politics of *wu wei* into our cities with "green cities programs." The Planet Drum Foundation in San Francisco, holds bioregional workshops to teach people about the native ecology of their region and works to restore the balance of life in our cities. Some of their ideas include: purifying city air by planting more trees, shrubs, and community vegetable gardens; creating better public transit systems; increasing our use of solar energy; initiating large-scale recycling programs; and setting up a special planning committee to consider the effects of all future decisions upon the ecosystem.[15]

The German Green Party practices ecological politics on a global scale. In March of 1983 twenty-seven members were elected to the

Bundestag, the West German Parliament. They entered the chamber carrying a large globe and the branch of a tree dying of pollution in the Black Forest.

Proclaiming "we are neither left nor right; we are in front," the Greens have not only influenced German politics but captured the imagination of the world. They appeal to our growing awareness that all life is intrinsically related. As Petra Kelly explains, "The spiritual content of Green politics . . . means understanding how everything is connected and understanding your relationship with planet Earth in daily life."[16] How closely this echoes the pragmatic spirituality of Tao.

Linus Pauling and Norman Cousins have seen greater cooperation and ecological awareness as paths to peace. Pauling proposes that "the great world problems be solved in the way that other problems are solved" through research. He urges people to cooperate in research for peace, "striving in every possible way to discover what the facts are, to learn more and more about the nature of the world, and to use all information that can be obtained in the effort to find the solution."[17]

Norman Cousins sees peace and ecology as "intimately related," for in the politics of peace we turn from destruction to creativity, "protect[ing] the conditions that support life." He views our ecological problems as an opportunity for international cooperation, a means to world peace. If we could only redefine our concept of security, he wrote prophetically in 1987, if the United States and the Soviet Union could "shift their gaze from each other to the need to make the planet safe and fit for human habitation, they may promote their own security even as they advance the common security."[18]

As I write this book, the gaze has shifted. The cold war is over. For the first time in my lifetime, perhaps the first time in this century, Americans have a vital opportunity to embrace a new paradigm of cooperation, to realize we are all neighbors on this planet. "Anything can happen now," a once-cynical friend told me the other day. "There's never been another time like it."

The realization grows as more people wonder "What will happen now?" We can fall backward into the old paradigm and postures of defensiveness or move forward into cooperation. We can stop using our technology to destroy life and chart a new path, providing food, shelter, clean air, and water for all, choosing to live in peace with our neighbors and the planet we call home.

Affirmation

I now know my life is peaceful and harmonious.

I feel my oneness with all life on this planet.

I communicate clearly, listen carefully, and respect the views of
others.

I cooperate more each day, living the wisdom of Tao.

I respect myself and the process.

I harmonize with nature and all others in my world.

I accept greater peace in my life now.

And so it is.

CHAPTER 23

THE TAO OF COMMUNITY

"The Tao person dwells in peace:
Reaching out
In a community of heart,
Regarding all that lives
As one family."

(Tao 49)[1]

REACHING out "in a community of heart," we affirm a new paradigm of cooperation. Beginning locally, extending globally, our relationships reinforce our entire world view. If they're hostile and competitive, we perceive the world as a dangerous place, reacting defensively, perpetuating cycles of violence. But if we live in an interdependent, caring community, then our world view, and consequently, the world we create will be peaceful. As we learn in this chapter, our local community is both means and end: a living symbol of the goal we seek.

In a single generation, increased mobility and new technologies have undermined community in America. The smaller businesses of the past didn't ask employees to "relocate." Most people grew up, found jobs, and married in the same town. Before the advent of the automobile, employees did not fragment their lives by living and working miles apart. Families lived closer together, in the same town, often under the same roof.

In earlier decades, families sat on the front porch, chatting with neighbors on a summer evening. Now they sit in front of the TV set. In fact, most Americans "know" the characters on TV sitcoms better than their own neighbors. As a result, we often feel alienated, powerless, and depressed. Clinging to the nuclear family, perhaps too tightly, we forget we're part of a larger human family.

The past fifty years have witnessed a mass movement from small towns to suburban tracts whose only gathering place is the nearest shopping mall. Every day millions of people stroll wistfully through the malls, looking for something that can't be bought, the community they've left behind them.

The Center for Conflict Resolution in Wisconsin blames the disintegration of community on America's commercial values, which pit people against each other in a frantic race to produce and acquire more.[2] For many, life seems a lonely game of survival in a brutal, Darwinian world. With its strong emphasis on individualism, American society has been arrested in adolescence, when the main task of life is to assert our independence. Many Americans suffer from chronic loneliness and frustration, unable to fulfill their destiny as human beings.

Life without community is both unhappy and unhealthy. Research has shown that constant interaction with strangers in crowded cities makes people mentally ill. A recent study indicates that 82 percent of the people in Manhattan are suffering from neurosis or psychosis. The U.S. Public Health Service reports that coronary heart disease is 42 percent higher in urban areas.[3]

This chapter will help us regain our vital sense of community by: 1) recognizing our interdependence, 2) strengthening our local community, 3) learning about collectives and co-housing, 4) supporting our natural habitat, and 5) reaching out to the larger human community.

Recognizing Our Interdependence

The first step in regaining our sense of community is to recognize our part in the larger whole. From frontier days Americans have cherished a myth of self-sufficiency, but in truth we are hardly self-sufficient. We're inextricably linked to one another by hundreds of interactions.

"Look around you," I ask people in my classes and workshops. "How many people have touched your life today?" The food we eat, the clothes we wear, the shoes on our feet link us in a bond of interdependence with nature and people we may never meet. We participate not only in the fragile web of life but in a vast network of craftspersons, farmers, inventors, artists, engineers, construction workers, writers, production workers, teamsters, and merchants. The list is endless. No person, no country in the world is independent. We're all linked in an ongoing exchange of energies. Our interdependence is a fact. Recognizing that fact and strengthening these bonds can promote greater peace for all.

Building Your Local Community

Communities come in different shapes and sizes, as radical as the latest New Age collective, as traditional as small town America with its Fourth of July picnics, county fairs, and town meetings. Community begins in your neighborhood, whether it's a town, city, or suburb. It's an extended family of people you can trust, folks you greet with a smile, neighbors who extend a helping hand, showing that life *can* be friendly, nurturing, and good.

Laurel's Kitchen, a natural foods cookbook, provides this recipe for a healthier world: "Suppose we were to commit ourselves to building up a *neighborhood* where we live: a kind of village where lives overlap and intermingle in a rich and productive way? What greater challenge to our creativity? Loneliness comes whenever we dwell on ourselves, and it leaves immediately once we start working for the welfare of others, beginning with those immediately around us."[4]

My own neighborhood, two miles from downtown Campbell, California, gives me a welcome sense of community after a nomadic childhood as a military dependent. My neighbors and I share flowers and vegetables from our gardens and water each others' plants when we're away. The people in the nearby health food store, library, and stationery shop know my name, and my auto mechanic has become a family friend. We exchange not only goods and services but good will, weaving the strands of our individual lives into a fabric of mutual care and support.

A local community creates a healthier world both personally and ecologically. People share rides and gardening tools, swapping home grown vegetables or starting community gardens. An informal bartering system begins. One neighbor does minor car repairs in exchange for festive meals. Another exchanges haircuts for household chores. A retired woman down the street trades home-baked bread for yardwork. Some families pass along their children's outgrown clothing, bicycles, and toys.

Some people find their primary community at home, others find it at work. Checking in each day over a cup of coffee, grabbing lunch or a snack together, people share ideas and common concerns. At the university where I teach, some friends commute sixty miles south from San Francisco or Berkeley, others drive thirty miles down from Palo Alto, and one friend drives ninety miles north from Pacific Grove. The rest live somewhere in between. Although we see each other mainly at work, we have a "long-distance community" that extends across many miles and uses phone calls to stay in touch.

Wherever you find it, your primary community is a group of people who care about each other, a network of love and support that makes the world a friendlier place.

PERSONAL EXERCISE

Take some time this week to evaluate your own community. Write down the answers to these questions.

1. Outside of your primary relationship, where do you feel a sense of belonging to a larger whole: in your neighborhood? at work? at church? in a community group? somewhere else?
2. What positive feelings does your community bring you?
3. What can you do to strengthen your current community, or, if you've moved or lost touch, what can you do to build one?
4. Take one step this week. It can be as simple as introducing yourself to a neighbor or calling up an old friend. Relationships are living, growing things. Do something to nurture yours every week.
5. Finally, consider your *natural* community—the native plants and wildlife that share your habitat. How much do you know about them? Find out what plants, birds, and animals are native to your area. Recognize your part in the network of life around you.

Discovering New Kinds of Communities

Hopeful individuals have lived in intentional communities for centuries. From St. Francis of Assisi and the religious communities of the Middle Ages to the Puritan and Quaker settlements in the new world, from Oneida and Brook Farm, to the most recent political collective or New Age venture, all such communities reflect people's attempt to structure their lives according to their beliefs.

The Findhorn Community in northern Scotland, was established on the simple principle: "Love where you are, love who you're with, and love what you do." Founded by Peter and Eileen Caddy in 1962, it has grown into a global village of over 225 residents from over twenty-five different countries. Each year thousands more visit its magnificent gardens and New Age conference center.

Love at Findhorn means care and commitment, which created the gardens, turning a former refuse dump in an old trailer park into an edenic profusion of vegetables, fruits, herbs, and flowers. Hundreds of varieties grow annually on soil composed primarily of sand and gravel. Findhorn residents find that even machinery works better when tended with love. The pipes, stoves, and boilers are all regularly cleaned and painted, even given names. At Findhorn respect for the individual is balanced by a larger cooperative vision in which all combine their talents for the good of the whole, living in harmony with nature and one another.[5]

The Philadelphia Life Center, a progressive political community in West Philadelphia, was formed in 1971 by people who believed "anyone seriously committed to changing our sick society must consider changes in personal life-style and interpersonal relations." From a group of thirty-five the Center has grown to over 125 people living in seventeen households, linked by a common commitment to nonviolent social change.

Most members work only part-time at outside jobs and live simply to free up time for political work. They run their households by consensus, share responsibility, and work to overcome sexism. Everyone takes turns preparing meals, cleaning, and doing home maintenance. Men and women bake bread, care for children, do carpentry and plumbing. The Center has its own food cooperative, community gardens, and political action groups as well as a press, New Society

Publishers, which prints books on nonviolence, communication, and social change.

Each year activists come to the Center from across the country and around the world to attend workshops on conflict resolution, strategy skills, street speaking, group dynamics, nonviolence, and direct action. The group has branches in cities throughout the United States and participates in an international peace network.[6]

Convinced that traditional housing isolates us from one another, a group in Denmark founded Trudeslund, a 33-unit co-housing development near Copenhagen. Each household has a private residence but shares a common kitchen and dining hall, children's play area, workshops, laundry facilities, and guest rooms. Although residents have their own kitchens, the common dinners have become an important part of community life.

Married women in America often find themselves working a double shift. After a hectic day at the office, they face a schedule of dinner preparation, child care, and household chores that leaves them exhausted. Authors Kathryn McCamant and Charles Durrett provide a refreshing contrast in their description of a co-housing community: "Anne is glad the workday is over. As she pulls into her driveway, she begins to unwind at last. . . Her daughter yells, 'Hi Mom!' as she runs by with three other children. Instead of frantically trying to put together a nutritious dinner, Anne can relax now, spend some time with her children, and then eat with her family in the common house. Walking through the common house on her way home, she stops to chat with the evening's cooks, two of her neighbors, who are busy preparing dinner—broiled chicken with mushroom sauce—in the kitchen. Several children are setting the tables. Outside on the patio, some neighbors share a pot of tea in the late afternoon sun. Anne waves hello and continues down the lane to her own house" where she can relax with her husband before dinner.[7]

The pace is relaxed, people look out for one another, and watch the children when they come home from school. Young parents never feel overburdened, old people are never isolated: they're part of an integrated, caring community. As of 1988, there were sixty-seven such communities, called *bofoellesskaber* ("living communities") in Denmark. The idea has spread to the Netherlands, Sweden, France, Norway, and Germany.

In the United States, shared housing has become an answer for

many single mothers who move in together to split the rent, then discover the advantages of community—sharing child care and household chores, companionship and support—they become an extended
family.

Supporting Your Natural Community

Lao Tzu tells us, "Harmony with nature means oneness with Tao."
(*Tao* 16). Tao people cooperate with the natural community around
them, respecting the other lives that share their world.

To support the local wildlife population, Oregon rancher Dayton
Hyde returned one fourth of his land to marshes. Today, the native
birds, fish, and small mammals are flourishing. His land is home to
rabbits, a herd of deer, even coyotes. The *Tao* teaches that whenever
we give, we receive in return. In Hyde's case, the additional water
produced twice as much grass for his cattle, and troublesome grass-
hoppers were virtually eliminated by the teeming bird population.
But the greatest joy of all, he says, is to share in the beauty of the
natural life around him. He has started a national movement, "Oper-
ation Stronghold," to help set up similar wildlife refuges around the
country.

We're never too young to begin cooperating with nature. A group
of children in northwestern Montana have formed a club, "Children
for Wildlife." Believing that people and animals should live together
in peace, members educate themselves and their neighbors about
local wildlife, conduct workshops and phone surveys, write government leaders, and monitor local wildlife. They help park rangers take
a census of wild mountain sheep, put up bluebird houses in local
fields, and teach their neighbors and friends that our efforts *can* make
a difference.[8]

PERSONAL EXERCISE: SUPPORTING YOUR NATURAL COMMUNITY

Urbanization eliminates natural habitats, endangering local wildlife.
We can help counteract the destruction by creating wildlife refuges in
our back yards. Even if your yard is small or nonexistent, you can put
water and bird feeders on your patio or windowsill. If you have a
large yard, you can provide your wild neighbors with all four of their
needs:

1. *Food*: Set out seeds and suet for birds, sugar water for humming-birds. If possible, plant berries and nuts for birds and small animals to feed on.
2. *Water*: All living things need water. You can buy a bird bath or make one by filling a pie plate with water. A small pond will attract birds, frogs, and turtles as well as larger animals.
3. *Cover*: Birds and small animals need protection from weather and predators. Squirrels and birds take cover in trees. Chipmunks and lizards use rock piles, rabbits prefer shrubs and dense brush, and tortoises burrow in the mud or deep grass. What can you add to your habitat to help local species?
4. *Nesting areas*: All wildlife need a protected area to raise their young. Mature trees or nesting boxes are used by squirrels and birds. Rabbits prefer low shrubs. Frogs, fish, and salamanders lay eggs in ponds, and many insects breed in the water.

Be a good neighbor to the natural community around you. Set up a backyard habitat. Get to know the names and customs of native birds and animals. Work to eliminate hazardous waste—poisons and plastics that endanger your wild neighbors and yourself.[9]

Reaching Out to the Larger Community

Building a broader community becomes a conscious effort for those who follow the Tao. By cooperating with nature and one another, we affirm essential bonds, without which our spirit withers and our world fragments into endless confusion.

We can extend these bonds and enrich our lives by reaching out in community service. Many people say they don't have time to get involved, yet these same people often complain of feeling isolated and lonely. Doris, who commutes four hours a day from her home in exclusive Carmel, California to her computer job in Santa Clara, laments the lack of community in her fast-track life. She says she has to work long hours to make ends meet and her schedule leaves her too exhausted to do anything else.

Instead of complaining, others are reaching out. Paula, a busy nurse and single mother, volunteers at a local shelter for the homeless. Her two teenagers often come along to help. She's found that reaching out gives them all a new perspective on life and has brought them closer together. My friend Andy moved here last year from Minnesota. Instead of getting depressed about spending Thanksgiving hundreds of miles from home, he volunteered to cook the holiday meal at a local soup kitchen.

Families often grow closer through shared service. Joanna Rogers Macy says she grew much closer to her daughter Peggy when they worked side by side to help save dolphins from being killed by tuna fishermen.[10] As the *Tao* explains, recognizing we're part of a larger whole makes our lives and our world more harmonious.

"The people of Tao transcend self
Through loving compassion
And find themselves
In a higher sense.
Through loving service
They attain fulfillment."

(TAO 7)

TAO QUESTION

Ask yourself, "What can I do to reach out to the larger community? Is there a cause you're committed to, a local service project that could use your help? Your energies and ideas can make a difference—in your life and your world.

Reaching Out to Support Your Global Community

In the past decade, people throughout the world have been reaching out globally, affirming our oneness in international peace vigils, grass roots movements from Band Aid to the Harmonic Convergence, and recent efforts to save the rainforests. The artificial borders between us melt away as we realize we're all neighbors on the same small planet.

Today our most complex problems involve the whole planet. Hunger, poverty, and pollution affect us all and require our combined energies for their solution. Tao people develop a holistic vision that cuts through the old boundaries of the past, leading to new insights, new solutions.

How do we develop this vision? Christer Jonsson, professor of international relations at Lund University in Sweden, says the best way is through crosscultural experience.

When Chris was eighteen, he spent a year in Texas as an exchange student. He and his "American brother" Mike formed a musical combo called "the Cosmopolitans." Chris played the piano, Mike played drums, and another friend, Gordon, played bass. Together they created harmony and expanded their sense of identity. Later Mike visited Sweden, went to school in Germany, and married a German woman. Gordon studied in Sweden and traveled throughout Europe. Chris became an expert on international relations, teaching and consulting all over the world. Being exposed to another culture at an early age made these three young men global citizens.

Chris believes in educational and cultural exchanges, especially for young people. His family has hosted Dutch exchange students at their home in Lund. His daughter Lena spent six weeks at a UNESCO International Summer Village in Mexico when she was eleven and is still in touch with friends she made there. Recently Lena and her brother Linus joined their parents for six months in California while Chris taught at Stanford University.

Citizen diplomacy, professional and educational exchanges build bridges of friendship and understanding across cultures, helping us "think globally" and recognize our part in the world community. Each year the Windstar Foundation in Colorado welcomes concerned citizens and international experts to explore global issues in their "Choices for the Future" symposium. Some people share their skills on a professional basis. Dr. Max Ibsen, a northern California pediatrician, spends several weeks each year treating children in Brazil, Honduras, Columbia, and Ecuador. After serving on the Ship Hope, and holding clinics in South American jungles, he's now a volunteer with Interplast, a group of doctors who perform corrective surgery on children in the third world. As a pediatrician, he helps prepare the children for surgery and monitor their recovery. He showed me some pictures of his young patients, his eyes shining with compassion, saying his greatest reward was to see a child smile.

Many people I know have spent their vacations as citizen diplomats, visiting other countries and building bridges of understanding. When Dr. Ibsen and his family visited the Soviet Union in the 1960s, he met a Russian pediatrician in an elevator and the two have corresponded ever since. Jeff Arnett, who teaches English at Santa Clara University, spent a month in Nicaragua and El Salvador on a visit arranged by Witness for Peace. Since returning home, he's given slide presentations about what he learned. High school teacher Bill Sullivan has worked in Cambodian refugee camps and on an agricultural cooperative in Nicaragua. An active member of Amnesty International, he works for social justice by writing letters during the school year and volunteering his time during vacations. [11]

An international experience permanently alters one's consciousness, making us more open minded, less judgmental. Never again do we fall into narrow-mindedness or xenophobia, believing our way is the only way. A person becomes not only more tolerant, but more innovative, able to see new solutions to longstanding problems. Leaders such as Willy Brandt, Bruno Kreiske, and Olaf Palme all had early international experiences. The young Brandt lived in Norway after World War I, Kreiske spent several years in Sweden, and Palme traveled in his youth throughout North America.

PERSONAL EXERCISE: THINKING GLOBALLY

Even if you can't travel extensively or live in another country, you can still develop your global perspective by following some of these suggestions.

- Become a host for people on educational or cultural exchanges in this country. Invite an exchange student to share your home or welcome visitors on short-term cultural exchanges.
- If you're not ready for a long-term exchange, invite a foreign student to share a meal. Call the international student club at the local college for a reference and enjoy a cross-cultural evening.
- Participate in a sister-cities program. Does your town have a sister-city somewhere else on the planet? Call your Chamber of Commerce and find out.
- Sign up for a foreign language class at the local community college. Learning another language teaches new concepts, new ways of perceiving.

- Attend international fairs and cultural activities in your area. Check your local newspaper for information.
- Check out books or videos from the local library about a country you're interested in. Learn its history and customs.
- Because the mainstream press tells us very little about people in other countries, seek out alternatives. Read the *Christian Science Monitor* and *World Press Review*. Consult the international news sections of the London *Times* or *Manchester Guardian* in the library. Find a good public radio station or listen to the BBC World Service on a short wave radio.

Educating ourselves about other countries is a vital part of becoming a global citizen. As we expand our sense of community, we see our world and its problems in a different light.

From the days of Lao Tzu to the complex, interdependent world of today, following the Tao means developing a sense of community with our neighbors near and far. The *Tao* upholds this vision in the model of a "small country," where needs and resources are balanced and life takes place on a human scale:

"Seek the small country
With small population,
Where people are neighbors
And life is in balance:
Nothing wasted,
Nothing lost
There people love life
And do not wander far
Despoiling the earth
With destructive machines.
Their weapons of war
Never used or displayed,
The people live simply,
Enjoy wholesome food,
And comfortable clothes,
The beauty of nature,
The pleasures of home;

Delight in life's rituals
And meaningful work.
Another country may be so close
That people can hear
The sounds of life
From a distant valley,
Weaving together
The music of peace."

(TAO 80)

It's a natural transition from the small country of Lao Tzu to the vision of our own small planet. Community begins locally, putting us in touch with ourselves and our neighbors near and far, linking us in an ever-expanding network that encircles the globe.

Separate, yet close enough to share the daily rituals of life, people hear "the sounds of life from a distant valley," feeling intimately at home with their world and one another. This is the Tao of peace.

Affirmation

I now know my life is peaceful and harmonious.
I see myself as part of a living community.
I affirm this oneness daily through cooperation, compassion, and service.
I think globally, act locally, reaching out to my community, near and far
I respect myself and the process.
I harmonize with nature and all others in my world.
I accept greater peace in my life now.
And so it is.

CHAPTER 24

CREATING TAOIST POLITICS

"Follow the Tao,
Cultivate its ways,
And find yourself at peace.
Cultivated in your soul,
The Tao brings peace to your life.
Cultivated in your home,
It brings peace with those you love.
Spreading to friends and neighbors,
It brings peace to your community.
Spreading through communities,
It brings peace to your nation.
Spreading through the nations,
The Tao brings peace throughout the world.
How do I know this?
Because it begins with you and me."

(TAO 54)

POLITICS is traditionally defined as "who gets what, when, how," the means by which a society allocates resources and values.[1] These means can take many forms. Most political power in the past was hierarchical, with the majority dominated by monarchies, oligarchies, or dictatorships. More recently, democracies have come on the scene, involving citizen participation in choosing their leaders. Policy decisions, however, remained in the hands of a select few. The *Tao* upholds a more cooperative political paradigm which works with the cycles of nature, benefiting from the contributions of *all* its members

Replacing hierarchy with cooperative cycles, the *Tao* asks us to take the lead ourselves. Creating Taoist politics "begins with you and me." If we want a more peaceful, cooperative world, we must live more peacefully ourselves. Then like the rings from a pebble thrown into a pond, our actions will flow outward, bringing greater peace to our world.

Creating Taoist politics means overcoming the psychic numbing and cynicism so prevalent in our society. We do this by 1) claiming our personal power, 2) leading from the grassroots, 3) practicing holistic politics, and 4) living the process every day of our lives.

Claiming Our Personal Power

The *Tao* reminds us that:

"Those who focus on Tao
Will be one with Tao.
Those who study its power
Will be powerful."

(TAO 23)

We've studied the cycles of Tao in our personal lives, nature, and society. All levels from the personal to the planetary echo this fundamental truth: that life is dynamic and interrelated. Herein lies our power to make a difference, for we participate in the continuous creation of the world.

Claiming our power means believing in ourselves and our own possibilities. Dag Hammarskjöld said, "Don't be afraid of yourself. Live your individuality to the full—but for the good of others. Don't copy others in order to buy fellowship or make convention your law."[2] We forsake the Tao when we imitate others.

Surrendering to external influences also undermines our power.

Losing their center, many people become compulsive consumers. Instead of seeking fulfillment, they fill themselves up, generating more than their body weight in garbage every month. The proliferation of trash in our world reflects a high degree of insecurity among our people.[3]

When we see ourselves as part of the oneness of Tao, recognizing all our actions have consequences, we claim our power. Affirming their power, the 1987 graduating class at Humboldt State University in northern California signed a pledge promising to examine the social and environmental implications of any job they applied for.[4]

Unlike Confucius, who upheld tradition, Lao Tzu appeals to progressive individuals who think for themselves, depart from convention, and seek the higher truth. He knew that new solutions rarely come from old leaders, entrenched in the status quo. Often they come from ordinary people who believe in their power to make a difference.

In rural Kentucky, Becky Simpson fought strip-mining companies to stop erosion and flooding, bringing hope to her small Appalachian community.

"I've seen a lot of human suffering all my life," she says, "And I hate it. There's better in the world for people." With a third grade education, six children to raise, and a husband blinded by disease, she began her work in 1977. Organizing her neighbors, she sued the mining companies to repair environmental damage and won. Then in 1982, she set up the Cranks Creek Survival Center, which provides thousands of people a year with food, clothing, schooling, and vocational counseling. Taking the center's literacy class to improve her writing, she lobbied officials in the state capital for government funding. Each day this diminutive woman in jeans and plaid shirt works in the center, distributing baskets of food, clothing, and hope for a better life.

In December 1982, radio talk show host Eddie Schwartz was outraged when he heard Chicago city government was cutting back funds to feed the homeless while spending $100,000 for New Year's Eve fireworks and holiday lights on city bridges. He shared his anger on the radio, challenging listeners to bring food to the station to make up for government cutbacks. Wondering if anyone would come, he sat out in front of the station all night broadcasting with a microphone—and collected 40,000 lbs of food.

"This is very much a grassroots event, a real blue-collar thing," he says. It's people helping people. Now any night in December, a line of cars, vans, and buses heads for Dearborn Street in the Loop, sometimes stretching as many as twenty city blocks, to donate food. In what has become an annual event, praised by city government, Eddie's food drive helps more than 800,000 hungry people a year during the winter holidays.[5]

Committed individuals are making a difference all over the planet. In July 1988, when botanist Paul Cox arrived for research in the village of Falealupo in Western Samoa, he was stunned to find loggers tearing down the rainforest. Knowing villagers had resisted loggers for generations, he asked why. Sadly, the chiefs said their local school had been condemned by the Samoan government, that they were forced to choose between their rainforest and their children's education.

To pay the $55,000 debt for building a new school, the desperate chiefs had signed an agreement with the logging company, which could harvest trees until the amount was paid off. Then they wept when they saw their trees cut down.

Cox took immediate action, sending his own check for $500 to the Bank of Samoa to cover that month's bill and promising to pay for the next six months. He estimated it would cost $1.83 to save an acre of rainforest, saying "What an incredible legacy we can leave the world with such a small amount of money."

After contacting friends and conservation groups, he presented the chiefs with a check for $45,000, the balance of their mortgage, thereby saving 30,000 acres of this rare paleotropical rainforest. For his actions, Cox was made an honorary "high chief" by the Falealupoans and honored by the king of Sweden, himself a donor, who invited Cox to visit his country.[6]

As these examples demonstrate, we can begin new positive cycles by claiming our power to make a difference and taking action.

PERSONAL EXERCISE

Take a few minutes now to develop your vision of a world at peace and commit yourself to taking the first step.

- Find a quiet spot where you won't be disturbed. Sit comfortably and tell your body to relax, shaking off the tension of the day.
- Close your eyes and take three slow, deep breaths, releasing with them any distracting thoughts. With each breath become more relaxed.
- Now ask yourself, "What is my vision of a world at peace? What does it look like? What does it feel like?"
- Think of what you've been doing lately. Ask yourself, "In my daily life, have I been creating a world of peace?" What about your interactions with the people in your life? Were they peaceful? harmonious? anxious? defensive?
- Think for a moment of a peaceful interaction and remember what you did, what peace felt like.
- Then think of a negative interaction. What could you have done to make it more peaceful? See yourself doing this now.
- Feel the sensation of peace within and around you. Affirm to yourself, "I am a powerful center of peace."
- Ask yourself what you can do to extend this peace into a wider sphere. See yourself doing this.
- Feeling yourself profoundly at peace, take another deep breath and come back feeling refreshed, centered, and renewed, ready to act on your vision.
- Write down any new insights that came to you during this process, and commit yourself to your own plan for creating a more peaceful world.

Following the *Tao*, we know that by transforming ourselves, we transform our world. Reaching out from our center of power, we can create new solutions, new possibilities.

Leading from the Grassroots

Lao Tzu's vision of personal power corresponds to a new direction in leadership as we approach the year 2000. Across America, Europe, and Asia, people are losing faith in traditional politics. Tired of waiting for leaders to solve their problems, they're taking the lead themselves. From Green politics in Europe to local concern about toxic wastes, garbage, and groundwater pollution in the United

States, grassroots leadership is working to promote social justice and preserve the environment.

Since 1980, Green parties have organized in sixteen European countries, affecting the political policies of the European Economic Community. Environmental advocates have emerged in Brazil, Argentina, India, Malaysia, Thailand, Indonesia, Kenya, Mexico, Ecuador, and other developing countries.[7]

The emergence of grassroots democracy and crumbling of centralized structures is described by John Naisbitt as one of the "megatrends" of our age. Ralph Nader sees it as a way to overcome cynicism, apathy, and feelings of powerlessness.[8] While the magnitude of global problems can paralyze our will, taking local action produces results and restores our faith. Here are some examples.

In the 1980s a network of women's groups and neighborhood associations in a poor district of Lima, Peru, planted a half-million trees and trained hundreds of local health workers. They built twenty-six schools, 150 daycare centers, and 300 community kitchens. Illiteracy there has fallen to 3 percent, one of the lowest rates in Latin America, and infant mortality is 40 percent below the national average. Grassroots political action has built a strong local community and a healthier life in what was once an area of extreme poverty.[9]

Often a small movement expands as people gain a greater sense of power and possibility. In 1965, a group of housewives in the Setagaya District of Tokyo formed a cooperative buying group which grew into a Seikatsu (consumers' club) with a membership of 1000. Buying directly from producers, members received discounts on produce and dairy products. Today the Seikatsu has 170,000 members and has become an active force for food safety and progressive political change.

In the 1970s, the club began buying organic rice and vegetables, concerned about dangerous chemicals in their food. Greater environmental awareness stimulated a member-led ban on synthetic detergents. Since government leaders ignored them, Seikatsu members ran for office in 1979 with the slogan, "Political reform from the kitchen." Today thirty-three members sit in local assemblies, committed to health and safety, environmental protection, peace, women's rights, cooperation, and greater citizen participation.[10]

Up until now, most political leaders throughout the world have been military officers or lawyers, schooled in war or the adversary system of justice. As grassroots leadership grows, we can expect new solutions, new possibilities for a healthier world. As more concerned citizens become actively involved, they bring insights from many walks of life—as teachers, artists, counselors, construction workers, engineers, parents, health workers, merchants, cooks, managers, musicians, and farmers, to name a few.

If our old leadership has failed us, the proliferation of grassroots movements upholds the promise of cooperation: that together we can create new harmonies and build a more peaceful world.

As we take the lead in our own lives, our own communities, we too become Tao people:

"By small actions
Accomplishing great things."

(TAO 63)

PERSONAL EXERCISE: MAKING IT HAPPEN

1. Commit to a goal. It can be global or local. Some examples: eliminating hunger, providing safe water or affordable housing, preserving rainforests, protecting an endangered species.
2. Focus on your goal. Write it down where you'll see it often. Meditate on it. Visualize the results you'd like to see.
3. Search for resources. Your reference librarian can help you find organizations with a common interest. Contact them for ideas and information.
4. Tell your friends about your goal. Some will offer support. Brainstorm with them. Ask if they have resources to share.
5. Watch your network grow as different lives and talents intertwine. Listen. Recognize that everyone has something valuable to contribute.
6. Meet with supporters and draw up a plan of action. Set short-term goals and an agenda, establishing who will do what. Meet regularly to check results.
7. Communicate often. Use notes, phone calls, even a newsletter to keep everyone informed and involved. Networks, like living things, need nurturing.

8. Don't argue over differences. Be open to new ideas, new possibilities, and watch things grow.[11]

Practicing Holistic Politics

The *Tao* teaches us to think holistically, reminding us that we're part of a much larger whole. Solving today's complex problems requires holistic vision. But some people cannot see that far. As you look around, you'll find some people thinking holistically, others caught up in the old fragmented vision, unaware of the consequences of their actions.

When *USA Today* asked a random group of Americans if they were willing to pay for cleaner air, many answers revealed limited vision. Marie, a retired secretary in New Jersey, said her taxes were too high already, that trucks and buses that pollute should pay the bill. Bob, a video producer in Florida, said his local air is fine, and "when you aren't the creator of a problem, you shouldn't have to pay the bill."[12]

People like Bob and Marie may not realize it, but they *do* contribute to the problem. We all pollute the air when we buy transported food and consumer goods, use styrofoam, drive cars, send or receive mail, read books, magazines, or newspapers. The list goes on. Anything heavily processed or transported over a long distance takes its toll on the environment.

Realizing that the production and distribution of their books depletes the environment, New Society Publishers initiated a "green tax," asking customers to offset environmental costs. Half the money goes for local environmental restoration, the other half for environmental education. Other socially responsible companies have recently added the "green tax" to their business plans.[13]

Seeing holistically, Tao people act with *wu wei*, cooperating with the natural world around them. Sometimes their actions seem a bit odd to conventional thinkers, but as Lao Tzu reminds us:

"When a conventional person hears about Tao,
He breaks into loud laughter.
If there were no laughter,
It would not be Tao."

(TAO 41)

One such exchange happened when President Carter called E.F. Schumacher to the White House in 1977 for a solution to rising inflation and unemployment. "I think you should plant more trees," he told the president.

When considered holistically, Schumacher's answer was more than a laughing matter. Trees enrich a society in many ways, not only by creating short-term jobs planting and tending them, but by collecting energy which can be used for fuel or building materials. Trees provide shade and shelter, purify the environment, supply us with oxygen, enrich the soil, and create a habitat for plants and animals.[14]

Seeing the larger picture, Tao people practice holistic problem solving, taking action with positive consequences on many levels. In rural Minnesota, a Vietnam vet named Jeff Steiner is planting trees for every dead and missing person in Vietnam, creating a forest as his own personal memorial. With thousands of small pine trees, he's affirming life, recovering from his own loss, and contributing to the ecology around him. His action is good personally and good for the planet.[15]

Another example of holistic politics, a UN project in Kenya, employs local women in reforestation work, paying them in corn and cooking oil. Before the project, the area suffered drought and soil erosion from overgrazing. Now the women are planting fast-growing drought-resistant trees and sorghum, contouring the land to help capture rainfall. The project offers positive contributions on many levels: hunger relief, restoration of the environment, equal opportunity for women, and training for a better life. It's good for the people and the environment, promoting balance and social justice.[16]

In a holistic approach to housing, builders in California's Santa Clara Valley are combining new homes with fruit trees in an innovative project called Lee's Orchard. Known as "the Valley of Heart's Delight," the area was once filled with orchards, but in recent years the environment has been assaulted by layers of concrete and new buildings supporting the burgeoning computer industry.

Cooperatively-owned and run by a hired operator, the orchard will help restore residents' kinship with nature as they watch the trees change with the seasons. The complex will also include a community pool and recreation building. A holistic approach to housing in the 1990s, the orchard will foster community, purify the air, produce local fruit for the area, and offer people a sense of peace.[17]

A cooperative approach to the world housing problem, Habitat for Humanity mobilizes volunteers and future residents as construction workers, literally putting their faith to work to build "a decent house in a decent community for God's people in need."

Providing homes for low income people throughout North America, Africa, and Central America, Habitat builds or renovates houses in partnership with local families and sells them the houses at cost. Funds, building materials, and volunteer work are donated by churches, community groups, and concerned individuals.

Habitat offers more than housing: cooperation, meaningful service, dignity for the poor, and hope for a more compassionate world. In 1965, Habitat's founder, lawyer and millionaire businessman Millard Fuller, gave up his practice and personal wealth to follow his soul. Moving to Koinonia village in Georgia, he rediscovered his Christian faith, then launched a housing project in Zaire. There Fuller and his family grew closer together, helping people not only build houses but restore their faith. Time and again people and materials appeared at just the right time, the answer to their prayers. Fuller's book *Love in the Mortar Joints* describes many such incidents and the support of volunteers whose love, he says, has become part of every building.[18]

Former president Jimmy Carter has his own holistic vision of peace. After an unsuccessful bid for a second term in 1980, he came home to Georgia to decide what to do. One project he chose was Habitat for Humanity. For the past few years, he and Rosalynn have pounded nails, laid floors, sanded, painted, and raised the walls of new homes, working side by side with future residents.

While other past presidents have been content to rest on their laurels, Carter remains committed to helping others with active, tangible work. "For me this is one of the almost perfect ways to put my religious beliefs into action," he explains, finding Habitat the kind of program "that can break down barriers and heal hate."[19]

Carter demonstrated the same holistic approach when setting up his presidential library. Instead of a storehouse for official papers, Carter envisioned a vital educational center where people could study new approaches to health, negotiation, and world peace. The Carter Center offers seminars on negotiation and mediation, reflecting Carter's belief in these principles as a means to greater peace, collectively and individually.

At a recent press conference, I asked him what private citizens can do to create a more peaceful world. He smiled, looking straight at me with those pale blue eyes of his. "There are principles in peace seeking—negotiation, mediation, arbitration—that apply to every person, even private life in a family. The same principles apply to international dispute resolution," he said, referring to recent books on the subject.[20] He encouraged private citizens to learn these principles and insist that their government use them as well.

Carter said he'd like to see America rely more on negotiation and diplomacy, becoming "a champion of peace" rather than relying on "belligerence or the injection of American troops in trouble spots around the world." "It's very difficult to wage peace; it's very easy to wage war," he said thoughtfully.

Waging war, we fall back into old dualistic habits, perpetuating cycles of defensiveness, aggression, and violence. Seeing problems holistically, practicing cooperation, we reach out in new directions, exploring the Tao's unknown potential of *wu*, taking what Christians call a "leap of faith."

Following the intangible wisdom of spirit isn't easy in a world which conditions us to accept only material realities. But as Carter says, there are principles that apply equally to individuals or nations, principles studied in our time by the Carter Center and recorded centuries ago by Lao Tzu:

"Principles of truth
Informing all creation,
The lessons of life
Inherent in Tao."

(TAO 21)

Living the Process

The *Tao* asks that we have the courage to live these principles. This is the ultimate message of Lao Tzu. In this crucial time of transition, when the old paradigm is winding down, we can create a new cycle of peace by living the Tao: at home, at work, in nature, and in the silence of our own hearts.

Can we follow the Tao? Only we can know. The principles are there but the way for each of us is unknown, uncharted. The possibilities are many; the choice is ours. As Dag Hammarskjöld said, "Life only demands from you the strength you possess. Only one feat is possible—not to have run away."

If you are called to live the Tao of Peace, you'll recognize the feeling Hammarskjöld recorded in his private journal, *Markings*:

"Thus it was.

I am being driven forward
Into an unknown land.
The pass grows steeper,
The air colder and sharper.
A wind from my unknown goal
Stirs the strings
Of expectation.

Still the question:
Shall I ever get there?
There where life resounds,
A clear pure note
In the silence."[21]

Following the Tao leads us into unknown territory, the area of *wu*. It is a path less traveled, less secure, but most needed. We have never been there. Few in the world have ever been there before. Yet our troubled world waits, the distant goal calls us, the path is at hand.

As we've learned in these pages, the path is the process. And we are the process. The process is Tao.

Lao Tzu tells us:

"Persevering on the path is strength.
To keep your center is to endure."

(TAO 33)

Persevere, the *Tao* reminds us, be strong and yielding as water. Remain open and centered, flexible as bamboo. Practice compassion. Honor the cycles within and around you. Seek harmony with nature and all others in your world. Then surely peace will fill your life and flow forth to heal this planet:

"Spreading through the nations,
The Tao brings peace throughout the world.
How do I know this?
Because it begins with you and me."

(TAO 54)

Affirmation

I now know my life is peaceful and harmonious.
Centered and powerful, I live my beliefs.
I lead from the grassroots, working for the good of all
I think holistically, act cooperatively, practice Taoist politics.
I always remember that life is a process.
I respect myself and the process.
I harmonize with nature and all others in my world.
I accept greater peace in my life now.
And so it is.

CHAPTER
NOTES
AND RESOURCES

Frontispiece Illustration: The Tao, the path of life, peace and illumination.

Notes to the Introduction

1. My own version of the *Tao Te Ching*, Chapter 62. Unless otherwise noted, all *Tao* quotes in the text are my version and will be cited by chapter numbers to facilitate comparisons with other translations.

2. *Lao Tzu: The Way of Life*, trans. R.B. Blakney (New York: New American Library, © 1955), Chapter 8, p. 60. Used by permission of the publisher.

3. R.L. Wing, translator's introduction, *The Tao of Power: A Translation of the Tao Te Ching by Lao Tzu* (Garden City, NY: Doubleday, 1986), p. 16.

Section I Illustration: *Te,* virtue or character, combining the characters for "to go," "straight," and "heart-mind." A person with *Te* lives wisely and authentically, expressing the power of Tao.

Notes to Chapter 1

1. Some of the ideas in this self-assessment were based on Louise L. Hay, *You Can Heal Your Life* (Santa Monica, CA.: Hay House, © 1984), pp. 19–20. Used by permission of the publisher. This book is an excellent resource for building self-acceptance.

Notes to Chapter 2

1. R.L. Wing, *The Tao of Power: A Translation of the Tao Te Ching by Lao Tzu* (Garden City, NY: Doubleday, 1986), p. 9.
2. In *Ordinary People as Monks and Mystics* (Mahwah, NJ: Paulist Press, 1986), Marsha Sinetar describes modern men and women who've chosen lives of contemplation, simplicity, and service, comparing them to traditional monks and mystics.
3. An earlier version of this story appeared as "A Strange Encounter," by Genevieve Farrow in *Science of Mind Magazine,* May 1989, pp. 3–5. Used by permission of the author and publisher. Subscriptions: $15/yr (12 issues) from Science of Mind Publications, 3251 W. 6th St., P.O. Box 75127, Los Angeles CA 90075.
4. My version was inspired in part by R.B. Blakney's translation, in *Lao Tzu: The Way of Life* (New York: New American Library, © 1955), p. 101: "But when you try and try,/ The world is then beyond the winning." Used by permission of the publisher.
5. Henry David Thoreau, *The Variorum Walden.* Ed. Walter Harding (New York: Washington Square, 1962), p. 67.
6. Witter Bynner, translator's introduction, *The Way of Life According to Lao Tzu* (New York: Putnam, 1944; renewed 1972), pp. 12–13.
7. Norman Cousins, *Human Options* (South Yarmouth, MA: John Curley and Associates, 1981), p. 66.
8. Gerald G. Jampolsky, M.D., *Teach Only Love: The Seven Principles of Attitudinal Healing* (New York: Bantam, © 1983), pp. 56–59. Used with permission of the publisher.

Notes to Chapter 3

1. My version was inspired by Tolbert McCarroll's translation, *The Tao: The Sacred Way* (New York: Crossroad, © 1982), p. 47: "Therefore the True Person embraces the One/ And becomes a model for all." Used with permission of the author.
2. Jean Shinoda Bolen, *The Tao of Psychology: Synchronicity and the Self* (San Francisco: Harper and Row, 1979), 95–96.
3. For the best discussion of physics and Eastern philosophy, see Fritjof Capra, *The Tao of Physics: An Exploration of the Parallels Between Modern Physics and Eastern Mysticism.* 2nd edition. (Boulder, CO: Shambhala, 1983). Excellent discussions of Cartesian dualism on pp. 22–24, particle-waves and probabilities on p. 81.
4. Fritjof Capra, *The Turning Point: Science, Society, and the Rising Culture* (New York: Simon and Schuster, 1982). Discussion of implicate order and the S-matrix theory on pp. 92–93, 95–96.

Notes to Chapter 4

1. My version of *Tao,* Chapter 45, inspired by R.L. Wing's translation in *The Tao of Power* (New York: Doubleday, © 1986), p. 45: "Clarity and stillness/ Bring order to the world." Used by permission of the publisher.
2. Joseph A. Grassi, *Changing the World Within: The Dynamics of Personal and Spiritual Growth* (New York: Paulist Press, 1986), p. 38.
3. Mark Satin, *New Age Politics: Healing Self and Society* (New York: Dell, 1979), p. 189.
4. Translation of *Tao,* Chapter 11 from *Lao Tsu: Tao Te Ching,* trans. Gia-Fu Feng and Jane English (New York: Alfred A. Knopf, Inc., © 1972), p. 11. Used by permission of the publisher.
5. Lin I-Ming, *Awakening to the Tao,* trans. Thomas Cleary (Boston: Shambhala, 1988), p. 12.
6. Louise L. Hay, *You Can Heal Your Life* (Santa Monica, CA: Hay House, 1987), p. 95.
7. Henri Maspero, *Taoism and Chinese Religion,* trans. Frank A. Kierman, Jr. (Amherst: Univ. of Massachusetts Press, 1981), p. 439.
8. For more inner peace breaks and daily exercises, see: Bob and Judy Cranmer's *The Thirty Day Peace Diet* (Cupertino CA: Right Brain Unlimited, 1988), available for $9.95 and 2.00 postage from Right Brain Unlimited, P.O. Box 160484, Cupertino CA 95016–0484.

Section II Illustration: *hsin,* the character for the heart-mind, the center of all feeling and motivation.

Notes to Chapter 5

1. Satin, *New Age Politics,* p. 189.
2. Chang Chung-Yuan, *Creativity and Taoism* (New York: Harper, 1963), p. 231.
3. My thanks to Rev. Carole Price of the First Church of Religious Science, 1195 Clark St., San Jose, CA, for interviews and discussions on inner peace from 1986 to 1989.
4. Gerald Kushel, *Centering: Six Steps Toward Inner Liberation* (New York: Times Books, 1979), p. 56.
5. From Jack Canfield's session at the Full Esteem Ahead workshop, October 1, 1988, in San Jose, CA. Used with permission. For additional self-esteem exercises, a curriculum guide, and self-help tapes, contact Self-Esteem Seminars, 17156 Palisades Circle, Pacific Palisades, CA 90272 (213) 454–1665.

6. Information from Mitchell Saunders, M.A., here and elsewhere from interviews during 1907 and 1988, used with permission Saunders is Director of Programs for California Leadership, 2700 Augustine Dr., Santa Clara, CA 95054.

7. R.B. Blakney, translator's introduction to *Lao Tzu: The Way of Life,* p. 47.

Notes to Chapter 6

1. Some of the material in this chapter appeared in an earlier form in "Stress Management for a Healthier World" by Diane Dreher, *Quality Living,* April 1989, pp. 17–18. A magazine devoted to helping people develop greater peace in their lives, *Quality Living* is available by subscription for $20 yr (4 copies) from Box One, Valle Crucis, NC 28691.

2. Norman Cousins, *The Healing Heart: Antidotes to Panic and Helplessness* (New York: Norton, 1983), p. 168.

3. Joanna Rogers Macy, *Despair and Personal Power in the Nuclear Age* (Philadelphia: New Society Publishers, 1983), passim.

4. Thomas Merton, *The Way of Chuang Tzu* (New York: New Directions, 1965), p. 155.

5. Grassi, *Changing the World Within,* p. 40.

6. Gerald G. Jampolsky, *Love Is Letting Go of Fear* (Berkeley: Celestial Arts, © 1979), pp. 85, 34. Used with permission of the author and publisher.

7. My thanks to Arlene Wiltberger, M.A., and Gay Leah Swenson, Ph.D., for an interview in San Carlos, CA, October 2, 1988. Arlene is a marriage and family counselor in private practice at 501 First Avenue, San Mateo, CA 94401. Gay is Director of the Carl Rogers Institute for Peace at the Center for the Studies of the Person, 1125 Torrey Pines Road, La Jolla, CA 92037 (619) 459–3861. She told me later that the workshop in question was a very successful gathering of fifty political and lay leaders from eleven countries, including President Oscar Arias of Costa Rica, 1987 Nobel Peace Prize winner.

Notes to Chapter 7

1. Quotes and information from Michael Reed Gach here and elsewhere from Michael Reed Gach with Carolyn Marco, *Acu-Yoga: Self-Help Techniques to Relieve Tension* (Tokyo: Japan Publications, 1981), a wonderful resource for balancing energies. Information about tension and fatigue on p. 160. Used with permission.

2. Gach, *Acu-Yoga,* p. 169; Hay, *You Can Heal Your Life,* 154, 158, 168, 176, 184.

3. Gach, *Acu-Yoga,* p. 154. Used with permission.

4. Holmes Welch, *Taoism: The Parting of the Way* (n.c.: Beacon Press, 1965), p. 71.
5. Maspero, *Taoism and Chinese Religion,* pp. 47–48, 326.
6. Maspero, *Taoism and Chinese Religion,* pp. 71–72.
7. Koichi Tohei, *Ki in Daily Life* (Tokyo: Ki No Kenkyukai, 1978), pp. 25–26.
8. Gach, *Acu-Yoga,* p. 161.
9. For this peaceful renewing posture, I am grateful to Michael Reed Gach. Used with permission from *Acu-Yoga,* p. 87. For more information about Gach's self-help books, acupressure workshops or trainings, contact the Acupressure Institute, 1533 Shattuck Ave., Berkeley, CA 94709 (415) 845–1059.
10. Indra Devi, *Yoga for Americans* (Englewood Cliffs, NJ: Prentice-Hall, 1959; New York: Signet, 1968), pp. 41–42. I am grateful to Indra Devi for introducing me to this exercise years ago.
11. Gach, *Acu-Yoga,* p. 223.
12. Da Lui, *Taoist Health Exercise Book* (New York: Quick Fox, 1974), p. 37.
13. The Chinese word for this power center is *tant'ien.* I have used the Japanese aikido term throughout the book because it is simpler and easier to remember.
14. Standing meditation here and elsewhere in the book used by permission from Janet Y. DeVore, R.N., a holistic healer and medicine woman who teaches acupressure, herbal healing, toning, drumming, shielding, and meditation at the Earth Woman Medicine Shield Center, 1032 Lovell Ave., Campbell, CA 95008. My gratitude to Janet for sharing her combined wisdom on healing from Eastern and Western traditions.
15. Al Chuang-liang Huang, *Embrace Tiger, Return to Mountain: The Essence of T'ai Chi* (Moab, UT: Real People Press, 1973), p. 177.
16. Da Lui, *Taoist Health Exercise Book,* p. 37.

Notes to Chapter 8
1. Arthur Waley, *The Way and Its Power: A Study of the Tao Te Ching and Its Place in Chinese Thought* (London: Allen & Unwin, 1956), p. 167.
2. Thoreau quotes from *The Variorum Walden,* pp. 68, 83.
3. Alvin Toffler, *Future Shock* (New York: Random House, 1970), pp. 4, 52–53.
4. Toffler, *Future Shock,* pp. 308, 314–15.
5. *The Writing of Chuang Tzu* in *The Texts of Taoism,* trans. James Legge (New York: Julian Press, 1959), pp. 623–24.
6. My version here is similar to R.L. Wing's translation in *The Tao of Power,* (New York: Doubleday, © 1986), Chapter 46, p. 46: "Therefore know

that enough is enough. There will always be enough." Used with permission of the publisher

7. Benjamin Hoff, translator's notes, *The Way to Life: At the Heart of the Tao Te Ching* (New York: Weatherhill, 1981), p. 73.

8. *Peace Pilgrim: Her Life and Work in Her Own Words,* compiled by some of her friends (Sante Fe: Ocean Tree, 1983), p. 51. For a copy of this book or more information about Peace Pilgrim, contact Friends of Peace Pilgrim, 43480 Cedar Avenue, Hemet, CA 92344 (714) 927–7678.

9. A summary of ideas from *99 Ways to a Simpler Lifestyle* by Center for Science in the Public Interest (Garden City: Anchor Doubleday, 1976), pp. xi–xii.

11. Kushel, *Centering*, pp. 30–31.

12. Some of my ideas for simpler communication are based on Duane Elgin, *Voluntary Simplicity: Toward a Way of Life That Is Outwardly Simple, Inwardly Rich* (New York: Morrow, 1981), pp. 170–71.

Notes to Chapter 9

1. Variations of this disidentification process are widely used in counseling. For more background and discussion, see: Roberto Assagioli, *The Act of Will* (New York: Viking, 1973), pp. 214–217.

2. My version was inspired by the beautiful translation of Brother Tolbert McCarroll, *The Tao: The Sacred Way* (New York: Crossroad, © 1982), p. 47. Used by permission of the author.

"Therefore the True Person embraces the One
    and becomes a model for all.
Do not look only at yourself,
    and you will see much.
Do not justify yourself,
    and you will be distinguished.
Do not brag,
    and you will have merit.
Do not be prideful,
    and your work will endure.
It is because you do not strive
    that no one under heaven can strive with you.
The saying of the Old Ones, 'Yield and Overcome,'
    is not an empty phrase.
True wholeness is achieved
    by blending with life."

Notes to Chapter 10

1. Maspero, *Taoism and Chinese Religion*, p. 73.
2. Chang Chung-yuan, *Creativity and Taoism*, p. 4.
3. Elgin, *Voluntary Simplicity*, p. 158.
4. Assagioli, *The Act of Will*, p. 206. For more integrating exercises, see also: Assagioli, *Psychosynthesis* (New York: Viking, 1971).
5. For an extensive discussion of the *anima* and *animus,* see: Carl Jung, "Marriage as a Psychological Relationship," in *The Development of Personality,* trans. R.F.C. Hull, *Collected Works* 17 (New York: Pantheon Books, 1954), p. 198.
6. For a discussion of the shadow, see: Carl Jung, *Man and His Symbols* (Garden City: Doubleday, 1979), pp. 168–76.

Notes to Chapter 11

1. Lin Yutang, commentary to the *Tao Te Ching* in *The Wisdom of China and India* (New York: Modern Library, 1942), p. 590.
2. The story is from *Peace Pilgrim: Her Life and Work in Her Own Words,* compiled by some of her friends (Santa Fe: Ocean Tree Books, P.O. Box 1295, Santa Fe, NM 87504, © 1982), pp. 61–62. Used by permission of the publisher and Friends of Peace Pilgrim, 43480 Cedar Avenue, Hemet, CA 92344. The name "Molly" is my addition.
3. Quote and description of *pu shih* from R.B. Blakney, commentary, *Lao Tzu: The Way of Life* (New York: New American Library, © 1955), p. 400. Used by permission of the publisher.
4. For a fuller description of Taoist self-discipline, see: Hua-Ching Ni, *Tao: The Subtle Universal Law and the Integral Way of Life* (Los Angeles: College of Tao and Traditional Chinese Healing, 1979).
5. Robert William Smith, Ph.D., "The Distinction Between Life as a Problem or a Mystery," course syllabus. Used by permission of the author.

Section III Illustration: The Chinese character for water, symbolizing the power and flexibility of Tao and the water cycle that supports all life on the planet.

Notes to Chapter 12

1. R.L. Wing, *The Tao of Power,* commentary to *Tao* Chapter 73, p. 73.
2. Taoist theory of correspondences discussed in Maspero, *Taoism and Chinese Religion,* pp. 339–40; Chang Chung-yuan, *Creativity and Taoism,* p. 138.

3. The ecological vision of St. Francis is described in Bill Devall and George Sessions, *Deep Ecology: Living as if Nature Mattered* (Salt Lake City: Gibbs M. Smith, 1985), p. 92.

4. Thomas Traherne, *Centuries of Meditations,* in *Seventeenth-Century Prose and Poetry.* 2nd ed. Ed. Alexander Witherspoon and Frank J. Warnke (New York: Harcourt, Brace, Jovanovich, 1982), p. 696.

5. John Donne, *Devotions Upon Emergent Occasions* (Ann Arbor: Univ. of Michigan Press, 1959), 108–09.

6. The Greenpeace Philosophy used by permission of Greenpeace USA and Canada. For more information about Greenpeace, contact them at 1436 U. Street NW, Washington, DC 20009 (202) 462–1177 or 578 Bloor St. West Toronto, Ontario Canada M6E 1k1 (416) 538-6470.

7. Discussion of *ying* from Lin Yutang, ed. *The Wisdom of China and India,* p. 587.

8. Thoreau, *The Variorum Walden,* pp. 98–99.

9. Dorothy L. Sayers, *Creed or Chaos?* (New York: Harcourt Brace, 1949), p. 47.

10. See, for example, R.G.H. Siu, *The Man of Many Qualities: A Legacy of the I Ching* (Cambridge: Massachusetts Institute of Technology, 1968), p. 7.

11. Chuang Tzu 7:4 in *The Wisdom of Laotse,* trans. Lin Yutang (New York: Modern Library, 1976), p. 148.

12. E.F. Schumacher, *Small Is Beautiful: Economics as if People Mattered* (New York: Harper & Row, 1973), pp. 38–39.

13. My version is close to the translation by R.L. Wing in *The Tao of Power,* (New York: Doubleday, © 1986), Chapter 46, p. 46: "Therefore know that enough is enough./ There will always be enough." Used by permission of the publisher.

14. Borneo story taken from G. Tyler Miller, Jr. *Living in the Environment.* 2nd ed. (Belmont: Wadsworth, © 1979), p. 92. Used by permission of the publisher.

15. John Seymour and Herbert Girardet, *Blueprint for a Green Planet* (New York: Prentice Hall, 1987), p. 73. For more information about rainforests, contact the Rainforest Action Network, 301 Broadway, Suite A, San Francisco, CA 94133 or the Environmental Defense Fund, 257 Park Ave. South, New York, NY 10010.

16. John Muir, *John of the Mountains: The Unpublished Journals of John Muir,* ed. Linnie Marsh Wolfe (Boston: Houghton Mifflin, © 1938 by Wanda Muir Hanna. Copyright © renewed 1966 by John Muir Hanna and Ralph Eugene Wolfe), p. 222. This quote and the one that follows reprinted with permission of Houghton Mifflin Company.

17. Some ideas in this quiz were based upon "Where You At? A Bioregional Test," by Jim Dodge, Leonard Charles, Lynn Milliman, and Victoria Stockley, published in *Coevolution Quarterly* No. 32, Winter 1981, p. 1. Used by permission of Jim Dodge and the publisher, now *Whole Earth Review.* Subscriptions $20/yr (4 issues) from *Whole Earth Review,* 27 Gate 5 Road, Sausalito, CA 94965. For more information about endangered species, contact The Nature Conservancy, 1815 North Lynn Street, Arlington, VA 22209 or The World Wildlife Fund, 1250 Twenty-Fourth Street NW, Washington, DC 20037.

18. See: Robert Aitkin Roshi, "Gandhi, Dogen, and Deep Ecology," first published in *The Mind of Clover,* © 1984 by North Point Press, Berkeley, reprinted in Appendix C in Devall and Sessions, p. 233.

19. John Seed, "Anthropocentrism," Appendix E in Devall and Sessions, *Deep Ecology* (Layton, UT: Gibbs Smith, 1985), p. 243. Reprinted by permission of John Seed and the publisher. John Seed's book, *Thinking Like a Mountain,* is available from New Society Publishers, P.O. Box 582, Santa Cruz, CA 95061–0582.

20. Muir, *John of the Mountains,* p. 439. Used with permission.

Notes to Chapter 13

1. For a discussion of dragon veins, see: John Blofeld, *Taoism: The Road to Immortality* (Boulder: Shambhala, 1978), p. 7.

2. For the best discussion of quantum physics and Taoism, see: Capra, *The Tao of Physics.*

3. Alan Watts, *The Way of Zen* (New York: Pantheon, 1957), p. 5.

4. Discussion of the "chill factor" on p. 141 and some excellent ideas for edible landscape from Robert Kourik, *Designing and Maintaining Your Edible Landscape* (Santa Rosa: Metamorphic Press, 1986).

5. Some ideas from this quiz were based on "Where You At? A Bioregional Test," by Jim Dodge, Leonard Charles, Lynn Milliman, and Victoria Stockley, first published in *Coevolution Quarterly* No. 32, Winter 1981, p. 1. Used by permission of Jim Dodge and the publisher, now *Whole Earth Review.*

6. For a brochure and information on local recycling centers, write the Environmental Defense Fund, Recycling, 257 Park Avenue, New York, NY 10010.

7. For a discussion of "Buddhist Economics" and reverence for trees, see: Schumacher, *Small Is Beautiful,* pp. 53–62.

8. For background information on the water cycle, I am grateful to my friend, environmental writer James P. Degnan. Information on the Ogallala Aquifer from John Seymour and Herbert Girardet, *Blueprint*

for a Green Planet (New York: Prentice Hall, 1987), pp. 22. This book is an excellent resource for living in harmony with the environment.

9. Information used with permission from the Mono Lake Committee, P.O. Box 29, Lee Vining, CA 93541. I'd also like to thank my student, Farah Chichester, whose oral report and unpublished paper, "The Beauty and the Beast of Mono Lake," Santa Clara University, March 1989, helped me see the problem more clearly.

10. Information on water pollution from Seymour and Girardet, *Blueprint,* pp. 24, 34–36.

11. Many of these recommendations are from Seymour and Girardet, *Blueprint for a Green Planet* (New York: Prentice Hall, © 1987), p. 33. Used with permission of the publisher. For excellent information on non-toxic soaps, cleansers, and other household products, see: Debra Lynn Dadd, *Nontoxic and Natural* (Los Angeles: Jeremy Tarcher, 1984).

12. Miller, *Living in the Environment,* p. 345.

13. Seymour and Girardet, *Blueprint,* p. 26.

14. Miller, *Living in the Environment,* p. 346.

15. Seymour and Girardet, *Blueprint,* pp. 24–25.

16. Many of these recommendations are found in Miller, *Living in the Environment,* p. 353. For more information on water and energy conservation, contact the Rocky Mountain Institute, 1739 Snowmass Creek Road, Snowmass, CO 81654.

Notes to Chapter 14

1. Capra, *The Turning Point,* p. 25.

2. Research on alar and other chemical additives was obtained from a 1989 Daminozide Press Release by the Environmental Protection Agency and the Natural Resources Defense Council. For further information, see: *Intolerable Risk: Pesticides in Our Children's Food,* a report by the Natural Resources Defense Council, February 27, 1989. The pamphlet and the results of more recent studies can be obtained from the Natural Resources Defense Council at 90 New Montgomery, San Francisco, CA 94105 (415) 777–0220.

3. Seymour and Girardet, *Blueprint,* p. 70.

4. Information from Stephanie Turner, "Guidelines for a Vegetarian Lifestyle" (Interview with Frances Moore Lappé), San Francisco *Chronicle,* March 15, 1989, Food Section, p. 3.

5. Quote from Lappé and statistics in previous paragraph from Turner, "Guidelines," above. For background information on world hunger, I'm grateful to Frances Moore Lappé for a telephone interview in 1987. For a thorough discussion of the relation of diet to world hunger, see

Frances Moore Lappé, *Diet for a Small Planet: Tenth Anniversary Edition* (New York: Ballentine, 1982) or contact Food First, the Institute for Food and Development Policy, 145 Ninth Street, San Francisco, CA 94103 (415) 864–8555.

6. See Dadd, *Nontoxic and Natural,* pp. 112, 241–42.

7. John Jeavons' *How to Grow More Vegetables Than You Ever Thought Possible on Less Land Than You Can Imagine* (Palo Alto: Ecology Action, 1974) is available from Ecology Action/Common Ground, 2225 El Camino Real, Palo Alto, CA 94306.

8. Information on Chinese agriculture from *Ecology Action/Common Ground Newsletter,* February 1976; other data from Jeavons, p. v. Peter Chan's *Better Vegetable Gardens the Chinese Way* and *Peter Chan's Magical Landscape* (Pownal, VT: Storey Communications, 1985 and 1988) are excellent guides to Chinese gardening methods.

9. Information on Richard Stevens from Patti Thorn, "Professor grows his groceries instead of grass," *Rocky Mountain News,* May 18, 1988, p. 52; reprinted in *The Orange County Register,* December 3, 1988, Home Section, F3.

10. Chan, *Magical Landscape,* pp. 6, 86–87.

11. Stu Campbell, *Let It Rot: The Home Gardener's Guide to Composting* (Pownal, VT: Storey Communications, 1975), p. 13.

12. Miller, *Living in the Environment,* p. 1.

13. Information from Earth Care Paper Company, *Recycled Paper Catalogue,* October 1988–September 1989, p. 11. This company (P.O. Box 3335, Madison, WI 53704) makes attractive stationery, business paper, cards, and gift wrap from recycled paper and lists information about pollution and recycling throughout its catalogues.

14. Seymour and Girardet, *Blueprint,* pp. 75, 77–79.

15. Earth Care, *Recycled Paper Catalogue,* p. 15.

16. Seymour and Girardet, *Blueprint,* p. 85.

17. Earth Care, *Recycled Paper Catalogue,* p. 7.

18. Campbell, *Let It Rot,* p. 19.

19. Seymour and Girardet, *Blueprint,* p. 29.

20. Seymour and Girardet, *Blueprint,* p. 30.

21. Miller, *Living in the Environment,* p. E120.

22. Some ideas from Seymour and Girardet, *Blueprint,* pp. 80, 92, and Mary Trahan, "Recycling at the Office," *Windstar Journal,* Summer 1989, pp. 26–28. Subscriptions $18/yr (4 issues) or included in annual membership, the Windstar Foundation, 2317 Snowmass Creek Road, Snowmass, CO 81654 (303) 927–4777. Over 900,000 tons of recoverable office paper are dumped into U.S. landfills annually. The Paper Stock

Institute of America (330 Madison Avenue, New York, NY 10017) will provide information on waste paper recycling agencies in your area.
23. Details from "Students give environmental lesson at U.N.," story from AP wire service, reported in the San Jose *Mercury*, May 2, 1989, p. 11A.

Notes to Chapter 15

1. Information from R.L. Wing, *The Tao of Power*, commentary to Tao, Chapter 17, p. 17.
2. For more information on Taoist masters, see Waley, *The Way and Its Power*, p. 161.
3. Hua-ching Ni, *Tao: The Subtle Universal Law*, p. 31.

Notes to Chapter 16

1. For further discussions of the relationship between the observer and observed in physics, see: Capra, *The Tao of Physics*, p. 141, and R.G.H. Siu, *The Tao of Science: An Essay on Western Knowledge and Eastern Wisdom* (Cambridge: M.I.T. Press, 1957), pp. 76–77.
2. A. Westbrook and O. Ratti, *Aikido and the Dynamic Sphere* (Rutland, VT: Charles E. Tuttle, 1970), p. 70.
3. Westbrook and Ratti, *Aikido*, p. 24.
4. *Elegant Choices, Healing Choices: Finding Grace and Wholeness in Everything We Choose* (Mahwah, NJ: Paulist Press, © 1988 by Dr. Marsha Sinetar), pp. 2–3, 22. Used by permission of the publisher.
5. Hua-ching Ni, *Tao: The Subtle Universal Law*, p. 128.
6. See: *The Writings of Chuang-Tzu*, in Legge, *The Texts of Taoism*, p. 314.
7. For a discussion of *hui* and celestial light, see: Maspero, *Taoism and Chinese Religion*, p. 284.
8. Details from *Elegant Choices, Healing Choices* (Mahwah, NJ: Paulist Press, © 1988 by Dr. Marsha Sinetar), pp. 13–15. Used by permission of the publisher.
9. My friend Rev. Genevieve Farrow affirms this principle of order in her counseling, classes, and workshops.
10. Details from "From a tragedy comes a hotel to help the poor, homeless," San Jose *Mercury*, November 11, 1988, p. 9B.
11. My thanks to Frank Olson, co-owner of Ernesto's in Los Gatos, CA, for his example and an interview in April, 1989.

Notes to Chapter 17

1. Huang, *Embrace Tiger, Return to Mountain*, p. 141.
2. Lui I-Ming, *Awakening to the Tao*, pp. 70, 81.
3. Yutang, *The Wisdom of China and India*, pp. 591, 622.

4. See Siu, *The Man of Many Qualities*, p. 68.
5. Bill Devall and George Sessions, *Deep Ecology*, p. 8.
6. Dag Hammarskjöld, *Markings*, trans. Leif Sjoberg and W.H. Auden (New York: Alfred A. Knopf, Inc.; London: Faber and Faber Ltd., © 1965), p. 13. This quotation and those which follow used with permission of the publishers.
7. Hammarskjöld, *Markings*, p. 13.
8. Hammarskjöld, *Markings*, p. 157.
9. Witter Bynner, trans. *The Way of Life According to Lao Tzu* (New York: Putnam, 1972), p. 101. © 1944 by Dorothy Chauvenet and Paul Horgan; copyright renewed 1972. Reprinted by permission of Harper & Row Publishers, Inc.
10. John Naisbitt, *Megatrends: Ten New Directions Transforming Our Lives* (New York: Warner, 1982), p. 181.
11. For information about Jimmy Treybig and Tandem Computers, I am grateful to Jeri Flynn, Manager, Financial Public Relations, Tandem Computers, Cupertino, CA.
12. Fritjof Capra and Charlene Spretnak, *Green Politics* (New York: Dutton, 1984), p. 195.

Section IV Illustration: The Chinese character for *tz'u* or compassion, the empathy of Tao which embraces all of life.

Notes to Chapter 18

1. My version was inspired by Tolbert McCarroll's translation in *The Tao: The Sacred Way* (New York: Crossroad, © 1982), p. 47: "Therefore the True Person embraces the One/ And becomes a model for all." Used with permission of the author.
2. Maspero, *Taoism and Chinese Religion*, p. 365.
3. For a discussion of synchronicity, see: Bolen, *The Tao of Psychology*, p. 36.
4. For a good discussion of Taoist religious background, see: H.G. Creel, *Chinese Thought from Confucius to Mao Tse-tung* (Chicago: Univ. of Chicago Press, 1953), p. 101.
5. Muir, *John of the Mountains* (Boston: Houghton Mifflin, © 1938 by Wanda Muir Hanna. Copyright © renewed 1966 by John Muir Hanna and Ralph Eugene Wolfe.) p. 320. Reprinted with permission of Houghton Mifflin Company.
6. For a discussion of Taoism and the peace movement, see: Herrymon Maurer, *The Way of the Ways* (New York: Schocken, 1985), p. 6.
7. Story about Buckminster Fuller from Amy Edmondson, "Peace 2010," *Windstar Journal*, Winter 1986, p. 24.

8. Satin, *New Age Politics,* p. 189.

9. Details and quote used with permission from "Two Billion People for Peace: An Interview with John Randolph Price," by John S. Niendorff © *Science of Mind Magazine,* August 1989, pp. 18–29. Subscriptions to *Science of Mind* are $15/yr (12 issues) from Science of Mind Publications, 3251 W. 6th St., P.O. Box 75127, Los Angeles, CA 90075.

Notes to Chapter 19

1. Information on *t'zu* and Taoism from Hoff, *The Way to Life,* p. 77.
2. For Chaung-Tzu's explanation, see: Book XXV in Legge, *The Texts of Taoism,* p. 555.
3. Erich Fromm, *The Art of Loving* (New York: Harper & Row, 1956), p. 1.
4. See Hua-ching Ni, *Tao: The Subtle Universal Law,* p. 126.
5. Carl Jung, commentary, *The Secret of the Golden Flower: A Chinese Book of Life,* trans. Richard Wilhelm (London: Kegan Paul, 1945), p. 96.
6. Information from an interview with Tina Clare at the Center of Light, Los Altos Hills, CA, May, 1989. Meditation adapted with permission from her audiotape, *Silence in the Heart: Meditations for Inner Growth and Relaxation* (Los Altos Hills: Clarity Productions, © 1989). For further information about tapes or classes, write Clarity Productions, The Center of Light, 12620 La Cresta Drive, Los Altos Hills, CA 94022.
7. Gerald G. Jampolsky, *Love Is Letting Go of Fear* (Berkeley: Celestial Arts, © 1979), p. 34. Used with permission of the author and publisher.
8. *Peace Pilgrim: Her Life and Work in Her Own Words* (Santa Fe: Ocean Tree Books, © 1982), p. 64. Used with permission of Ocean Tree Books, P.O. Box 1295, Santa Fe, NM 87504 and Friends of Peace Pilgrim, 43480 Cedar Avenue, Hemet, CA 92344. I am grateful to Peace Pilgrim for introducing me to this powerful lesson of rechanneling the anger energy.

Notes to Chapter 20

1. Merton, *The Way of Chuang Tzu,* p. 43.
2. *Chuang Tzu* in Legge, *The Texts of Taoism,* p. 326.
3. Details of the incident and quote from Robert Hunter, *Warriors of the Rainbow: A Chronicle of the Greenpeace Movement* (New York: Holt, Rinehart & Winston, © 1979), p. 339–40. Used with permission of the author.
4. Schumacher, *Small Is Beautiful,* p. 60.
5. For further discussion see: Maspero, *Taoism and Chinese Religion,* p. 227.
6. For the source of this quote and an excellent discussion of energy and ecology, see: Miller, *Living in the Environment,* p. 39.

7. Capra, *The Turning Point,* p. 279.
8. For further information on carrying capacity, see: William Catton Jr., *Overshoot: The Ecological Basis of Revolutionary Change* (Urbana: Univ. of Illinois Press, 1980).
9. For a discussion of world population control and peace, see Robert Muller, "Global Cooperation," *Windstar Journal,* Summer 1989, p. 15.
10. Welch, *Taoism,* p. 33.

Section V Illustration: The Chinese characters for abundant peace and security, the result of living the Tao.

Notes to Chapter 21

1. For a discussion of this process, see: Leroy H. Pelton, *The Psychology of Nonviolence* (New York: Pergamon, 1974), pp. 191ff.
2. Chuang Tzu in Yutang, *The Wisdom of Laotse,* p. 54.
3. For a discussion of *Te* in conflict resolution, see *The Taoist I Ching,* trans. Thomas Cleary (Boston: Shambhala, 1986), p. 219.
4. Hunter, *Warriors of the Rainbow* (New York: Holt, Rinehart & Winston, © 1979), pp. 252–53. Used by permission of the author.
5. For more information on Amnesty International, contact the national office, 322 Eighth Avenue, New York, NY 10001 (212) 807–8400.
6. Pointers for witnessing based on advice from the Society of Friends. For more information from the Friends Committee on National Legislation, contact them at 245 Second St. NE, Washington, DC 20002 (202) 547–6000.
7. Thoreau, *Walden and Civil Disobedience,* ed. Sherman Paul (Boston: Houghton Mifflin, 1960), p. 245.
8. Excerpted from "Letter from a Birmingham Jail," by Martin Luther King, Jr. Copyright © 1963, 1964 by Martin Luther King, Jr. These quotes and the one that follows used by permission of Joan Daves.
9. King, "Letter from a Birmingham Jail." Used with permission (see above).
10. Mohandas K. Gandhi in *Gandhi on Non-Violence: Selected Texts from Mohandas K. Gandhi's Non-Violence in Peace and War,* ed. Thomas Merton (New York: New Directions, 1965), p. 67. For a discussion of Gandhi's tactics, see: Timmon Milne Wallis, *Satyagraha: The Gandhian Approach to Nonviolent Social Change* (Northampton, MA: Pittenbruach Press, 1985), pp. 29–33.
11. Hammarskjöld, *Markings* (New York: Alfred A. Knopf, Inc.; London: Faber and Faber Ltd., © 1965), p. 114. Used by permission of the publishers.

12. Merton, "Introduction," *Gandhi on Nonviolence,* p. 14.

13. Anders Boserup and Andrew Mack, *War Without Weapons: Nonviolence in National Defense* (New York: Schocken, 1974), p. 14.

14. Gene Sharp, "Investigating New Options in Conflict and Defense," in *A Peace Reader: Essential Readings on War, Justice, Non-Violence, and World Order,* ed. Joseph Fahey and Richard Armstrong (New York: Paulist Press, 1987), p. 115.

15. Information on the Danish resistance from an interview with William J. Stover, Ph.D., former U.S. diplomat and professor of international relations, and Christopher Kruegler and Patricia Parkman, "Identifying Alternatives to Political Violence: An Educational Imperative," in Fahey and Armstrong, *A Peace Reader,* p. 253.

16. Account of nonviolent resistance among German ranks from Haridas T. Muzumdar, "Gandhi's Nonviolence," originally published in *Friends Journal,* reprinted in Fahey and Armstrong, *A Peace Reader,* p. 217, 218. Used by permission from *Friends Journal.* Subscriptions $18/yr (12 issues) available from 1501 Cherry Street, Philadelphia, PA 19102–1497 (215) 241–7280.

Notes to Chapter 22

1. See Riane Eisler's excellent book, *The Chalice and the Blade: Our History, Our Future* (San Francisco: Harper & Row, 1987). Further information, workshops, and study guides are available from the Center for Partnership Studies, P.O. Box 51936, Pacific Grove, CA 93950.

2. Anthony Donovan, *World Peace: A Work Based on Interviews with Foreign Diplomats* (New York: Anthony J. Donovan, 1986).

3. Information from William James Stover, Ph.D., political scientist and former Foreign Service officer, and John Spanier, *Games Nations Play.* 6th ed. (Washington, DC: CQ Press, 1987), pp. 634–72.

4. Quote from "A Split at the Razor's Edge" by John Hubner, *West* magazine, San Jose *Mercury News,* April 30, 1989, p. 17.

5. Discussion of *sheng jen* in Blakney, *Lao Tzu: The Way of Life,* p. 41. Quote from Macy, *Despair and Personal Power,* p. 45. For a discussion of listening and conflict resolution, see: Arnold Gerstein and James Reagan, *Win-Win: Approaches to Conflict Resolution* (Salt Lake City: Gibbs M. Smith, 1986).

6. Lewis M. Andrews, Ph.D., *To Thine Own Self Be True* (New York: Doubleday, 1987), pp. 3–5, 91–92.

7. For a discussion of Rogerian communication, see: Carl R. Rogers, *Becoming Partners: Marriage and Its Alternatives* (New York: Delacorte Press, 1972). Further information on Rogerian communication in inter-

national peace work available from the Carl Rogers Institute for Peace, Center for Studies of the Person, 1125 Torrey Pines Road, La Jolla, CA 92037 (619) 459–3861.

8. David P. Barash, *Sociobiology and Behavior.* 2nd ed. (New York: Elsevier, 1982), p. 437.

9. From interviews with Barbara Warner, Santa Clara, CA, December 1987, and Gertrude Welch, San Jose, CA, April 1987; "US–Soviet Student Exchange Employs Art for Peace's Sake," San Jose *Mercury News,* May 10, 1989, Extra 3, p. 9; discussions with Jane Curry, Ph.D. and Linda Filley at Santa Clara University, May 1989.

10. My version was inspired by Tolbert McCarroll's translation, *The Tao: The Sacred Way* (New York: Crossroad, © 1982), p. 47: "Therefore the True Person embraces the One/ And becomes a model for all." Used by permission of the author.

11. Based on ideas from *Building United Judgment: A Handbook for Consensus Decision Making* (Madison: Center for Conflict Resolution, 1981), pp. 8– 9. For this and other materials on consensus and conflict resolution, contact the Center for Conflict Resolution, 731 State Street, Madison, WI 53703 (608) 255–0479.

12. From a discussion on consensus and cooperatives in William Valentine and Frances Moore Lappé, *What Can We Do?* (San Francisco: Institute for Food and Development Policy, 1980), p. 14.

13. Quote from Gary Snyder, *Turtle Island* (New York: New Directions, 1974), p. 99. Cory Wade's *July in Georgia* is available from Wisbeck, England: Red Candle Press, 1990.

14. Chief Seattle's Message to President Pierce, 1854, in Fahey and Armstrong, *A Peace Reader,* p. 195.

15. For more about "green cities programs," see *A Green City Program* by Peter Berg, Beryl Magilavy, and Seth Zuckerman (San Francisco: Planet Drum Books, 1989) available from the Planet Drum Foundation, Box 31251, San Francisco, CA 94131. San Francisco Friends of the Urban Forest (512 2nd Street, 4th floor, San Francisco, CA 94107 (415) 543–5000) will provide information about the significance of trees in balancing our ecosystem, and help you form green action groups in your area.

16. Quote from Petra Kelly and information about the Green Party from Capra and Spretnak, *Green Politics,* p. 55.

17. Information from a phone interview with Linus Pauling in December, 1986 and his book *No More War!* 25th anniversary edition (New York: Dodd, Mead, 1983), p. 193.

18. Information from an interview with Norman Cousins at UCLA in July

1988 and from his book, *The Pathology of Power* (New York: Norton, 1987), p. 193. Cousins is president of the World Federalist Association, which works for world peace through world law. For further information, write the W.F.A. at P.O. Box 15250, Washington, DC 20003.

Notes to Chapter 23

1. Opening quotation from Tao chapter 49 based on *The Wisdom of Laotse*, translated and edited by Lin Yutang. Copyright © 1948 by Random House, Inc.:
   "The people of the world are brought into a community of heart,/ And the Sage regards them all as his children," p. 231. Reprinted by permission of the publisher.
2. *Building United Judgment*, p. 15.
3. Research by Anne and Paul Ehrlich in Satin, *New Age Politics*, p. 38. For a discussion of the psychology of community, see: M. Scott Peck, *The Different Drum: Community-Making and Peace* (New York: Simon and Schuster, 1987).
4. Quotation and information in the bartering paragraph which follows are from Laurel Robertson, Carol Flinders, and Bronwen Godfrey, *Laurel's Kitchen: A Handbook for Vegetarian Cookery* (Petaluma: Nilgiri Press, © 1976), p. 61. Used by permission of the publisher. This book has since been replaced by *The New Laurel's Kitchen* (1986), published by Ten Speed Press, Box 7123, Berkeley, CA 94707.
5. Information from Peter Caddy's workshop in San Jose, CA, Sept. 1986, and Eileen Caddy, *Foundations of Findhorn*, ed. Roy McVicar (Forres, Scotland: Findhorn, 1978). For more information write Findhorn, The Park, Forres, IV36 OTZ, Scotland.
6. Information about the Philadelphia Life Center from Suzanne Gowan et al, *Moving Toward a New Society* (Philadelphia: New Society Publishers, © 1976), pp. 284–96. Used with permission of the publisher. The book may be ordered from New Society Publishers, P.O. Box 582, Santa Cruz, CA 95061 (408) 458–1191.
7. Quotation and information about Danish co-housing communities from *Co-housing: A Contemporary Approach to Housing Ourselves* (Berkeley: Ten Speed Press, © 1988 Kathryn McCamant and Charles Durrett), used by permission of the publisher. The book is available from Ten Speed Press, Box 7123, Berkeley, CA 94707 1–800–841–2665.
8. Information from Champions of Wildlife, a video produced by the National Wildlife Federation. For the video and related material, write the National Wildlife Federation, 1400 16th St. NW, Washington, DC 20036–2266 or call 1–800–432–6564.

9. Information from the booklet, *Invite Wildlife to Your Backyard,* available from the National Wildlife Federation, address cited above.

10. Macy, *Despair and Personal Power,* p. 54. Each year commercial tuna fishermen kill over 100,000 dolphins in their nets. To help save the endangered dolphins, contact the Earth Island Institute, 300 Broadway, #28, San Francisco, CA 94113 (415) 788–3666.

11. "Choices for the Future" information available from the Windstar Foundation, 2317 Snowmass Creek Road, Snowmass, CO 81654–9198 (303) 927–4777. My thanks to Max Ibsen, M.D., Jeff Arnett, and William Sullivan for conversations and interviews during 1988–89. For more information on citizen diplomacy, contact the Institute for Soviet–American Relations, 1608 New Hampshire Ave. NW, Washington, DC 20009 or Witness for Peace, P.O. Box 33273, Farragut Station, Washington, DC 20033.

Notes to Chapter 24

1. Quote from Harold D. Lasswell, *Politics: Who Gets What, When, How* (Magnolia, MA: Smith, 1936). This reference and other political advice by William James Stover, Ph.D., of San Jose, CA.

2. Hammarskjöld, *Markings* (New York: Alfred A. Knopf, Inc.; London: Faber and Faber Ltd., © 1965), p. 53. This and other quotations in this chapter used by permission of the publisher.

3. Andrea Cohen-Kiener makes this claim in "Smaller and Simpler Is Safer, Saner," written for the Hartford *Courant,* printed in the San Jose *Mercury News,* May 5, 1989, p. 7P.

4. For information about the student pledge (p. 88) and other ways to live a more balanced life, see: Bill Devall, *Simple in Means, Rich in Ends* (Salt Lake City: Gibbs Smith, 1988).

5. Stories about Becky Simpson and Eddie Schwartz from "You Just Have to Try," copyright © 1989 by Michael Ryan, first published in *Parade Magazine,* May 28, 1989, pp. 40–43. Reprinted by permission of the publisher, author, and the author's agents, Scott Meredith Literary Agency, Inc.

6. Information and quote from "How One Rainforest Was Saved" by Nancy Perkins in *Greenpeace,* May/June 1989, p. 16. Used with permission of *Greenpeace.* The magazine (4 issues) is available for $20/yr or more donation to Greenpeace, 1436 U. Street NW, Washington, DC 20009.

7. For more information on global grassroots movements, see: Alan B. Durning, "Grassroots Groups Are Our Best Hope for Global Prosper-

ity and Ecology," originally published in *The Progressive*, April 1989, reprinted in *Utne Reader*, July/August, 1989, pp. 40–48.

8. See Naisbitt, *Megatrends*, pp. 97, 129, and a 1982 interview with Ralph Nader quoted in Macy, *Despair and Personal Power*, p. 131.

9. The Lima project is described at length in Durning, "Grassroots Groups," p. 42.

10. Information about the Seikatsu from David Morris, "Political Reform from the Kitchen," *Building Economic Alternatives*, the membership magazine of CO-OP America, Summer 1989, p. 3. Used by permission of CO-OP America, which offers members environmentally safe products produced by cottage industries and third world cooperatives. For more information, write CO-OP America, 2100 M Street NW, # 310, Washington, DC 20063.

11. Some ideas in this exercise inspired by suggestions in Arnold Gerstein and James Reagan, *Win-Win: Approaches to Conflict Resolution* (Salt Lake City: Gibbs Smith, 1986), p. 99.

12. Survey from "Voices: Are You Willing to Pay Higher Prices for Clean Air?" *USA Today*, Tuesday, June 13, 1989, p. 10A.

13. For more information on the green tax, contact New Society Publishers: 4527 Springfield Avenue, Philadelphia, PA 19143, or the Finger Lakes Green Fund, P.O. Box 6578, Ithaca, NY 14851 (607) 387–3424.

14. The story about Schumacher from Byron Kennard, *Nothing Can Be Done, Everything Is Possible* (Andover, MA: Brick House Publishing, 1982), p. 145.

15. Information about Jeff Steiner from the CBS Evening News, May 1989.

16. Information about the reforestation project from Barbara Howell, "Seedlings of Survival," from *Christianity and Crisis*, September 16, 1985, p. 349. Used by permission of the publisher. Subscriptions $24/yr (19 issues) available from *Christianity and Crisis*, 537 W. 121st Street, New York, NY 10027.

17. Information on Lee's Orchard from "Back to Basics: Homes Within an Orchard," by Alan Hess, San Jose *Mercury News*, May 7, 1989, p. 1P.

18. Information on Habitat for Humanity from "Sharing the Vision" and *Love in the Mortar Joints* by Millard Fuller and Diane Scott (Piscataway, NJ: New Century Publishers, © 1980), used by permission of the publisher. The book may be ordered from New Century Publishers, 220 Old New Brunswick Road, Piscataway, NJ 08854, or Habitat for Humanity International, Habitat and Church Streets, Americus, GA 31709–3498 (912) 924–6935. For local Habitat branches and projects in your area, consult your local phone directory.

19. Quote from "Carter Finds Fulfillment in Providing the Poor Modest,

Low-cost Homes," by Sunny Merik, editor, *The Los Altos Town Crier,* April 1989. My thanks to Sunny Merik for sharing her ideas on cooperation and peace.

20. Some helpful books on the subject are Gerstein and Reagan, *Win-Win,* cited above, and Roger Fisher and William Ury, *Getting to Yes: Negotiating Without Giving Up* (New York: Penguin, 1983). Quotes from Carter are from a press conference at De Anza College, Cupertino, CA, May 6, 1988. For more information about the Carter Center and its programs, write the Office of Public Information, The Carter Center, One Copenhill, Atlanta, GA 30307 or call (404) 331–0296.

21. Hammarskjöld, *Markings,* pp. 8 and 5. Used with permission.